YIDDISH LITERATURE IN AMERICA: 1870-2000

Selected, Edited, and with an Introduction
by
Emanuel S. Goldsmith

Translated by
Barnett Zumoff

with
Shane Baker, Emanuel S. Goldsmith, Chava Lapin,
and Jeffry Mallow

Ktav Publishing House, Inc.
Jersey City, New Jersey

Library of Congress Cataloging-in-Publication Data

Yidishe literatur in Amerike 1870-2000. English. Selections
  Yiddish literature in America, 1870-2000 / selected, edited, and with an introduction by
Emanuel S. Goldsmith ; translated by Barnett Zumoff [et al.].
      p. cm.
  "This English abridgement of ... contains approximately one-fourth of the content of the
original two-volume Yiddish text published by the Congress for Jewish Culture in 1999
and 2002"-Pref.
  ISBN 978-1-60280-133-2
  1. Yiddish literature--United States. 2. Yiddish poetry--United States. 3. Jews--United
States--Literary collections. I. Goldsmith, Emanuel S., 1935- II. Zumoff, Barnett. III.
Title.
  PJ5125.Y5313 2009
  839'.14--dc22

                        2009033977

Published by
KTAV Publishing House, Inc.
930 Newark Avenue
Jersey City, NJ 07306
Email: bernie@ktav.com
www.ktav.com
(201) 963-9524
Fax (201) 963-0102

Publication of this volume was made possible
by generous contributions from

The Mlotek Family Foundation for Yiddish Culture
and
The Congress For Jewish Culture

Contents

Preface

Seventy years ago, the poet A. Almi described Yiddish culture as "an empire of scattered, beautifully blossoming islands...cutting through the great ocean of peoples and cultures/ and its tongue—the beautiful, tender, mellifluous Yiddish/ resounding proudly in the chorus of tongues." To aficionados of Yiddish, the revival of interest in the language today is nothing less than a miracle. The demise of Yiddish has been predicted with regularity for several centuries, the great centers of Yiddish culture were brutally destroyed in our time, and the younger generation in America, Israel, and elsewhere is largely unfamiliar with the language.

Nevertheless, the fact of the matter is that Yiddishism, an ideology that came to the fore at the time of the First Yiddish Language Conference in Czernowitz, Bukovina, in 1908, is far from dead. As a matter of fact, the two major events of modern Jewish history, the Holocaust and the establishment of the State of Israel, have made Yiddishists more determined than ever to secure a future for the beloved "mother tongue." In the words of Golda Meir, "Once it was assumed that Yiddish represented the Diaspora and anti-Zionism, while Hebrew represented Israel and Zionism... There is no longer a battle between the languages...The spirit of the murdered millions lives in Yiddish culture. We dare not commit the offense of not having provided our youth with a deep attachment to those millions and to the great cultural treasures they created."

In 1939, eleven million Jews, scattered throughout the world and constituting some 65-70 percent of the world Jewish population, spoke the language that originated with French and Italian Jewish settlers in the Rhine valley between the eleventh and thirteenth centuries. Yiddishism consciously attempted to secure a position of primacy for Yiddish and Yiddish culture at the dawn of the twentieth century. Yiddishists generally viewed the emergence of Yiddish as the most significant manifestation of Jewish vitality in the modern world. They saw the Yiddish language as the living bond that united Jewry and thwarted the corrosive effects of dispersion, minority status, and assimilation.

The Yiddishists in America and elsewhere have remained the only organized Jewish trend to publicly acknowledge the incontestable value of the Yiddish language and literature as depositories and wellsprings of Jewish peoplehood and Jewish values in modern times. With all our respect for Hebrew and its ability to link us with ancient glories, and with all our admiration for the revival of spoken Hebrew, we must assert again and again that the creativity of the Jewish people did not cease in the Biblical or Rabbinic periods. We must also remember that the attempt to revive Hebrew included more than a little self-deprecation and desire to sever ties with what were considered to be the despicable Jews of the *galut* and their culture. Yiddish, on the other hand, is indeed what Hyman Bass called "the fullest, most complete, and most faithful path to our people, because it represents the most complete development of the creative forces in Jewish life; because it brings us the sincere love of Jewish generations that yearned and struggled; because Yiddish connects us with Jews of other communities; and because Yiddish is the vehicle of the historical experience of a thousand years of Jewish life."

In Yiddish literature, perhaps even more than in Hebrew literature, we can discover the full richness of Jewish life throughout history and in all parts of the globe. Yiddish literature, according to Mordkhe Shtrigler, "is the only place where all Jewish life-styles have been preserved. Neither modern Hebrew literature nor latter-day rabbinic writings have preserved the breath of life and the complete picture of hundreds of years of Jewish existence. Whoever wishes to know the Jew of many generations and to read the biography of his people will be unable to do so without Yiddish literature."

Yiddish literature has bestowed a rich heritage upon the Jewish people. As Yudl Mark puts it: "It gave us the Jewish person in all his incarnations and transmigrations. It gave us the monologues of the Jewish person with himself as well as his dialogues with his own soul. Here the Jew was absolutely honest with himself. He spoke about both light and shadow, about his healing faith and his wounding, burning doubt. Modern Yiddish literature is the long road of the Jew to himself. 'Know yourself' and 'reveal yourself' are its commands...Modern Yiddish literature is a deeply national

Jewish literature. It is more national than Jewish literature of any other period or of any other language ever used by Jews."

Today, more than ever, Judaism needs Yiddishism. Now, more than ever, the survival of the Jewish people requires openness and responsiveness to all Jewish generations and to the totality of our heritage. Once again the stone that the builders of Israel rejected must become the chief cornerstone. As Yehoyshua Rapoport reminds us: "The life that took place in the Yiddish language has in large measure disappeared. But that life survives in the language itself. That is why Yiddish must now be cherished and protected even more than when it was alive. Yiddish must be preserved so that the cultural treasure which it possesses in the liveliest and most contemporaneous format does not disappear."

Even the secularism or anti-clericalism of Yiddishism, despite its misreading of Jewish history, has a role to play in the present. It can serve to remind modern Jews, who tend to see authentic Eastern European Jewry in one-dimensional religious terms, of the complexity of European Jewish society. Jewish pluralism was already in the making in Eastern Europe in the nineteenth century, and new forms of Judaism were aborning. *Tshuve*, return to Judaism, can legitimately take many forms.

Even since the Emancipation and the Enlightenment, the Yiddish language and literature have helped sustain Jewish identity and have helped bring new life and new hope to our people. Now Yiddish and Yiddish literature must call upon all organs of Judaism and the Jewish people to rally to their aid and help preserve the culture that has given life to generations of the dry bones of our people the world over. When Judaism needed Yiddish, Yiddish was there. Now, when Yiddish needs Jewry and Judaism, they must be there for it. The task of Yiddishism today must be to get all sections and branches of our people to help support Yiddish language and culture. Yiddish linguistic and cultural content must become part of the educational program of all Jewish schools, organizations, and social agencies. Yiddishism must no longer content itself with being a trend—it must become part of the Jewish consciousness of every Jew. Speaking Yiddish and reading Yiddish can no longer be the primary goals of Yiddishism. Only the recognition of Yiddish culture as an essential component of Jewish identity for all Jews will suffice.

The goal of a revitalized Yiddishism can be nothing less than the fulfillment of the Prophet's words: "Your sons shall build once more the ancient ruins, and old foundations you shall raise again. You shall be called the repairer of ruins, the restorer of wrecked homes." (Isaiah 58:12)

This English abridgement of *Yiddish Literature in America, 1870-2000* contains approximately one-fourth of the content of the original two-volume Yiddish text published by the Congress for Jewish Culture in 1999 and 2002. If some readers are encouraged by it to peruse the Yiddish texts, the editor and translator will have been amply rewarded for their efforts.

Emanuel S. Goldsmith

Introduction: American Yiddish Literature and Jewish Continuity

by Emanuel S Goldsmith

Throughout the ages, imaginative writing played a major role in shaping the Jewish self-consciousness of most Jews. The Jewish self-image was traditionally the projection of poets and philosophers, artists and dreamers. It was the construction of *ba'aley aggada,* masters of Jewish lore—the weavers of parable, metaphor, paradigm, and myth. In modern times, the role of the *ba'aley aggada* and the later *paytanim*, or liturgical poets, was assumed by the poets and fiction writers of our people, particularly those who did their work in Yiddish and Hebrew.

One of the major functions of literature is to convey the historical meaning of a civilization by crystallizing its self-expression. For one hundred and thirty years, Yiddish literature in America escorted, comforted, and inspired American Jewry on its adventure in freedom. It captured the changing image of the Jewish people all over the world, both because of the centrality of American Jewry in Jewish life of the past century and because the Yiddish writers of America overwhelmingly remained faithful to the mission of Yiddish literature as a whole: to responsibly mirror, interpret, and advance the life of the Jewish people.

Creative writing in Yiddish in America was always a social act fraught with both nationalistic and spiritual overtones, no matter how vocally such links were denied. Just as modern Hebrew, with its biblical and religious echoes, compels its writers to confront a legacy they may consciously seek to disavow, so Yiddish, with its deep Jewish associations and nuances, forbids spiritual and national amnesia or anonymity. It is not surprising that in his attempts to liberate American Jews from traditional Judaism, the Yiddish-writing philosopher and political activist Khayim Zhitlovski, at the

1

turn of the century, advocated writing Yiddish in the Latin rather than the Hebrew alphabet.

Yiddish has no more been able to liberate itself from the implications of its role as the language of traditional Torah instruction and the "God of Abraham" prayer regularly recited by Jewish women at the conclusion of the Sabbath than modern Hebrew has been able to disassociate itself from its role as *leshon hakodesh*, the language of the sacred texts and prayers of Judaism. The conscious bastardization of the Yiddish language by the American Yiddish press was no more successful than the similar attempts of Soviet bureaucrats to strip the language of Jewish associations and have it serve communist aims. The deeper levels of meaning in Yiddish words, phrases, and idioms continued to haunt both American and Soviet Yiddish writers and draw them ever closer to the inner needs of the Jewish people.

The Pioneers

Elias Shulman, Kalmen Marmor, and other historians of Yiddish literature in America trace its origins to the writings of Yankev Tsvi Sobel, who published a slim volume of Hebrew and Yiddish poems in 1877. Sobel was also the author of *The Three Principles of the Torah* in verse, subtitled *A World of Confusion*. In the latter poem, he warned his people against the dangers of assimilation. The Torah's three principles, he said, were: abstention from superstition, the practice of tolerance and humanism, and the elimination of poverty. If Jews would but unite, abandon fanaticism, and drive poverty from their midst, no enemy could ever defeat them.

Both Sobel and Elyokum Tsunzer, the *badkhn* or wedding rhymester, who came to America in 1889, were traditionalist Jews who had become *maskilim*, advocates of the modernization of Jewish life. Both preached agrarianization, both were influenced by Hebrew-writing socialist such as Shmuel Liberman and Moyshe-Leyb Lilienblum, and both bewailed the lot of the Jewish peddler in America. Tsunzer was the better poet, his poems representing the transition from primitive folk rhyme (set to his own music) to poetry. The work of these early writers was associated with the conservative wing of the American Yiddish press, which sought to preserve traditional Judaism in America and was obsessed with Jewish identity and *ahavas yisroel*, themes to which Yiddish poets far removed from the world of tradition would return half a century later.

N.B. Minkov estimated that in the 1880s and 1890s there were one hundred and fifty Yiddish poets in America. They wrote about nature and love, on the one hand, and about poverty and protest on the other. It was the social motif and the revolutionary outlook, however, that dominated this poetry. Radical freethinkers, socialists, anarchists, and others conveyed to the Jewish masses, in verse as well as in prose, their message of a working-class solidarity that transcended all national and religious divisions. Jewish labor proclaimed the Yiddish poets its spokesmen and transformed them into culture heroes. The wealthy Jews and the observant traditionalists, who joined together in cynically accusing the union organizers of being tools of the Christian missionaries, could not but be envious that the better poets always seemed to be found in the radical camp.

The socialist and labor poets, however, were not devoid of Jewish national feeling. Despite their conscious disavowal of Jewish nationalism and religion, there were striking conscious as well as subconscious allusions to the Jewish heritage and the Jewish plight in their poems. "What good is life beneath the whip of tyrants, without freedom or rights?" chanted Dovid Edelshtat. "How long will we continue to be homeless slaves?" In his *My Will*, the poet, who died of tuberculosis in 1892, at the age of twenty-six, asked his comrades to bury him beneath the red flag of freedom, sprinkled with the workingman's blood:

O dearest friend, when I have left this world,
bring to my grave our flag of red—
the freedom flag, the flag unfurled,
besplotched with blood of workers dead.

And there beneath the banners hanging,
sing me my song, my freedom-song,
my song that rings with fetters clanging,
the song of slaves, of human wrong.

The greatest of the Yiddish labor poets was Moris Rozenfeld (1862-1923). A poet of the working class, Rozenfeld was also an intensely Jewish poet. The national motif and religious sentiments expressed themselves in some of his best loved poems. His social and national poems were both reactions to Jewish homelessness and suffering. In his poem *Di Royte Behole* on the fire in the Triangle Shirtwaist Company in New York in 1911, in which 146 workers, most of them young Jewish girls, lost their lives, he wrote:

> *Kindle the* yortsayt *candles in the Jewish streets.*
> *This catastrophe is the catastrophe of the Jewish masses,*
> *of our benighted and pauperized masses.*
> *The funeral is ours, and ours the graves.*

Language Consciousness

Rozenfeld wrote of Jewish wandering, of life in the ghetto, of the solidarity of the Jewish people, and of the dream of Zion restored. His poems dealt with Jewish sorrows and Jewish hopes. He wrote of Moses and the prophets, and of Theodor Herzl, who had just come on the scene.

Many of the Jews who came to America from Eastern Europe did so with the hope of escaping the narrowness of *shtetl* civilization. Often this meant severing all links with Jewishness. Together with Rozenfeld and the poet and Bible translator Yehoyesh, Avrom (Walt) Lyesin (1872-1938) kindled Jewish pride and helped forge the national identity and self-awareness of the American Jewish community. Arriving in America in 1897, he became the outstanding Jewish national poet in the Yiddish tongue. In his poem *Yiddish* (1922), Lyesin reached heights of prophetic exaltation. At a time when the language seemed doomed to extinction in America, he had a vision of its luminous significance in the heritage of generations:

> *I come to you, my child, from the silent exile,*
> *from crowded, sealed-off ghettos.*
> *I possess only the beauty of pious prayers,*
> *I have naught but the loveliness of martyrdom.*
> *And if I have no lightning-flashes that blind one,*
> *or flaming sun-like words that perform miracles,*

I do have the sparkle of starry legends,
the precious moonlight of the spirit.
From Worms, from Mainz, from Speyer,
from Prague and Lublin to Odessa,
one fire continued to burn,
one miracle continued to glow.
Wherever mortal enemies lay waiting
and death was ready nearby,
there, alone and in sorrow
I accompanied your parents.
For hundreds of years together,
we faced every danger.
I forged through the generations
the wonder of willpower and woe:
to live for sacred teachings
and die for them with strength.
If pure holiness
reflects only from torture and pain,
then I my child, am the one for you,
I am your holiest one.

(Yidish)

Although he was already well known in Europe, it was after his arrival in the United State in 1908 that Avrom Reyzn (1876-1953) came to be acknowledged as one of the leading Yiddish poets and short-story writers. Reyzn, whose writing went through several fascinating metamorphoses, made Jewish poverty a symbol of the universal condition, and made Yiddish poetry the recorder of the full gamut of Jewish and human experience.

In our noisy land,
on roads without end,
we go about silently,
pensive and longing.
Some suppress their woe,
but it is suppressed anyway.

In his heart each
has brought his home along.
In the tumult and confusion,
each sees above himself
his own bit of sky.

(*In Undzer Land*)

Rebel Spirits

Homesickness and longing for the old country were also expressed in the work of Moyshe-Leyb Halpern (1886-1932), the greatest rebel of American Yiddish literature.

Joy blessed by God reigned at home and in the street.
Children played with their fathers' long beards.
Over ancient tomes, singing and always in deep thought,
sat gentle young people day and night.
Young girls sewed phylactery-bags of gold and silk
and all the girls looked as pure as stars.

(*In Der Fremd*)

Halpern's stature has continued to grow since his untimely death at the age of forty-six. His influence on Yiddish poets everywhere has been enormous because he brought a new, liberated diction and style to Yiddish poetry. This, together with his strong individuality and his powerful, earthy Jewishness, made him one of the leading Yiddish poets of all time. Halpern could also be devastatingly critical of the old country and the old way of life—and this too is highly characteristic of American Yiddish literature and of the American Jewish community as a whole.

Halpern was one of *Di Yunge*, the young rebels who after 1905 brought a new sophistication and refinement to Yiddish writing in America. "*Di Yunge*," writes A. Tabatshnik, "were not so much exponents of a new ideology as of a new psychology. Something took place in Jewish life at that time, something matured socially and culturally that made the rise of poets like *Di Yunge* inevitable. They felt differently, saw differently, heard differently."

In the poetry of the sensitive and lyrical Mani Leyb (1883-1953), a new type of person emerges in Jewish life. The individualism of Mani Leyb, and of *Di Yunge* generally, was based on a very intensive, more acute way of feeling; on a highly refined sensibility and openness to experience.

In poor houses there is so much beauty;
faith ennobles hungry lips.
In its abject smallness, the hand that is beaten
keeps all doors open for an even poorer neighbor.
Beside the cold fire of the dying coals,
around the table, heads leaning on elbows,
ears perked and old greybeards speaking
words of wisdom, sorrow, and imagined miracles.
And above all heads—the silent one, the liberator.
He emerges from the talk and sits in their midst.
The thin coals flicker with new fire
and redden all the heads and beards carved out of the fire.
(In Hayzer Oreme)

Mani Leyb's enduring historical accomplishment for Yiddish literature was "the purification of the dialect of his tribe." He established boundaries for Yiddish poetry that helped lift it to new levels of aesthetic accomplishment and refinement. In Tabatshnik's formulation, "he purified Yiddish poetry of prosaisms, jargon, and poor taste."

Jewish survival and the preservation of Jewish religio-cultural distinctiveness were major concerns of Y.Y. Shvarts (1885-1971), another member of *Di Yunge*. Shvarts translated numerous masterpieces of medieval and modern Hebrew literature into Yiddish and wrote narrative verse about America and the American Jewish experience. His skillful poems about the American landscape, about Jews and Blacks in Kentucky, and about his Lithuanian childhood assure his place among the outstanding Yiddish writers of America.

Poet of Accountability

Another early member of *Di Yunge*, who was to become a central figure in the history of Yiddish literature and in the culture of the Jewish people, was H. Leyvik (1888-1962). Leyvik, who inherited the mantle Y.L. Perets had worn in Europe, became the poet of ethical sensitivity and moral responsibility in Yiddish literature. His poems and plays revolve around the themes of guilt and forgiveness, accountability and humanity, messianism and mission as individual, collective, and universal experience. "What is sorrow?" he asked, and answered: "Sorrow is responsibility for everything, for everyone, for all times." The very first poem he wrote in America (in 1914) already contained motifs to which he continued to return throughout his life. In January 1940, when reports of Jews compelled to wear yellow armbands in Europe reached America, images from that first poem came back to haunt the poet:

> *The first snow fell today*
> *and children are sledding in the park.*
> *The air is filled with joyful shouting.*
> *Like the children, I too love white snow.*
> *Most of all, I love winter days.*
> > *(Somewhere far, somewhere far,*
> > *a prisoner lies alone.)*
> *True God of Abraham, Isaac, and Jacob,*
> *punish me not for this old love of mine.*
> *Punish me for not shaping*
> *a Moses from the meager New York snow,*
> *for not making a Mount Sinai from the snow*
> *as once I did in distant years of childhood.*
> > *(Someone wanders in the snow*
> > *strewn all about.)*
> *Punish me for not actually wearing*
> *the six-towered Star of David and*
> *the round emblem of the yellow badge*
> *to strengthen Israel in the hangman's land,*

to praise and glorify
the arm that wears the honor of this ancient seal
in every country of the world.

(*Lider Vegn der Geler Late*)

After the Holocaust and years of struggle with self-incrimination and guilt for not having been in Treblinka with his martyred brethren, the original vision helped Leyvik search for meaning in his people's suffering.

In Quest of Modernity

The rebellion of *Di Yunge* sparked another rebellion—that of the *Inzikhist* or Introspectivist-Imagist writers of the 1920s and 1930s. Where *Di Yunge* had taken Russian, French, and German poets as their models, the *Inzikhists* took American poets, and especially Walt Whitman, as theirs. To the *Inzikhists*, it also seemed that *Di Yunge,* despite their outstanding achievements in developing Yiddish poetry, had limited themselves to traditional form and content. The time was ripe, they felt, for more experimentation and more outspoken individuality than *Di Yunge*, in their quest for delicacy and refinement, had permitted themselves.

The chief theoretician of the *Inzikhists*, and a major voice in American Yiddish literature, was Arn Glants (1889-1966), whose pen name was A. Leyeles. Even before the organization of the *Inzikhist* group, Leyeles had published a volume of experimental poems with the telling title *Labyrinth*. In the 1930s, he created the persona of Fabius Lind, the poet's alter ego, whose very name symbolized the mature, intellectual, sensitive and activist, modern Yiddish writer, alive to both the modern world and his traditional culture. What is especially exciting about Leyeles' poetry is the fact that it was always on the move—probing, feeling, experimenting. It is the poetry of the modern Jew in quest of the totality of modernity while loyal to his people, his culture, his faith, and himself.

Leyeles' poems record the entire adventure of Yiddish literature in twentieth-century America, and they reflect and ponder the odyssey of the Yiddish language the world over in modern times.

Our poem of a sevenfold heaven,
our poem—nourished with the dew and poverty of every land,
can it not once again irrigate every soil?
Behold, we have gone far beyond A, B, and C.
Our poem—a blade of grass, a little flower yesterday,
is now a rare and lovely growth.

(Tsu Aykh Dikhter Yidishe)

Yankev Glatshteyn (1896-1971), an early colleague of Leyeles', was the twentieth-century poet of Judaism *par excellence.* There was no aspect of modern Jewish experience that did not find expression in his deeply thought poems. Glatshteyn brought to Yiddish poetry complete self-iden-tification with Judaism and the Jewish people, humanitarianism, wisdom, humor, and genius. His work is a culmination of all that is admirable in modern Yiddish verse. His poems about Rabbi Nakhmen of Bratslav, his odes to Yiddish, and his poems of the Holocaust, of Israel reborn, and of American Jewry are among the major documents of the Jewish people's tribulations and transcendence in the modern world.

Erets Yisroel, you are the Bible-come-true of a little schoolboy
above whose head all has been fulfilled.
Sing, Jewish daughters, in the vineyards; all has been fulfilled!
From early childhood he was shown signs and wonders.
His teacher Daniel never stopped
reciting triumphant verses,
but he never understood a word.
Now he sees the light of day.
It really did not take very long
for the hour and its aftermath to arrive.

(Bist Geshen, Bist Gevorn)

Y.Y. Sigal (1896-1959) and Arn Tseytlin (1898-1973) were, like Glat-shteyn, writers whose scope of activity was defined by their Jewishness. Sigal was obsessed with Jewish uniqueness, with the *shtetl,* and with *kha-sidizm.* He was the poet of longing for the past and hope for the future. Speaking in God's name, Sigal appropriated for himself the role of the prophet, visionary, and seer in Jewish tradition. "The artist must prophesy, not in the sense that he foretells things to come but in the sense that he tells his audience, at the risk of their displeasure, the secrets of their own hearts..Art is the community's medicine for the worst disease of the mind: the corruption of consciousness." (R.G. Collingwood).

Who is as strong and powerful
as you, my beautiful little trampled people?
Who is like you, who may be compared to you, Israel?

*   *   *

You are as eternal
as the eternal heavens.
You are as enduring as time itself.
Sacred is the soil
of your generations and your cemeteries.
Yisroel sheli—*you are my people, Israel.*
I believe, I believe, I believe in you, my people.
(A Bletl Fun Got's Sidur)

Despite the so-called 'secularism' of modern Yiddish literature, religion and religious motifs occupy a prominent place in it. There is scarcely an important Yiddish poet who has failed to take up this theme in his work. Where Y.L. Perets, in Europe, had spoken of Yiddish literature as a substitute for a national territory, the American Yiddish essayist and literary critic B. Rivkin spoke of it as a substitute for religion in the modern world.

Tseytlin and Grade

The work of Arn Tseytlin was completely suffused with the religious quest and with the doubts and conflicts of the religious soul. Philosophically and theologically more avant-garde than any other major Yiddish poet in the years following the Holocaust, Tseytlin's forays into the world of tradition, into the liturgical mode, and into the mythologies and vocabularies of *kabala* and *khasidizm* were journeys into the past by a highly sophisticated artist who recast the precious ore of a hoary antiquity into the startling and grotesque designs and structures and structures of the contemporary imagination.

Tseytlin was a mystical poet in the tradition of William Blake, Meister Eckhart, Solomon Ibn Gabirol, Nakhmen of Bratslav, and Avrom Yitskhok Kuk. Like them, he was forever in search of the other side of things, the eternal in the temporal, the cosmic in the earthly. He sought contact between the material and the spiritual, the revealed and the hidden, the human and the divine. Tseytlin's metaphysical probings often collided with his grotesque humor to produce statements typical of modern Jewish religious sensibility.

> *I defy death with all my might—*
> *death is nothing but a name.*
> *Are the six million really dead?*
> *They are an ever-present flame.*
> *My generation, you say is in retreat;*
> *I say: Not so! In* netsakh yisroel
> *the past and the present meet.*
> *Even in despair, there is a Levite's song—*
> *just listen for the tune.*
> *We shall all be there soon—*
> *the road from prophet to sabra isn't long.*

*   *   *

> *"Jew" and "stop" can't ever unite, never will—*
> *the meaning of Jew is anti-end.*
> (*Dialog Tsvishn Mir Un Mayn Atsves*)

Another major, unique voice in American Yiddish literature was Khayim Grade (1910-1982), who arrived in the United States after the European Holocaust. An accomplished novelist whose works vividly depict the world of the common folk of his native Lithuania and of the students of the Lithuanian yeshivas, Grade wrote poetry while in the United States that dealt primarily with the Holocaust and the rebirth of Israel. In classical lines reminiscent of the Hebrew poetry of Khayim Nakhmen Byalik, Grade captured the profound reactions of a modern Jew to these two crucial events of modern Jewish history. He saw the mission and purpose of his life and work in the recording for posterity of the travail and glory of his people.

> *Though a stranger in the world, my life has a purpose:*
> *I live so that I may revive the dead.*
>
> (*Geheyme Gest*)

Despite the fact that Yiddish literature in America was written in a lonely, nearly ignored language, it created great values. "The Yiddish writers here," wrote Glatshteyn, "raised Yiddish to the highest heights, as if to protect themselves from shallowness and escape the continuous funereal echo of dying…Out of apathy to language, Yiddish literature in America created language-consciousness, and for a declining generation it created a beautiful linguistic instrument." The Yiddish writers of America helped preserve and stimulate loyalty to the Jewish people and to Jewish religious and cultural values and ideals.

Stress on Individuality

It is also in American Yiddish literature that the awareness of individuality first surfaces in the collective Jewish consciousness in America. The Yiddish writers celebrated individuality and concretized it as a major component of modern Jewish identity. Although Judaism and individuality are far from incompatible, independent thought and feeling were discouraged in traditional Jewish society.

Individuality was as rare in Yiddish poetry as in Yiddish fiction until the emergence of Edelshtat, Rozenfeld, the later Yehoyesh, and *Di Yunge* in America. In American Yiddish literature, the modern Jewish individual *qua* individual and *qua* Jew comes into his own. "The function of literature, through all its mutations," writes Lionel Trilling, "has been to make us aware of the particularity of selves and the high authority of the self in its quarrel with its society and its culture. Literature is in that sense subversive."

In giving voice to the emergence of the sensibilities and conflicts of individuality in modern Jewish life, American Yiddish literature has both reflected and participated in the creation of that individuality. The changing image of the Jewish people in American Yiddish literature is the image of the Yiddish writers themselves. Creative writing may actually be said to have but one hero—the author himself.

American Yiddish literature provides the most complete, most condensed, and most authentic record of the changing image of American Jewry and of the Jewish people as a whole in the twentieth century. It is a complex and often bewildering image. The horrors of persecution and physical annihilation on the one hand, and the process of identity-erosion and language-assimilation on the other, wreaked havoc upon the thousand-year-old Ashkenazic Jewish civilization. Yet what was essentially a scattered, backward, medieval people at the dawn of the century attained national self-consciousness, forging a this-wordly political and cultural identity that is one of the wonders of Jewish history.

Together with the emergence of the modern Jewish religious movements, the rise of Jewish socialism, Zionism and the Hebraic renaissance and the birth of Israel, and the flowering of modern Yiddish literature and culture all over the world in the first half of the twentieth century are miracles of Jewish creative survival. The significance of Yiddish culture in the totality of the Jewish experience and in the vastness of the 4000-year-old Jewish heritage is still only vaguely realized. But the magnitude and significance of the Yiddish cultural achievement have made it an absolutely vital and essential dimension of modern Jewish continuity. It is the Jews' map and compass between the Scylla of all the antiquated, anachronistic forms of Jewish identity and the Charybdis of individual and collective self-denial that inevitably leads to anomie and spiritual self-destruction.

Dovid Edelshtat (1866-1892) and three of his contemporaries, Yoysef Bovshover, Moris Vintshevski, and Moris Rozenfeld, were known as the "proletarian poets" because their poems were heavy on social, political, and economic protest. Though all were fine poets, they were sometimes mocked by other poets as mere propagandists; the poet Zisho Landoy referred to them as "the rhyme section of the labor movement." Ironically, Edelshtat's premature death was due to tuberculosis, known as "the workers' disease." Many of his songs were set to the melodies of Russian folksongs and are still sung today.

~

Dovid Edelshtat

In Battle

They hate us and drive us all 'round the earth,
they plague us, oppress us, and more,
because we can value the true worth
of people who suffer and are poor.

They shoot us and hang us, where'er we be—
they hound us from birth to our graves.
But truth for all workers we will see,
and freedom for all the wretched slaves.

And they cannot frighten us any more—
we fear neither prison nor death.
We're ready to fight in the last war—
we'll fight to our final struggling breath.

Though they forge us fetters of strongest steel
and tear off our limbs from the whole,
it's only our bodies they can steal,
but never our holy human soul.

O tyrants, the flow'rs wake from coma now—
immortal they bloom near and far.
The petals' exciting aroma,
is spreading to everywhere you are.

They bloom in each man's thoughtful, open mind
who loves justice, truth, and the light.

15

The blessings of Nature urge mankind
to battle, to struggle for the right,

to free from their pain all the tyrants hate,
to free them from hunger and cold —
for mankind a Heaven we'll create,
a world free and beautiful and bold,

a world where there'll be no more shedding tears,
nor innocent blood more will flow,
where man's hope will shine through the ages,
and love there forevermore will glow.

You tyrants—you think you can kill us all,
but new fighters soon will be born.
we'll fight and we'll stand straighter, taller,
and freedom will have a bright new morn.

Wake Up!

How long, O how long, will you keep being slaves
and wearing the shameful steel chains?
How long will you heap all the glorious riches
on those who have robbed you of your bread?

How long will you stand with your heads bowing down,
abased, with no home, full of pain?
The day has now dawned, just wake up — you will be then
aware of your mighty, steely strength!

Achieve all your freedom, on barricades fight.
Declare war on tyrants and kings!
Your courage, decisions, my brave fighting comrades,
will bring you the victory you crave.

Your chains and their thrones both will soon disappear
beneath blows from brave workers' swords.
With sweet-smelling flowers and sun's golden radiance,
our freedom will beautify the earth.

The world then will live, love, and blossom again,
and glow in a bright golden May.
My brothers, enough of your bowing to tyrants,
now swear that you all will soon be free!

The chime of our freedom is ringing out now—
assemble the long-suff'ring slaves.
Inspired, fight the battle, my fearless dear brothers —
redeem all your holy human rights.

My Will

O dearest friend, when I have left this world,
bring to my grave our flag of red —
the freedom flag, the flag unfurled,
besplotched with blood of workers dead.

And there beneath the banners hanging,
sing me my song, my freedom song —
my song that rings with fetters clanging,
the song of slaves, of human wrong.

I'll hear it even though I'm in my tomb,
my freedom song, my song so true.
I'll shed hot tears from earth's cool womb
for all the slaves, Christian and Jew.

But when I hear the clanging swords so brave
in final battle for the right,
I'll sing to all from out the grave
to give them courage for the fight.

Elyokum Tsunzer (1836-1913) was renowned as a *badkhn*, or wedding jester, and indeed was often nicknamed Elye Badkhn. However, many of his poems, such as the one printed here, had quite serious themes.

∾

Elyokum Tsunzer

Return to Zion
(fragment)

Lift up thine eyes round about and behold: All these gather themselves together and come to thee (Isaiah 49:18)

What do I see through the windowpanes?
They're flying toward me like doves —
my Joseph and my Benjamin are knocking on my door!
O Heaven, God, the wonder!
For I am seeing my children,
the most beloved, the most faithful, coming back to me!
You've been gone so many years
that I thought I was lost,
a desolate widow whose table was deserted.
How have things gone with you
since they captured you?
How are Judah and Ephraim? Tell me about them!

Come back, years of long ago!
I've become young,
I discard my sorrow—
come here, my silk dress!
My house becomes full again,
my heart and limbs grow lighter —
many of my children are coming back with joy!
Tears of joy are flowing —
let me hug you, kiss you.
rest your bones with me, beloved guests —

You'll receive every pleasure from me.
You'll know no strange tables, only your mother's hospitality!

These young people
will be blessed by the world.
They've abandoned houses, possessions,
glitter, happiness, and influence.
Educated persons,
highly civilized,
they want to be sacrifices for the entire people!
They've decided,
despite all their regrets,
to remove all the stones
that block their way—
to bear difficulties
like those in Moses' time.

And their names shall remain,
with Ezra's,[1]
till the final days.

---

[1] Ezra the Scribe, 5th century B.C.E. Generally credited with compiling the Hebrew Bible into its present form.

Yoysef Bovshover (1872-1915), also one of the "proletarian poets," was an anarchist, as was Edelshtat; their two colleagues, Rozenfeld and Vintshevski, were socialists. He wrote a famous poem eulogizing Dovid Edelshtat, which established him as Edelshtat's successor in anarchist circles.

~

Yoysef Bovshover

A Song to the People

Raise your eyes, O people so lonely and poor —
raise your eyes to the East, West, North, and South,
and see the gathered treasure, the fruits of your labors,
and the left-over riches from previous generations.

Raise your eyes and see on the ocean the golden ships,
and see in the forests the smoke from locomotives,
and see how they soar and come quickly from a distant region
and bring to our land products and merchandise to trade.

Raise your eyes and see the great walled factories
where workers saw and plane and weave and sew and knit,
and forge and file and turn and carve and smooth and polish,
and make the merchandise and make the riches for human use.

And see the dumb robots, the giant iron slaves,
that spare human strength and help create the riches.
And see how the wild, mighty force of Nature is subdued,
for deep is human intelligence and full of secrets.

And to the distant, blooming, merry fields raise your eyes
and see the golden stalks standing there, bowed down with their weight,
and see the beautiful gardens and the trees hung with fruits,
where birds fill the branches, fill the air with song.

And see how the juicy wine grapes are trodden in the cold,
how wine is poured into casks to get older and tastier

so it can later fizz in goblets to gladden the human heart,
awakening hope and love, chasing pain and woe.

And see how all of Nature is ready to sweeten your life
and fulfill demands in your breast and strivings in your heart.
Courageously, in gigantic multitudes, stretch out your skinny hands.
Enough of being robbed! Enough of being deceived!

Raise your eyes, O people — come out of your dark tombs.
Raise your eyes to the East, West, North, and South
and take the inherited riches and the fruits of your labor,
and while creating—live,
and while enjoying—create in the freer generations!

Avrom Mikhl Sharkanski (1869-1907) published his first book of poetry at the age of 22, and continued to publish poems, humorous pieces, and other articles in various Yiddish periodicals. He also wrote for the Yiddish stage: his first play, in 1894, was *John the Baptist*, which was highly acclaimed.

~

Avrom Mikhl Sharkanski

Old Nekhama

What's bothering old Nekhama?
What does she lack, the aged mama?
She's with her children now!
From Lithuania, her rich children
brought her here
and truly appreciate her.

She traveled joyously —
she'd yearned for many years
to see her sons and grandchildren!
So what can be lacking to a mother
who is together with her children?
What terrible thing has occurred?

How can mama be satisfied?!
Her sons are no longer Jews —
not a Yiddish word is heard!
They don't live with Jews,
so how can Nekhama like it —
how can she stay there?

They never open a prayerbook,
they sing only Gentile songs
and speak only the Gentile tongue.
The grandchildren don't know the Hebrew alphabet —
that cuts her heart like a knife!
Oh! — How can she ignore that?!

Her clever grandchildren
think she is crazy
and silently mock her.
Of what use is the old grandma
who thinks only of the next world?
What is her craziness to them?

And she, our aged Nekhama,
the faithful, gentle mama,
often sits and silently weeps.
She yearns for years gone by,
regrets that she came,
and wants only to die.

Ab Kahan (1860-1951) was the Founding Editor of the *Forverts*, the world's leading Yiddish newspaper, and remained its editor for more than 50 years. Though that position was his principal claim to fame, he was also a fine essayist, critic, and novelist, in both Yiddish and English.

$\sim$

Ab Kahan

I Go to Visit the Belzer Rebbe
(From the book *Pages From My Life*)

The path to the rebbe's 'court' was very muddy. It had probably rained a lot in Belz earlier, and the little streets were full of ruts. We had to proceed very carefully because there were puddles there. Poor people ran after me on all sides. I had prepared myself with pockets filled with various coins, copper and silver, but no paper money. I came to a large *shul* that was filled with *khasidim*. It was very messy inside and the air was stale. A few of the Jews were walking around talking quietly to themselves, others were silent, and still others were conversing with one another. Two of the *khasidim* are engraved in my memory because of the nervous restlessness of their movements. They were walking around together, saying or singing something with a quiet melody. They walked slowly but their bodies and faces expressed haste, strain, and impatience. It seemed to me that they were on fire with religious fervor, burning with it but trying at the same time to suppress it so it wouldn't look as if they were showing off the intensity of their ardor.

* * *

To see the rebbe, naturally, one first had to go to his chief administrator. I found him there in the *shul*. From everything I had heard about the administrators, who play the role of 'prime ministers' to the *khasidic* rebbes, I had put together the following portrait: a man who understands affairs, a man of character with a self-satisfied expression on his face and a wily look in his eyes. On my way to the administrator, I was thinking that everything usually comes out just the opposite of what you expect, so he too would probably not be exactly what I had pictured in my mind. My expectation, however, was not fulfilled — the administrator was exactly as I had imagined him: a strapping, well-fed man who wore a fur hat and had red cheeks and a commonsensical expression on his face.

He was standing and conversing with someone. I introduced myself to him. I told him my real name but not the real place I came from. I had been told that they were not very gracious towards Yiddish newspapers in the Belzer 'court' (probably a Yiddish newspaper had attacked him) and I therefore believed that to introduce myself as the editor of the *Forverts* would not be a good idea. On the other hand, to introduce myself as a business-man wouldn't be a good idea, either — according to what I had heard from my fellow-traveler, the man from Hungary, they knew a lot more about business in the 'court' than I did, so if I were to try to pass myself off as a merchant I would make a bad impression. In brief, I felt that it would be more comfortable to come as a journalist, and if it didn't pay in Belz to be a Yiddish newspaperman, I would declare myself to be a correspondent for English newspapers.

I don't remember how it came out — I introduced myself to the administrator as a Jew who lived in England and was connected with English newspapers in New York as their London correspondent. The administrator looked me over with his wise eyes and cross-examined me strenuously. The story I told him went smoothly — I played my role convincingly and it worked. The administrator had respect for a Jew who was a correspondent for English newspapers published in America. He began to speak to me with a friendly tone. Other *khasidim* came in, all of them wearing tall fur hats, and they all started asking me questions:

"From London?"

"A correspondent?"

"For American newspapers, but not Yiddish ones?"

"From London, not from America? But they speak English in America don't they?"

One man asked whether I knew Yankev Gordin, who had visited Belz a few years earlier. I told him that he had been dead for three years already.

"Blessed be your true words," he said, with pious surprise. "He was a nice man, but what sort of business is that for a Jew, writing stories for the theater! Feh!"

The administrator grimaced, as if to say 'You talk too much!'

I offered him an American five-dollar bill, but he wouldn't take it.
"That's not necessary," he said, waving the bill away with his hand.

*   *   *

I don't remember the details, but they took me into the rebbe's house and immediately closed the door behind me, explaining that if they left it open all sorts of people would rush in, some looking for advice, some for a cure, and some for a prayer.

On the opposite wall there was another door. I couldn't see the chief administrator any longer. I found myself in a large room that at first gave me the impression of an anteroom, but it contained two beds that were partly curtained off. As was later explained to me, this was the bedroom of the rebbe and his wife. I had to wait, so meanwhile I looked everything over. There was a half-open wardrobe in which the rebbe's clothes were hanging, his best frock-coats as I later learned. I was astonished by them, so old and poor did they look, and an odor of mildew came from the closet as if it had never been aired out.

Finally, the second door I mentioned opened, and three men came in with a fourth man. It immediately became clear that the fourth man was the rebbe. He was a man of about sixty, with one bad eye. He was dressed as a poor burgher, or, more accurately, a poor congregant. He was wearing an old satin frock-coat and a high fur cap on his head. The three men, the administrators, looked even poorer than he did. They sat down. Since they didn't ask me to sit down, I took a chair myself and started to sit down, but two of them immediately rushed over to me and held me back by both arms so I wouldn't sit down yet. I was holding an umbrella in my hand, and one of the men took it from me and set it down in a corner.

The rebbe wiped his hand on a towel and said a blessing. When he finished, he greeted me and asked me to be seated.

One of the three administrators had a bad ear. It was stuffed with a piece of cotton and was running. The piece of cotton was flecked with fresh yellow spots and was filthy. The rebbe turned to me with questions, and the administrators kept mixing into the conversation. The rebbe's speech was slightly distorted — he didn't actually stammer, but his words came out haltingly as if he did. By his manner and the style of his remarks, he made a good impression on me, and as far as I could judge in the half-hour I spent with him, he seemed to be a straightforward, orderly person and really experienced. But this was all quite preliminary and based on little knowledge.

Two boys appeared, the rebbe's grandchildren. One was about ten and the other was about twelve. Both wore yarmulkes and both had side-curls. They sat there the whole time we were talking and never took their black eyes off me, but quietly, with respect, in a dignified way.

"Where are you from?" the rebbe asked me, in a friendly and respectful way, but at the same time with the tone of a man who was more used to getting respect than giving it. He was very gentle about this, however; he was not full of himself or overbearing.

"From London," I answered.

"They've told me that you write for newspapers in New York. You live in London and you write in New York? How come?"

I explained to him that I was a correspondent, that I sent in my articles by mail. On hearing that, he nodded, as if to say: "Yes, yes, I understand now. Did you think I wouldn't?"

"For English newspaper?" he asked.

"Yes, for English ones."

"For English newspapers!" he repeated, with respect. "But you're a Jew like other Jews, isn't that so?"

"Of course I'm a Jew like other Jews, but I've been living in England for a long time already."

"And where do you come from originally?"

"From Vilna"

"Vilna? A Jewish city! A fine city!"

I began to ask about his views concerning political matters. In Galicia, there was a constant question whether Jews should vote to support the Poles or the Ruthenians. For that reason, it was of interest to me to find out what he had to say about the issue. To tell the truth, it seemed curious to me even to put such a question to an old-fashioned Jew of that type. My interview with him seemed to me like some sort of joke. And indeed, about politics in the usual sense of the word he knew very little, though more than I had expected.

"I tell the Jews to go along with the government" he said (he meant the overall Austrian government, the monarchy.) "Our government is good to the Jews, so we should support it. The Zionists want us to oppose it; they say that Jews should show courage. But we say that all of that is just politics. When the time comes that we have to show courage, we'll show courage. The Zionists have their politics and we have ours. Our political viewpoint today is that Jews should keep their heads bowed down." (In saying this, he was quoting a well known passage from the Talmud.)

"They say that we always stand with the Poles because they are the stronger. That is not true — we just think it is better for the Jews. If we knew it would be better for the Jews to go along with the Ruthenians, we would vote to support Jewish candidates who favor the Ruthenians. We have just one rule: do what is best for the Jews."

Speaking about Zionism in general he said:

"They are destroying Judaism. They create Jewish schools in which they teach Gentile subjects. They say that a good Pole doesn't necessarily have to be a good catholic, by which they mean to imply that one can be a faithful Jew and not believe in Judaism. I, however, say that a Jew who doesn't believe in Judaism is no Jew."

He asked about America. It was my impression that he had no clear conception that England and America were far from one another. I said that I had been in America a few times. He asked about our Jewish immigrants and made the following comment in that connection:

"For my part, there shouldn't be any immigrants, because the immigrants abandon the Jewish spirit (those were his words — in my notes about the conversation, I made the following comment: He had probably heard the expression "Jewish spirit" from someone and liked it, because he used it again and again.) The immigrants go to America to take care of bodily needs; they abandon their wives and live with other women; anything goes."

He said a few words about Roosevelt. He praised him, but he had no clear concept of the man or his politics. To maintain the conversation, I asked how he knew all that and whether he read newspapers. To this, the adjutant with the bad ear responded:

"No, the rebbe doesn't read any newspapers—no newspapers comes into the house."

On the table there lay a volume of the Talmud. The rebbe tapped it with his finger and said:

"When one spends whole days on such difficult matters, smaller things have no importance. One doesn't have to study about them at all — one understands them automatically."

Speaking about America again, he asked me how I knew so much about what was going on there. He had forgotten what I had told him, that I had been in America a few times; apparently that had made no impression him. He had no clear concept whatever about the difference between England and America. If there was a big ocean between them, how could I be now in England and now in America? He was foggy about that.

"First of all, one reads things in the newspapers, and secondly, in my business I have occasion to be in America from time to time," I explained again.

I explained to him about the Jewish workers in America, that they were organized "so they wouldn't be deceived or swindled," as I put it.

"Do they strike?" he asked. "What do they want? To be paid higher wages? Nothing wrong with that! There's a shortage of workers here —- is there is a shortage in America too? They work too hard there, isn't that true?"

"Yes, it's true."

I tried to elicit from him an opinion about capital and labor, about the rich and the poor. That, however, was impossible. To my first question in that direction, he answered as follows:

"All are children of the same Lord of the Universe. If a virtuous Jew owns a factory, he pays good wages, and if a Jew tortures his workers, he is an evil person."

He quoted a passage from the Bible, or perhaps from the Talmud, that one must treat a worker well.

That was the clearest answer I was able to get out of him in relation to the matter of labor. I asked him the same question in another form, in the hope that I might draw him a bit deeper into the matter, but he wouldn't allow it. One could see that he had an instinct that told him when it was better for him to wiggle out of giving an answer, and he had had a lot of experience in that regard. People of various classes had spoken to him and had tried to confuse him into rendering an opinion about various dangerous issues, and he was therefore proficient and quick at giving non-responsive answers.

Nevertheless, in the final analysis he didn't give me the impression of being a sly person. On the contrary, I even found him sympathetic. If he had been a crafty person, a bit false, at least a few Jews would not have loved him, but as far as I was able to ascertain, everyone truly loved him, not only with a love born of their religious fervor toward a 'Godly man' but simply as a person as well.

When my visit was over, one of the three administrators accompanied me to the exit and locked the door behind us. A group of Jews who had been waiting outside marched up on the off chance that they might be able to get in somehow, but they weren't allowed to enter.

*   *   *

Outside, all kinds of people surged toward me with outstretched hands. I stepped to one side to write down my interview with the rebbe and everything that had happened in that connection. The beggars didn't interrupt me. They looked at me respectfully and curiously as I was writing in my notebook.

When I was finished, I distributed a large number of coins and started back to my inn, striding across the foot-bridges over the puddles and the mud.

The number of Jews who were begging for aid grew larger. My stock of coins was finally exhausted. I explained that I didn't have any more, and that later, at the inn, I would give out the rest. I pleaded with them to let me go alone. I didn't find it easy, but I finally got them not to run after me. There was just one exception, a deaf-mute. He didn't understand my hints and he wouldn't let me alone. He followed me through the whole maze of muddy little streets and alleys, running after me and shouting to me in his nerve-shattering mute style. When I reached the inn, I got some coins from the innkeeper and satisfied him.

Later, the innkeeper, his son, and a couple of neighbors came into my room. They all asked about my visit to the rebbe. A crowd gathered, and I'll never forget the excited face of a middle-aged Jew as I was telling them what the rebbe had said.

"Understand me, he has a pure mouth," he commented. "A word of his is not like a word of mine. Whatever he says comes to pass."

He then started telling something about the Trisker rebbe, that he was an extremely holy man, a sort of god.

"He doesn't eat and he doesn't sleep, the Trisker rebbe. Is it any wonder then that such a person can turn the world upside down?"

The innkeeper and others of those present interrupted his words with paeans to the Belzer rebbe till they finally outshouted him. The *khosid* who was excited about the Trisker rebbe then asked me:

"Is it true that in America they eat the "third meal"[1] at home and not in *shul*?"

I confessed that it was true, upon which he exclaimed with venomous sarcasm:

"So what kind of meaning can that have? What do you have there, theater? Singing and eating the third meal[2] at the rebbe's table is the greatest joy. What is theater? A Gentile disguises himself as a Jew and a Jew as a Gentile, an old man disguises himself as a young man and a young man as an old man. A fine how-do-you-do!"

Later, in the evening, a fairly intelligent Jew came in who interested me with his wise words. He didn't strike me as a man who laughed at the rebbe; on the contrary, he spoke of him with real respect. However, it seemed to me that he respected the rebbe because he was used to doing so, the way, for example, that a Jew who has long since forsaken religion still can't eat anything *treyf*[3]. He told me about the various types of "residents," *khasidim* who constantly sat with the rebbe. One was lazy, so he just sat there and didn't bother to rack his brain about earning a living — let his wife worry about that! In the rebbe's house, he ate prepared food, sang, and told stories with other 'residents'. Another one had a troublesome wife, so he was running away from her.

After that a Jew came in who used words like "capacity" and "abstract" in his speech. He confided a secret to me, that he smoked on the Sabbath but believed in the rebbe.

[2] A meal that is eaten in the afternoon, before the evening prayers
[3] Non-kosher

"How are those thing consistent with each other?" I asked.

"My belief is not a simple one," he explained, "it's a higher level of belief. If I smoke on the Sabbath, that's contrary to simple belief, but my soul rises to higher levels of belief, and there the ordinary Torah mitzvas and sins have no meaning."

I told him that his answer was incomprehensible to me, upon which he remarked:

"If you were to settle here among us and live here for a few weeks, you'd understand. You can't understand such things just by hearing them"

From what I learned subsequently, the *khasidizm* considered him half-crazy.

Very late at night, a Jew came in who declared that since I wanted to know about the various residents, about what sort of people they were (so someone had told him), he could explain it all to me for a few guldens. We bargained and settled for one gulden (two kronas), and he started speaking. He just chattered, in a curious, tumultuous manner that confused him more than me.

"Do you know what a 'character' means?" I suddenly addressed him.

"No," he answered, "what does it mean?"

"I'll explain it to you. You want to tell me about the various residents, about what sort of person each of them is, isn't that right? That means that you want to tell me what type of character each of them is. So now you know what a character means."

"Yes, now I understand."

"Well let me tell you that the most interesting character of all the characters is you yourself."

I saw that he still didn't understand what a character was, but I paid him the two kronas nevertheless. He took the silver coins, wished me all the best, and left.

Moris Vintshevski (1856-1932) was the most politically active of the four "proletarian poets," and was sometimes called "the grandfather of Jewish socialism." As a poet, he was both militant and sentimental; some of his characters were a blind fiddler, a tattered beggar, and a girl who sold her body to make a living.

⮂

Moris Vintshevski

Three Sisters

In England's a city called Leicester,[4]
in London's a square by that name.
Three sisters work there in the square,
and all have achieved certain fame.

The youngest sells flowers all day,
the second sells laces for shoes,
and late in the night comes the eldest —
her body she lets men abuse.

The younger ones look at their sister —
no hatred at all in their eyes.
The world and the town and the square
all three of them strongly despise.

At night when the younger ones reach
their nest, as they call their poor place,
they secretly moisten the flowers
with tears running down from their face.

[4] Pronounced "Lester"

Yankev Gordin (1853-1909) was the first great dramatist in Yiddish literature. He wrote original plays in Yiddish and also translated and adapted many plays from other languages into Yiddish, most notably *The Yiddish King Lear*. *Mirele Efros* was his most popular play, and is considered his masterpiece.

Yankev Gordin

Mirele Efros
(Excerpt from Act III)

Characters in order of appearance:

Shalmen: Previously Mirele's long-time business-manager

Mirele Efros: Well-to-do dowager businesswoman and benefactress of Grodne's Jews and institutions

Sheyndele: Yosele's wife

Makhle: Mirele's long-time maid and (previously) housekeeper

Yosele: Mirele's elder son

Donye (Daniel): Mirele's younger son

Shalmen: A blessed good afternoon to you, Mirele. It's a rare privilege to see you. Come, come—have you rejected the rest of the world? Look at her! Woe to my soul, what you look like! Whatever is the matter with you?

Mirele: Sit, sit. Makhle, let's have some more chairs. What has brought you to me? I thought that Grodne had long forgotten that Mirele ever existed . Sheyndele, perhaps you could have some whisky and snacks brought in. Shalmen is a very special guest to me. How are you, my good and loyal old friend? I feel as if I haven't seen you in ages.

Sheyndele: Mother-in-law, we have no whisky in the house. You know

34

that Yosele doesn't drink, so for whom should I keep whisky in stock?

Shalmen: Why go to all that trouble? You know what we've come for—our community has finally decided to build a Jewish hospital, you know, and, well—who else among us has such a warm heart and such a generous hand as Mirele Efros? So we've come to you before anyone else. Ha, ha, ha. We expect a substantial contribution from you—like a few thousand.

(Mirele is seated, sunk in thought.)

Sheyndele (to herself): He should have come with a sack.

(Yosele stops her from speaking.)

Makhle: Dear Father in Heaven, save her from shame!

Mirele: A substantial contribution, eh? I don't know. You understand—business is slow. But I certainly won't let you leave my house empty-handed.

(She climbs out of her easy-chair and slowly approaches her children.)

Mirele: Yosele, give me two hundred-ruble notes. I don't want anyone to know what is going on here.

Yosele: No need even to say it, mother dear. (He extends his hand to the till, but Sheyndele covers it with her arm.)

Sheyndele: Ha! Very necessary, their two hundred rubles! Two hundred pox I'll give them!

Donye: (Sarcastically) It's very necessary to waste money for fanatic purposes!

Mirele: Children, I beg you. Don't shame me in front of strangers. You know that I haven't asked for anything for myself, and I won't. But now, on this occasion….(She trembles with agitation. Yosele hides his face in his hands.)

Sheyndele: (Sweetly) Mother-in-law—take my advice: get rid of your foolish grandeur and childish arrogance, I say.

Mirele: I'm not interested in hearing what you have to say. (Looks at her) Out of here, everybody, out!

(Yosele starts to get up, but Sheyndele prevents him from leaving. Donye remains seated.)

Mirele: I mean, if you have no business here, you may leave. But if you want to stay, stay.

Donye: We certainly will stay here.

(Mirele returns to her easy-chair and almost falls. Makhle catches her.)

Makhle: (Quietly) Mirele, don't be angry with me. You know, of course, that I've saved up 126 rubles. What do I need money for? After all, I'm just an old woman! (Pulls out a knotted cloth full of banknotes.)

Mirele: Yes, you are right. Give me your money, lend it to me. Nobody has to know about my humiliation. (Takes Makhle's money.) Gentlemen, you mustn't be upset with me. I can't make a major contribution, just a hundred. (She hands him a 100-ruble note. One of the townsmen tucks the money into his pocket. Mirele seems lost in her own thoughts.) No! Forgive me! Give me back the money! I was about to commit the most terrible wrong. Makhle saved that money with bitter sweat and blood, and I was going to play the role of Lady Bountiful at her expense because I was ashamed to tell the truth. No—my daughter-in-law is right. I have to discard my foolish grandeur and childish arrogance.

Sheyndele: The days when hundred-ruble notes were tossed in the mud are over.

Mirele (reclaiming the money): Yes, my friends, those times are over. Mirele Efros is now very poor herself. It is possible that I may soon have to turn to you. I'll come asking for charity. Makhle—take your money. We shouldn't borrow when we are not sure where the repayment will come from.

(All the townsmen stand up, stunned.)

Makhle: Lord strike me dead if I understand what makes you tick!

Shalmen: You understand, gentlemen, that Mirele Efros is joking. Ha, Ha! What do you mean, you have no money? Why I myself owe you hundreds and hundreds.

Mirele: You, Shalmen? How come?

Shalmen: Now, now. Stop joking with us. Here's a hundred on behalf of Mirele Efros. Come, gentlemen, let's go. (Quietly to Makhle: I'll be right back.) (Sharply) Have a good day, Mirele, and stay well.

The townsmen (leaving): Confound it, Shalmen. What's going on, eh?

Shalmen: Goodness only knows. Don't you know Mirele? Probably some sort of joke, a whim. Never mind—let's go! (All exit)

Sheyndele (sweetly): You feel rotten, I bet. Never mind—it will pass, and the hundreds will stay in our pockets. Much better.

Mirele: I've often wondered how there could be men so malicious as to raise a hand against their wives. Now I realize that there are women to whom one can speak only with a stick. (She stamps her cane.) With you there is no alternative.

Yosele: What are you saying, mother dearest? Who would dare raise a hand against my Sheyndele? She is my wife, she is my Shloymele's mother, she is the mistress of this house.

Mirele (sadly): There! He does remember: she is the mother and the mistress of this house. And who I am you've all forgotten. Let's assume that I am not the mistress here; I actually abdicated from that role myself. But am I then no longer mother either? Who took that title away from me? Ha! People pretend. They manage to forget quickly what the earth covers up. Sadly for me, I've been forgotten even before the earth covers me.(Makhle starts to cry.) Makhle, I beg you—please don't cry, because it won't take much for me to burst into tears like a child. (Chokes on her tears.) Oy Makhle—my heart, my heart! (Falls against Makhle's shoulders.) I won't expose my stricken heart in front of strangers. (Proudly) Come— help me get out of here. (Makhle leads her and both exit.)

Donye: Oy, do I ever love these female hysterics and soap operas. Fui! (Exits.)

Sheyndele: Look how downcast he is! Why is your brother not one bit troubled?

Yosele: I ache for her old, gray head. Sheyndele, you know how dear you are to me, but still, often when I see how much pain my mother is suffering because of you I hate myself for giving in to you. I hate you for that quality, and I often think I'm your mortal enemy!

Sheyndele (coquettishly): Really? You're my mortal enemy? Come on, I want us to become friends again. (Takes his arm and walks with him.)

Yosele: What diabolical power these women possess! Who invented them to trouble us? Oy, I shouldn't know from you! (Both exit.)

Makhle (Opens the door carefully): How clever she is about leading people around by the nose! Her kind will never be an abandoned wife. Reb Shalmen will be back soon. He won't begin to believe that Mirele's home has been transformed into a charnel-house. Here he comes!

(Sheyndele sneaks in and eavesdrops.)

Shalmen: God help us! What's going on in this house, Makhle? Why didn't you let me know sooner?

Makhle: She made me swear not to tell anyone, not even you. And then today she went ahead and spilled the beans herself. Oh Shalmen—what our Mirele is forced to endure here! They've stripped her of everything, from head to toe. They've robbed her; she hasn't a penny to her name—not to save her life! You know how she can't stand a dirty house, or clutter and bustle. She's used to eating meals at a regular hour, with everyone at the table together. Now meals are sometimes at two, sometimes at three, and sometimes at four. Everyone is served separately. There are always dirty dishes in the dining-room. She's lost her appetite. She doesn't eat, she doesn't drink, and she doesn't sleep a wink all night. Whenever I wake up during the night, I hear her moaning, poor dear!

Shalmen: Makhle, what are you saying? I don't understand. Woe is me!

Makhle: And the things that happen here every day! They insult her, they treat her worse than a servant. The daily hollering, cursing, threats, arguments! And they've come to blows here, too. Oh Reb Shalmen, I don't know how she'll be able to stand all this.

Shalmen: I knew that she had handed over her possessions to the children, but no one could have imagined that she, Mirele Efros, would be the victim of so much sorrow and shame in her old age? Alas! (He wrings his hands.)

Makhle: You don't know the half of it! Day-in, day-out, her daughter-in-law, that bitch, sucks the life out of her. I don't know where Mirele finds so much patience. Her only comfort is her grandson, Shloymele. She takes him in her arms, talks to him, hugs him to her bosom, and sinks into a reverie.

Shalmen: And you, Makhle—you've been able to watch it all and remain silent? I hope God won't punish you for that. Makhle, I won't allow Mirele to suffer so harshly. And to you I say: Fool, fool, fool! (Exits, to Mirele.)

Makhle: And what do *you* think? Was I a fool to keep quiet?

Sheyndele: You'd better continue to keep your mouth shut in my house! Do you hear me, you rotten hag, you gossip-monger? If you tattle about what happens at home, I'll kill you! I can't throw you out because I'm not ready to get divorced from Yosele over you, but I'll beat the hell out of you! Bulletins? Gossip? There, take that! (Strikes Makhle.)

Makhle: Heaven help you, Sheyndele. What are you doing? God help you! (Her gray hair creeps out of her kerchief.)

Sheyndele: So complain about me to Shalmen! Go on—complain! (Continues to beat her. Mirele appears, with Shalmen behind her.)

Mirele (very agitated—bangs the floor hard with her cane): What are you doing? Who do you think you're beating? Against whom do you dare to raise your disrespectful hand? You'd beat an old woman? You'd beat Makhle, my Makhle, my only friend in the world? Beat *her*? Alas! Up to now, nobody in this household has even insulted a servant, and you dare to beat Makhle?

Sheyndele: I'll beat her every day till she learns who the boss is in this household. It's nobody's business who I used to be—I want respect from everyone, just as you do.

Mirele: *You*'ll beat *her*? *You*?

Sheyndele: Yes, I! If she doesn't like it here, she can leave!

Makhle: Mirele dear, it's not right for you to suffer even more because of me. It would be better if I left. You'll manage without me somehow. What can we do?

(Yosele runs in.)

Yosele: Hey! What's going on now? What a day this has been! God in Heaven!

Mirele: Not a thing. You run an aristocratic house now, you've turned your husband into a dandy, and everything else is so grand— but the house is filthy, you yourself are up to your neck in mud, and you beat the maids. That's who you are, my aristocrats!

Sheyndele: Really? You don't like the match? Have the wagons hitched up and go home!

Mirele: Precisely. I don't like the match. Makhle, run and call Shalmen back to me. Hurry! (Makhle exits.) Yosele, the two of us can't live together in this house. It's impossible. I want you to divorce her this very day! Give her a divorce—do you hear me? There's no other solution. (Bangs her cane on the floor.) A divorce, a divorce!

Yosele: Mother dear, what are you saying? God help you!

(Sheyndele laughs.)

Mirele: Scared you, didn't I? Ha, ha, ha! I'm only fooling. I know it's easy to divorce an old mother, but nobody divorces a young wife, and a pretty one to boot, so I'm leaving this place. (Shalmen arrives, with Makhle.) Here's Shalmen. I'll be done with this right away. Hear me out, Shalmen— I have a very important request of you. For 35 years you worked in my household; now permit me to serve in yours! I have no other choice. I don't want to die in the street, so I'll go and work for you.

Shalmen: Work for me? What are you talking about? I'll be like a father to you and you'll be like a child to me. We're simple folk, but we know how to appreciate a person. Work for me? Woe is me! Don't you know that if you'd just say the word, the firm of Mirele Efros and Shalmen could do outstanding business.

Mirele: Mirele Efros is not about to compete with the firm of Yosl and Daniel Efros. No—I want to work for you. Without work I get depressed, I go out of my mind. As long as my old eyes are still able to see, I'll keep your books. After that, Shalmen, I'll do whatever you tell me to do.

Shalmen: Whatever I tell you to do? Oy! Stop it! (Wipes away his tears.)

Mirele: Enough! I don't want to, I can't, and I don't have to tolerate this any more. Mirele Efros has not yet fallen so low as to let people walk all over her. Love for children and maternal feelings also have a limit. I'm leaving right now. Just a minute (Pokes around among her things.)

Sheyndele: With her, who knows? She could do it, too! Yosele—don't let her. Can you imagine what people will think of us?

Yosele: I'm afraid it's already too late. Sheyndele—what will become of us now?

Makhle: Every corner of this house will weep and wail. (Mirele approaches her, carrying a small bundle.)

Mirele: See, Shalmen? Thirty-some-odd years ago I entered this house with many things, with many fond hopes and expectations . Now I leave with only some undergarments and one dress, without hope, without expectations. I came here to live and I leave here to die. How did Job put it? God has given and God has taken away. (All are weeping. Sheyndele wipes away a tear.)

Sheyndele: Dear mother-in-law, don't do this. I beg you. Forgive me. Oy, such a disgrace! Yosele won't survive it.

Yosele: Mother dearest, don't leave us. If not for our sake, stay for our child's sake. You love our child so much!

Mirele: No! It's too late now. Mirele Efros does not stay on after she decides to leave. I cannot stay any longer. Yosele— give Shloymele a kiss for me, and if you want to be a good boy, send him to me sometime. I'm leaving. Let the whole world know the truth. Am I supposed to hide my disgrace, hide what has happened till now? Am I supposed to fool the world and tell lies? No way! That I've done it up to now was a mistake on my part and a weakness. Indignity continues to exist only because it is denied. Shalmen, give me your hand. I'd much rather be a servant in a strange home than a fool in my own . Well, Makhle? What will you do?

Makhle: Don't worry, Mirele. Reb Shalmen will certainly let me come and visit you sometime.

Shalmen: Don't be silly, Makhle. What do you mean? Do you think you won't be able to earn your bread in my house? It's quite all right—we are not aristocrats. Come, Mirele, Makhle, come with me Old soldiers don't abandon their general at a time of misfortune. (Shalom and Makhle lead Mirele away.)

Mirele: Take care, children. I don't know whether my foot will ever cross this threshold again. I'm going. (Starts to go.) My old friends are leading me. Sure, it would have been more appropriate for me to be carried out of here in a coffin—it is terribly unfortunate when a person outlives her time, but until God sends us death, we must live. One consolation remains, however: though I've lost my children and everything else, I still have a few good friends. (Starts to go. At the door, she turns around and scans the house.) Makhle, you know how dear all this is to me, but I feel that now I'm looking at it for the last time. Who could have believed that I, that both of us, in our old age…..Yosele, be well! (Exits with Makhle and Shalmen.)

Yosele (drops into a chair): Mother, mother! Woe is me!

(Sheyndele weeps.)

CURTAIN

Moris Rozenfeld (1862-1923) was probably the finest as well as the most popular of the "proletarian poets." His poems were dominated by a tone of pity and lamentation for toiling workers who were prisoners of their machines and never got to see their children during waking hours. In contrast, he was very hopeful of the Zionist dream. Many of his poems were put to music, often composed by the poet himself, and are still sung frequently.

∾

Moris Rozenfeld

A March Of Exile

With wander-staff in hand,
without a home, without a land;
without helper or friend along the way,
with no tomorrow, no today;
not at a measured pace, but chased,
stayed at night, at dawn we raced;
always woe, woe, woe,
always go, go, go,
always stride, stride, stride,
while we have our strength and pride.

Our strength ground to dust,
our Torah mocked by the unjust;
there's danger in our name,
and sorrow in our fame;
our genius is a sin,
our abilities — we cannot win;
always grave, grave, grave,
always slave, slave, slave;
always seek, seek, seek
the blessings in curses our enemies wreak.

And so it is as years go by,
time passes, generations fly.
No hope, no goal draws near,
we're wrapped in horror and in fear.

We wander the world, again and again,
we go from agony to pain.

Always tread, tread, tread—
always beg, beg, beg.
Always need and want, man and boy,
and till death no happiness enjoy.

Kaddish
(A memorial poem for my beloved only son)

A golden lock, a picture, and a book I see —
that's all that remains of my boy,
my boy who was my pride and joy,
and since his death, the world is cursed for me.

The lock reminds me of his lovely head;
the picture shows his lovely face, its pallor;
the book recalls his spirit of youthful valor;
but he's fallen out of life's sweet bed.

It's mine—keep this legacy for me;
fate has left me nothing more.
I see Death and recall life again,
the life that lives in my pain.

My Little Boy

I have a darling little boy,
a lovely son so fine,
and when I see him, seems to me
the whole wide world is mine.

But seldom, seldom do I see ˙
my lovely boy awake,
I see him only when he sleeps —
it makes my poor heart break.

My work drives me away by dawn —
I get home late at night.
A stranger to me is my boy —
a stranger to my sight.

I come depressed and sad back home —
the darkness there abounds.
My wife so pale then tells me how
he plays, with joyous sounds,

How sweet he speaks, how wisely asks;
"O mother, dearest ma—
when will he bring a penny home
for me, my darling pa?"

I hear his words and rush to heed —
yes, yes, it has to be!
My father's love burns bright in me —
my child just has to see!

I stand right near his little bed
and listen quietly.
His lips move now, he's dreaming sweet:
"Dear pa, you've come to me."

I kiss his dear blue eyes just once —
they open and see me.
They see me standing next to him,
but sleeping soon is he.

"Your daddy's here, my darling son —
a penny here for you."
Again he's dreaming, oh so sweet:
"Dear pa," he says anew.

I stand there feeling sad and blue —
I'm bitter to the core.
"When you awake, my dearest son,
you'll find me here no more."

My Resting-Place

Don't look for me where myrtle's greening —
you won't find me there, my dear.
At my machine, where life's lost meaning —
here's my resting-place, I fear.

Don't look for me where birds are singing —
you won't find me there, my dear.
A slave am I whose chains are jingling —
here's my resting place, I fear.

Don't look for me where fountain's splashing —
you won't find me there, my dear.
Where tears are flowing, teeth are gnashing,
here's my resting place, I fear.

And if you truly, deeply love me,
come to me, my sweet, my dear,
and bring your glow to skies above me —
help me rest, I'll rest right here.

In the Catskill Mountains

O you ancient, unconquerable witnesses of immortality,
elevators of the spirit, crowned with eternity and strength,
on whose back eagles,
flying through the air and soaring to the skies,
rest from their cloud-journeys;
O you worthy, holiness-breathing tribunes where God dwells,
and from whose horrifyingly gigantic heights
the creation-fresh balsamic winds of life blow;
O you angels'-ladders, as big as souls
and rising to anonymous heights —
mountains!
A little grain of dust,
meaningless as a dream
from your own exalted time
and fearsome almighty-ness;
a piece of dust,
just a destructively cutting piece,
I gape at your thought-provoking,
age-old, secret-hiding,
border-mocking incomprehensibility.
In your titan's-breast roots,
the centuries, and your ignoring, freezing stony coldness
towards mankind's momentary tumults
make the unsteady, billowing spider-webs
of our philosophies tremble —
and yet, you mountains,
you are, in the end,
just overgrown heaps of earth;
and though you outlive worlds,
you must remain chained and immobile,
with no choice and no alternative,
a clumsy, helpless mass
strictly bounded by your deep valleys,
determined by fate;

and you cannot prevent my eternally active hand
from digging into your treasure-filled hearts,
dark as tombs,
and you must quietly and patiently
let my insect's feet
walk on your eternally covered heads,
gray with the years.

* * *

My parents walked on you,
and my children and my children's children
will also climb your heights,
till eternity.
And as you are eternal, O mountains,
so too is immortal and everlasting
that which is eternally human:
brilliant, striving, unconquered Man.

Sholem Aleichem (pen name of Sholem Rabinovitsh) (1859-1916) was the greatest and most beloved humorist and storyteller in Yiddish literature, and is also considered a major figure in world literature. He was sometimes called "the Yiddish Mark Twain." His work combined an awareness of underlying tragedy with a will to extract joy and laughter from every event—laughing through tears, as it were. *Motl, Cantor Peysi's Son*, the hero of the story printed here, was one of his most popular literary creations.

~

Sholem Aleichem

The "Four Questions" Of An American Boy

"Daddy, I want to ask you four questions. The first question I want to ask is : *ma nishtane halayle hazeh*— why is this night different from all other nights in the whole year?"

Shebkhol haleyles—for on all other nights in the year we eat whatever we want: A Jewish steak, pork chops, fish with horseradish, oysters, noodle pudding, or pumpkin pie. *Halayle hazeh*—on this night of Passover, we eat only matzo and bitter herbs. And if we want to eat something non-*peysakhdik*[5], my mother has told us, we can go to a restaurant on Broadway, because in her house, she says, things are strictly *peysakhdik*. Everywhere, in every corner, things are kosher and clean. The house shimmers and sparkles, and we have just bought brand-new dishes from the store. The furniture has been redecorated, the doors have been washed, the windows have been cleaned, and the woodwork has been revarnished. Sadie the maid has been koshered. An odor of heavily peppered fish rises from the kitchen. There's a smell of goose-fat. They've made pancakes and blintzes with the soup, and home-style *kneydlekh*, *khremzlekh*, and *falirtshikes*. They've suddenly told us to put on our hats, seated us at the table, and put in our hands little prayer-books and hagodes for us to look into. So we sit like dummies and watch, like the rooster in the B'nei Odom prayer[6].

"What sort of comedy is that? What's the name of that play?"

* * *

---

[5] Suitable for eating on *peysakh*, i.e. free of leaven
[6] The prayer used in the ritual of *shlogn kapores*

"Now I've asked you one question, Daddy, and I want to ask you the next question:

"Why did Mama send our Christian cook away for all of *peysakh*? Why are we so ashamed of our holiday?

"Are we ashamed that we freed ourselves by our own efforts from our exile in Egypt, and that from slaves, Gypsies, we became a people?

"Are we ashamed of Moses' Bible?

"Are we ashamed of our Holy Temple, which was, they say, a temple, a house of God for all people?

"Are we ashamed of our kings, who distinguished themselves not only with war and bloodshed? They, it is said, also wrote unusual books and sang lovely songs, the Psalms.

"Are we ashamed of our prophets, who didn't hesitate to point out the errors of even the greatest person, even the king himself, and to tell him the truth right to his face?

"Are we perhaps ashamed that our parents allowed themselves, they say, to be slashed and cut to pieces, burned and roasted, hanged and drowned, and to watch as their children were killed before their eyes, and to jump into the fire to sanctify His name, all the while shouting: 'Hear, O Israel...!

"Is that what we are ashamed of?"

* * *

"Now I've asked you two questions, Daddy, and I want to ask a third question:

"Why did you send us to a school to learn only English, and forget to teach us Yiddish, our own language, or Hebrew, the language in which the Bible was written, the language that the prophets spoke, the language in which, they say, there is a rich and beautiful literature"

"Why did we memorize the history of all peoples, the old ones and the new ones, but omit the history of one people—our own Jewish people?

"Why are we clear about the geography of the whole world, but cannot describe the land of our ancestors, Israel?

* * *

"Now I've asked you three questions, Daddy, and I'll ask you the fourth question:

"Why do we know when it's Christmas, Washington's Birthday, Lincoln, Birthday, Decoration Day, and Thanksgiving Day, but we don't know when it's *khanike*, what *purim* is, when it's *sukes*, and what *peysakh* means?

"Why do we know who Shakespeare, Milton, Longfellow, Dickens, Thackeray, Poe, and Mark Twain were, but not who Yehuda Halevi, Gordon, Levinson, Abramowitz, Bialik, and many other poets and writers of ours were?

"Why and why and why? Why should I have to ask you any questions at all?"

* * *

"I've asked you four questions, Daddy. Now I ask you to give me an answer to my questions. And if you can't give me an answer to my questions, I'll give you the answer myself: We were slaves[7]......

The Parting Of The Reed Sea
(from Motl, Cantor Peysi's son)

A.

I had begun to tell you about the punishment we received *yom kipur* morning, on the ship *Prince Albert*. It was an ugly punishment. We'll remember it all our lives.

It started with a small thing. The night before, right after *kol nidre*, what looked like a little cloud, a black, dense cloud, became visible on the horizon. My friend Mendl and I were the first ones to see it, because while all the other Jews were still below, weeping and reciting passages from the Psalms after *kol nidre*, we, Mendl and I, were strolling around the ship.

---

[7] The classical answer to the *Four Questions* in the *peysakh hagode*

Then we retired to a corner of the deck and sat down without saying a word. It was quiet and warm, and we were feeling good but slightly sad. What Mendl was thinking, I don't know. I was thinking about God, who sits up there in Heaven. How great He must be for everything to be His! And what does He think when He hears so many Jews reciting the Psalms, praising Him, and pouring out their hearts to Him? Mama says that He hears and sees everyone, and that He knows everything, even what I am thinking secretly at this moment. If so, it's not good, because I've just been thinking about a delicious apple, a sweet pear, and at least a swallow of water. Cold water. The potatoes are giving me heartburn, but I am not allowed to drink. Who would drink water on *yom kipur*, after *kol nidre*? My brother Elie would kill me. He wants me to fast till the following evening. My mother said "We'll see". Meanwhile, she was looking for me all over the ship and couldn't find me. A sailor pointed out to her where Mendl and I were sitting, at the bow. "Motl, Motl," she yelled. "What is it, Mama?" "What do you mean, what is it? Go to bed! We have to get up early tomorrow, have you forgotten? It's a sacred day!" I really didn't want to, but one must go to bed.

B.

The next day, when we got up in the morning, the sky was completely overcast. The sea was angry and threatening. The waves rose higher than the ship and tossed the *Prince Albert* around like a splinter, a toy. The sailors started running back and forth like poisoned mice. The stewards held onto the railings. The passengers walked close to the walls and fell at almost every step. Suddenly there was a downpour of rain. Thunder-claps came rolling, one after another (God is riding on his chariot—and on *yom kipur*, no less!). One lightning-flash after another lit up the dense black clouds for a moment. The *Prince Albert* groaned, rolled, and pitched. The rain lashed us. What kind of flood was this? After all, God had sworn that He would never again loose a flood on the world!

"The Parting of the Reed Sea", said my brother Elie. And our friend Pini agreed: "Yes, it's the Parting of the Reed Sea." That was the first time the two of them had agreed on anything. The phrase "Parting of the Reed Sea" had made a hit with both of them. Each of them kept getting up, looking out, and then saying: " It's the Parting of the Reed Sea." Then he would lurch to one side of the ship and vomit up his guts, and would be seen no more. Who could think about praying or about *yom kipur*? They had even completely forgotten where in the world they were.

C.

Brokhe was the first in the family to begin. She started screaming that she was going to die any minute! Then she started cursing my brother Elie for talking her into going to America. She had known beforehand that America is Siberia. Worse than Siberia! Siberia is like gold in comparison with America! Mama wanted to defend her son. She started to lecture Brokhe that a person has to be able to bear anything, because it is an act of God, a sign. "As is written in the Torah...", but she couldn't say what was written in the Torah, because she suddenly got so nauseated that she almost fainted. Looking at her, Pini's wife, Taybl, also started to faint. So Pini said: "The women are just putting on an act for you, a comedy!" He stuck his hands in his pants pockets, tilted his hat to one side, and said: "Silly girls! Foolish ones! Why, I ask, should it bother me if the sea rages and the ship rolls about? A person, a thinking creature, will find a solution. When the ship tilts one way, I tilt the other way. That's called balance."

And, tilting back and forth, Pini demonstrated 'balance' to us. When my brother Elie also became nauseated and both of them started to vomit everything they had eaten, the other passengers did likewise. Each one barely dragged himself to his bed and fell onto it like a sheaf of hay. Only then did the real hell of the 'Parting of the Reed Sea' begin.

D.

I and my friend Mendl held out longer than anyone else. Mendl had a 'remedy' provided by an emigrant who was traveling with us and was constantly giving us advice. This emigrant was a 'smoked pipe'[8] as he described himself. He had sailed back and forth across the ocean to America

---

[8] An experienced person

three times, so he had a 'remedy': for the ocean. The remedy consisted of sitting outside on the top deck, thinking about the width of the ocean, not its length, and not thinking that you're riding a horse but rather that you're riding on a sled on the snow. In the end, however, the emigrant, the 'smoked pipe', was lying on his bed like a dead one, and I and my friend Mendl got wringing wet from the rain. We couldn't get to our beds on our own—people took pity on us and led us to our resting places.

E.

How long did the 'Parting of the Reed Sea' take? A day or two or three— I don't know. I've forgotten already. I know only one thing—once we got up from our beds, it was a joy to be alive! The sky became clear, like spun gold. The water was like glass. The *Prince Albert* raced along, scrubbed and spruced up, and its wheels cut through the water, foaming, frothing, and spraying water in all directions. The passengers came alive. Everyone, young and old, went outside into the warm sunlight, into the beautiful, bright world. Someone passed the word that they would be able to see land any minute. From a distance, it looked like a dot—a large, yellow dot. The dot kept getting bigger and broader. We could see ships in the distance, innumerable ships with tall, thin masts. All our trouble was quickly forgotten. The passengers all dressed up in holiday clothes. The women got all dolled up. My brother Elie combed his beard. Brokhe and Taybl put on their veils. My mother put on her silk Sabbath kerchief. My friend Mendl and I didn't have anything to put on, and there was actually no time—any minute we were about to sail up to the shores of America. Our eyes lit up and we felt great, just the way the Jews must have felt after the 'Parting of the Reed Sea.' We had an urge to sing a song of praise.

F.

"Sholem Aleichem to you, Columbus! Greetings, you free country, you golden, happy land!"

That's how our friend Pini greeted the new land. He tore off his hat and bowed down. And since, as you know, he was nearsighted, he didn't notice that a big, sweaty sailor with a red, sooty face was running past him, and he bumped right into him. That is to say, the tip of our friend Pini's nose hit the sooty sailor's face right between the eyes. Fortunately, the sailor was a good-natured fellow, not a nasty guy. He looked at our Pini, with his bruised nose, smiled, and muttered something under his breath. It was apparently a curse in English.

G.

Suddenly, a tumult arose. "Third-class passengers" someone said, "please go down to your compartments and stay there." First he said it nicely, then angrily. Whoever didn't hurry to comply got a jab in the behind. Everyone was there, young and old: Jewish men, women, and children; Gentiles; Turks; Gypsies. The air was extremely stuffy. They locked the door and hung an iron chain across it. Only through the windows could we see what was going on outside. We had never felt so bad as now. We looked like prisoners to one another.

"Why? For what reason?" my friend Mendl complained to me, and his eyes were burning, shooting sparks of fire.

H.

It turned out that we had indeed arrived already, arrived in America. What then? The passengers in first and second class were allowed to descend a long ladder with perhaps a hundred rungs. And what was to become of us? We were in America, after all!

"Heaven help us," a Jewish tailor from Haysin called out. He was actually not a bad fellow, but a bit of a nuisance. He was all dressed up, saw through everything, thought an awful lot of himself, and loved to be contrary. He only had to hear what you said to say just the opposite. There had been several run-ins between him and my friend Pini—my brother Elie had been barely able to pull them apart. The tailor had vowed that he would not say another word to Pini because Pini had insulted him. He had called him all sorts of ugly names: "tailor boy", "patch-maker," and "poor excuse for a tailor," and had asked him how much left-over material he had stolen in his lifetime. Now, when they had imprisoned us, the tailor from Haysin suddenly started to talk. And in Hebrew, no less!

"*Ma onu? Ma koykheynu?*—What are we ? What's the meaning of our life?" "*Moshul kakheres hanishbor*— They are treating us like garbage, if you'll excuse the comparison. When you bring in garbage, you can't ignore it."

Our friend Pini attacked him. He said it was a very poor analogy—that when you talked about America you should wash your hands first. And he kept pouring out his pretty words, as Pini can. He couldn't bear to hear a bad word against America.

The tailor from Haysin answered that he was saying neither good things nor bad things about America. He was just against the idea that everything was good and beautiful and fine—Heaven help us, we wouldn't be allowed to get off the boat so fast!

Pini lost his temper and shouted:

"What will they do with us? Preserve us with salt?"

"They won't preserve us with salt" said the tailor from Haysin bitterly, enjoying himself. "They'll take us to a place they call 'Ellis Island', and there they'll lock us up like cattle in stalls till our friends and acquaintances remember to come and get us."

Pini practically jumped out of his skin:

"He's some piece of work, this guy! This tailor-boy knows better than anyone about people's heavy hearts. He thinks he's more experienced even if he's not older! We too know that there is a Castle Garden, I mean an Ellis Island, but I haven't heard anybody say that Ellis Island was set up to hold people like cattle."

The more he talked, the angrier Pini got. He walked up to the tailor from Haysin as if he intended to tear him to pieces. The tailor got frightened and moved away, saying:

"Hah! Just look at him! We've hurt his feelings—bad-mouthed his America! Big deal! When we're a few hours older, we'll be wiser."

Khayim Zhitlovski (1865-1943) was the principal theorist and architect of Yiddishism, and was one of the organizers and guiding spirits of the famous 1908 Czernowitz Conference on Jewish Language.

~

Khayim Zhitlovski

What Is Assimilation?

On the face of it, it's extremely embarrassing to ask such a questions in these times. Who doesn't know what assimilation is? Who doesn't know that assimilation is the antithesis of nationalism, its worst enemy, against which it must carry on the bitterest struggle?

Yes, that is true, but nevertheless the following situation often occurs: Two nationalists of two different tendencies are arguing about the most important problem, how to respond to the Jewish national question. Both are secure in their hatred of assimilation. Both may be convinced initially that they have a common enemy that they must combat: assimilation. But if they go a bit more deeply into the tools for combating it, it turns out that they find themselves forced to accuse each other of assimilationism!

"I don't understand it," an opponent of mine once said to me, "I don't understand how you, who call yourself a Jewish nationalist, can be an adherent of 'Jargonism.' Isn't the jargon that the Jews speak a German dialect? Is it not a product of the assimilation process that the Jews underwent in the Middle Age in the German countries? Is it not the embodiment and symbol of assimilation? Don't we have to look upon the Yiddishists as assimilationists? Isn't our Hebraism the only way of shaking off the last traces of assimilation?"

Another opponent of mine, also a devoted nationalist, also a mortal enemy of assimilation, expressed himself in a conversation to the effect that he sees nothing wrong if we American Jews start to speak English and completely forget our Yiddish. Why not? English is a very cultural language and could so easily be accepted by the Jewish people.

"What do you mean!" I protest, "That is pure assimilationism"!"

"What assimilationism? Who's talking here about no longer being Jews? We have to see to it that every Jew is permeated with the great traditions of his wonderful past, with the exciting ideas of his brilliant future in a land of his own. We have to see to it that he absorbs into himself, with all his spiritual energy, that wonderful past and strives toward that exciting future. We can achieve better through cultured, rich English than with poor, crippled Jargon. And once we have achieved it, what bullets of assimilation will be able to strike us?"

Very often in the nationalist literature, one can encounter the idea that Jews cannot assimilate in any case. Consider this: despite the fact that in many West European countries Jews have, in their external lives, become completely the same as their surrounding neighbors, they still swim around on the surface, "like oil on the water." For example, the small group of Italian Jews, who speak Italian, are patriotic Italians, and consider themselves members of the Italian people, are still a separate Jewish group to which anyone can point with his finger.

Here are three cases with three different interpretations of assimilation: In the first case, which considers the Yiddish language as a product of German assimilation, an assimilated Jew is one who has taken on a foreign language. In the second case, it is one who gives his soul to the foreign nation, who does not live with the ideals of his own history. In the third case, a Jew is truly assimilated only if he has completely lost his Jewishness, and even his Jewish appearance, so that he can no longer be distinguished in any way from the surrounding populace.

It is clear that something here is not clear. The three quite separate cases can indeed be encompassed within a single concept, but there is a great difference in how you apply it. Different interpretations of assimilation lead to different programs for combating it. It is therefore necessary to clarify the matter, if for no other reason than to know who is who, and who can join whom against whom.

One can best learn about the essence of assimilation from those practical experts who concern themselves with it 'wholesale'. I mean those peoples who have taken on the task of assimilating other peoples. They exist, thank God, in considerable number. The Russians russify, the Germans germanize, the Poles polonize, the Hungarians magyarize, etc. They all see to it that they assimilate those parts of the population of their countries that belong to other peoples.

What do they mean by assimilate? When have they reached their goal?

It may be that they would want all the 'foreign' portions of their populace to be swallowed up without a trace by their people, but they don't need that final goal of the assimilation process. It doesn't bother the Russian assimilators that the Poles and the Finns remain in the places where they live, keep to themselves, and bring children into the world who have all the physical and mental signs of a Pole or a Finn. The russifyer wants only one thing: that the Pole or Finn stop speaking Polish or Finnish and start speaking Russian. That is the only task of the Russian assimilator. Russifying some region or some portion of the populace means making the entire life of the region or portion of the populace play itself out in the Russian language.

And all the other assimilating peoples set themselves the same goal. When the Prussian germanizers, with the help of the Prussian government undertook to buy up all the districts in Prussian Poland and settle them with Germans, they were motivated by the fact that the Poles were unwilling to become germanized, to accept the language of the people into which they were supposed to become assimilated.

The russifyer, germanizer, polonizer, etc. demanded only one thing from the 'foreigners': change your language to mine, accept my language — then you'll be mine.

And it's no wonder that he is so 'modest' in his demands and is satisfied with that 'little bit'. A people is an organism that creates human culture. The culture expresses itself on all sides and in all manifestations of the life of the people, in all its thoughts, feelings, aspirations, and accomplishments. But most important of all are the thoughts, because "the basic thing is the initial thought" — everything that people do must start as a thought before it can become an accomplishment. But the thought is always expressed in particular words, and the words belong to a particular language.

Language, therefore, is the substance of culture. Everything in culture is built by language and from language. If humanity should accept a single language for everyone, then there would develop a single, general-human culture and peoples would disappear as separate culture-creating organisms.

This is not the place to go into whether that is possible or whether it would be a joy or a catastrophe. I myself think it's impossible, and that it would be a catastrophe for human progress. But that's not what we're talking about now. It's more important now for all of us to understand why the assimilator is satisfied with the 'little bit' of language. Once he has devoured the language of a people, he has devoured the substance with which a people can create its culture. If he binds a people to him with the threads of his language, he seats it at the spinning-wheel on which the culture of his people is spun.

Assimilators of Jews the world over have always understood that, and understand it very well now too. The Orshanskis in Russia in no way wanted the Jews to mix completely with the Russian people; they wanted only to 'russify' us, i.e., to make us start to think and speak in Russian. By that alone they were assimilators. And if they had achieved their ideal, if we had exchanged our language for Russian, we would then have been assimilated, just as the Jews in Germany, France, Italy, England, and Holland are already assimilated.

National assimilation is language assimilation. National struggle is language struggle. That's how the world understands it, that's how it turns out according to the logic of the national problem. Does that means that we Jews who speak Yiddish are assimilated Jews? Yes, very definitely! Once upon a time, we assimilated into the German people of the Middle Ages, but we left Germany. The language that we took over from the foreigner became our own; it acquired its own image and became something quite different from the German language. Germans can no longer create their German culture in it, but Jews can and do express their cultural life and creativity in it. It has therefore become the Jews' language, the substance of the Jews' culture, i.e. the essence of its individuality as a people in the world.

Attacking that language, therefore, means attacking Jewish individuality. This enormously important fact has long since penetrated the consciousness of our people. It gave its language the name Yiddish (Jewish)—that means that our people knows and feels that there is only one people in the world that uses that language as a substantive basis for its culture—the Jewish people.

That is inherent in the term "Yiddish" that the people has created. Our people is not guilty of creating the ridiculous curse-word "Jargon." The libelous "Jargon," as a name for our language, was thought up by educated people, assimilationists, whatever the mask behind which they hide.

Assimilation in our life is therefore the process that wants to abolish Yiddish and exchange it for some other language. Only against assimilation do we nationalists have to fight. It makes no difference to us which language wants to devour the basis of our life and creativity, and with what pretensions it comes to us.

Assimilation is everything that leads to the disappearance of Yiddish. Our national struggle is a struggle for everything that strengthens the position of Yiddish.

Avrom Lyesin (pen name of Abraham Walt) (1872-1938), in addition to being one of the finest poets in Yiddish, was the editor of *Di Tsukunft*, the world's premier Yiddish literary magazine, for about a quarter of a century. His poem *Yiddish*, printed here, is an acknowledged world masterpiece.

~

Avrom Lyesin

Yiddish

In sleepless nights she used to come to me
with her dear grace.
Where she came from
has remained her secret.
In the quiet pre-dawn hours,
she'd come in gently trembling —
a whisper of some sort of prayer,
a shimmer from some sort of glow.
Her eyes would shine to me
with a soft, trusting light.
She'd lay her hand on my head
and cool my fevered brow.
The room would turn white and peaceful
at her wondrous touch
when the two wings on her back
shimmered with whiteness.
I'd hear her voice,
beautifully melodious,
like the voice of my mother
reading from the Yiddish Pentateuch on Sabbath,
long ago:

"I don't come to you radiant with God's word,
as my sister used to long ago,
sanctified by ancient, glorious times,
with lightning and thunder in her voice.

"I don't come to you, as she did, from a sunny height,
reflecting the purity of the blue heavens.
I don't have the softness of green meadows
or the wild, desolate beauty of proud mountain-cliffs.

"I come to you, my child, from silent exiles
in crowded, sealed-off ghettos.
I possess only the charm of pious prayers,
only the beauty of dying to sanctify God's name.

"Though I don't carry within me the blinding lightning
or the flaming sunbeams that perform miracles,
I do carry the sparkle of starry legends,
the precious moonlight of the soul.

"From Worms, from Mainz, from Speyer,
through Prague and Lublin to Odessa,
a single flame kept spreading,
a single miracle.
Our mortal enemies always hovered there —
thousand-eyed Death lurked nearby.
There, desolate and sorrowful,
I accompanied your ancestors.

"I endured every danger with them
for hundreds of years,
and I absorbed their rage and sorrow.

"I forged, through the generations,
the miracle of will-despite-pain,
to live for sacred teachings
and die steadfastly for them.
If pure holiness
reflects only from torture and pain,
then I, my child, am the one for you —
I am your holiest one.

"Though God's presence hasn't revealed itself to me,
nor have I experience prophetic visions,
the lust to sin
of the priest who shamefully kneeled before Baal
is also foreign to me.

"And though foreign to me is the enthusiasm of the victor
whom history has wreathed with sunbeams,
so too is the cruelty of the warrior
who lives by the bloody sword.

"I haven't had titans
who sparkle to the heavens like lonely icebergs in the sky,
but our entire people has been purified by misfortune
and sanctified by pain.

"I used to absorb the blood and tears
and the cries of pain,
and the more I heard the agonized cries of martyrs,
the holier I became.

"I've sung a song of Torah
to a child in his cradle —
after that, the melody resounded
in his soul, all his life.
I used to glow in hearts
when the reader spoke from the lectern,
and shout exultantly
when the *magid* preached.
I sent along fervent prayers
with Jewish mothers —
I prepared great, silent martyrs
with holiness,
led them through their hours of darkest need
with the women's Bible,
and lovingly adorned those heroic deeds

that they call living.
A treasure for the people
was preserved in me:
the folk-soul, fresh and pious,
an incomparable, immeasurable treasure.

"And furthermore, my child,
carry on the teachings of generations,
altered though they may be,
to live and die for sacred teachings
and to be a stubborn people of martyrs.

"If you seek to brighten the ghettos with beauty,
then know that no beauty is as beautiful
as the beauty of human souls often is
and the beauty of the folk-soul itself always is.

"Look for that quiet beauty in me,
and do not fear that someday I'll be gone.
Will even the people live forever?
Will even life itself live forever?

"As long as I'm so dear to you, my child,
and as long as we're still together here,
and as long as the fire still burns in your blood,
don't let the hour of inspiration go by."

That's how she used to speak,
and everything was brightened by her love.
In her call, I would hear
the sorrow of the world calling.
And then, in the quiet, exalted dawn,
something would happen:

I'd feel enlightened
and I'd see hidden wonders;

pure and illuminated in white,
my song would rise for her;
timely words would rise and fall,
syllable after syllable,
and I'd break out into tears
of loving, creative joy.

Weeping, I'd swear to her
to remain a link in the chain —
to carry on farther and farther through the generations
the miracle of will-despite-pain,
of living for sacred teachings
and dying steadfastly for them.

New York, 1922

Kalmen Marmor (1876-1956) was a distinguished essayist and one of the earliest historians of Yiddish literature in America. He was for a time the editor of the Labor Zionist *Der Yidisher Kemfer*, but was also fascinated for a time by the Communist international dream. His autobiography contained a wealth of reminiscences about personalities in Yiddish literature that he had known.

~

Kalmen Marmor

The Beginning of Yiddish Literature In America

The wave of immigration from Russia, accelerated by the Tsarist pogroms against the Jews in 1881, changed the character of the Yiddish speaking community in America. The new immigrants never found occupations other than peddling—they were drawn into various American industries. There the former artisans, tradesmen, store-clerks, yeshiva students, university students, and teachers were transformed into workers and cogs in the machine—into industrial proletarians. This transformation entailed enormous suffering for those transformed. At the same time, however, the strength to unite in the battle to improve their lives was born. The only thing they needed was to become conscious of their strength so they could fight and win.

The new circumstances evoked 'new singers' with 'new songs.' A new Yiddish literature began to be created, based on a new way of life in an environment that was free of the feudal restrictions of the old country. Its writers were recruited from the kind of intellectuals who, in the old country, would have written in Hebrew or the local language, but not in Yiddish. In the new world and under the new circumstances, however, they drew close to the Jewish working masses. They became progressive and socialistic builders and creators of the Yiddish literature and press, which Jews had not had previously. The new life of the Jewish masses as industrial workers working for wages in factories and shops required a press that was quite different from that which could have been created publicly under the semi-feudal regimes in the Eastern Europe of the 80's. The political freedom to speak and write without a censor, to present political and economic demands, and to strike and demonstrate, was a new development for both the Jewish masses and the Jewish intellectuals.

It was an enormously difficult task. Even those that were more or less acquainted with the literature of the folkist *Maskilim* could not use it as a model. The *Maskilim* fought against tax collectors and insurers, but here it was necessary to come out against the entire system of living at someone else's expense. For that it was easier to find a model in the social prophets of the Bible than in the Hebrew and Yiddish literature of Eastern Europe. They had to create something new that would be suitable for Jewish industrial workers. This made those creators pioneers of a new Yiddish poetry and a new Yiddish prose.

Outwardly, the early Yiddish literature in America did not represent a direct continuation of the Yiddish literature of Eastern Europe, but rather of that which arose in the small community of Jews who had emigrated to England. The Yiddish writers there were influenced by international sources. They found their models in the progressive and revolutionary writers of the industrial worker- masses in England, France, and Germany.

This was not because these pioneer Yiddish workers were not acquainted with the old Yiddish cultural legacy or had rejected it. The classical Yiddish writers of Eastern Europe would also have had to follow their path if they had come to England or America in the 80's. Their urgent need to improve and beautify Jewish life would have made them express themselves in a different form and context than in the old country. Life in the industrial democracies with their Jewish shop- and factory—workers doubtless dictated that the Yiddish classic writers speak to their people in a new way, for in that sense (i.e., the need to work for the welfare of the Jewish folk-masses), the beginning of Yiddish literature in America, as was the case earlier in England, was a continuation of its progressive creations in the old country.

Those who laid the foundations of the progressive literature in the old country were inspired by social ideas. At first, the most important thing for them was to clean out the medieval dust from Jewish life; later, under the influence of the new social trends in the world, they became permeated by the protests against oppression and injustice. They drew frightful pictures of those who lived on "the blood of the poor" (little people, such as tax collectors, marshals, usurers, and all sorts of other "blood-suckers"). They became masters at depicting the pity-evoking image of Jewish poverty, the wretched "beast of burden" that was tortured by his own people and strangers. However, they saw no way out of that situation.

The exploited small merchants and self-employed artisans could not unite in common action against their oppressors. There was a good reason why their 'awakeners' had to flee from the field of battle.

Uniting became possible for the first time with the development of Jewish organized labor in England and America. Jewish organized labor, its trade-unions, its workers' education associations, clubs, and libraries, and other cultural institutions solidified the people and created a Jewish social consciousness that provided continuity to Jewish national life, even though it tended toward internationalism.

The actual creator of Yiddish culture in America, and thereby also of Yiddish literature, was Jewish organized labor; its pioneering worker-poets and socialist propagandists became the foundation-layers of American Yiddish literature. These pioneers, with few exceptions, not only were socialists, in the broad sense of the word, but were also inspired by powerful Jewish national feeling. They were permeated by the need to enlighten the Jewish masses and raise them to a higher cultural level.

The horrible situation of Jewish labor in the 80's moved the Yiddish pioneers to devote themselves principally to social motifs. The Jewish sweatshop-bosses exerted all their strength to prevent the organizing of Jewish labor. Their nationalistic-orthodox press and religious leadership sought to frighten the young Jewish workers into believing that belonging to a union and fighting for better working conditions was a sin against God. They branded the socialist speakers and writers as Christian missionaries, and the trade unions as missionary societies.

The participation of these so-called Jewish nationalist and orthodox leaders in the agitations and false accusations by the sweatshops-bosses against their organized Jewish workers further deepened the chasm between them and the Jewish labor movement. In that atmosphere of exacerbated class warfare between Jewish organized labor and the bosses, there could not be any talk of national relatedness between the oppressive bosses and their enslaved workers, between well-to-do Jews and poor Jews. Vastly more important was the enlightenment of the broad masses of Jewish workers about the great significance of international solidarity between the workers of all nations. Jewish organized labor and its pioneers from the

Yiddish literature and press, despite their strongly Jewish national feelings, accepted the new slogan: "All workers are comrades" (motto of the Jewish tailors' union in London in the 70') instead of the old one: "All Jews are brothers", which was a mockery in the mouths of oppressive Jewish sweatshop-bosses, so-called Jewish nationalists, and the religious.

For the same reason, those literary pioneers who had had considerable faith in the Judaism of the simple folk fought against it bitterly when it became a harmful weapon in the hands of the bosses against the interests of Jewish workers.

* * *

As already mentioned, the intellectual forces of Jewish wage-laborers in American obtained great assistance in their difficult task from the Jewish proletarian culture-center in London. Industrialization of the immigrant Eastern European Jewish masses began in London as far back as the early 70's. There attempts were made at that time to organized them into trade unions. The London of the 70's was also influenced by the first propagandist for socialism among the Jews, Aaron Lieberman (1843-1880). He organized a Jewish socialist association and a tailors' union, as early as the summer of 1876.

Aaron Lieberman was a brilliant stylist in Hebrew. He was a contributor to the socialist publications of the 70's in Russian and German. He turned to the Jewish masses in Yiddish. At that time, he had nowhere to print his Yiddish pieces. His London comrades knew about them, however, and were influenced by him to try their hands, too, at writing in Yiddish.

From one of Lieberman's stories, *Mayse Sotn* (A Diabolical Deception), which exists only in manuscript, it can be seen that he wrote fine Yiddish for that time. Here is a description by him of how primitive people lived before the Devil seduced them into chasing after money:

"People all live as brothers. Each of them busies himself with his heart's desire, insofar as his strength and understanding permit. This one plans and seeks a piece of land, that one trims fruit-trees, another one fishes, and still another one grazes cattle that he has domesticated. Some cleverer ones undertake to make life easier or more satisfying."

What Aaron Lieberman couldn't accomplish in the 70's, his comrades and followers began to bring to realization in the 80's. The most important of them was Morris Vintshevski (1856-1932), who came to American from London as a political refugee in 1879. In his Lithuanian homeland in Kovno, he wrote poems in Hebrew. Working as a book-keeper in a bank in Konigsberg, he was drawn into the German Socialist movement. He wrote political articles and serials in Hebrew and German at the time, and sometimes in Yiddish too. He made contact with Lieberman's socialist magazine, *Ha-emes* (The Truth), and when the latter ceased publication, Vintshevski edited a magazine in Hebrew in Konigsberg. When the German government promulgated its anti-socialist law in 1878, Vintshevski was arrested, found guilty and deported. In London, he lived at first from his private means, but after 1880 he again became a book-keeper in a bank. In 1884, when the Social Democratic Federation was founded in London, Vintshevski grew close to its leaders, especially William Morris and Karl Marx's daughter Eleanor and her husband. In that same year, Vintshevsky helped found in London the weekly Yiddish magazine *The Little Polish Jew*, of which he became editor. He began to write his labor-poems, which became a model for America as well. His first labor-poem was a free translation from an English poem, *The Song of the Shirt*, by Thomas Hood, but it sounds like an original creation in Yiddish.

For a while, Vintshevski depicted only the loneliness of self-employed artisans, such as seamstresses, shoe-shine boys, homeless girls who sold matches, and other such figures of a modern big city. Most of his images were universal, and were not limited to the immigrant population. On the contrary, he depicted mostly the poverty of the native English worker masses, whom he had seen die of hunger and cold in their wealthy Fatherland no less frequently than the immigrant toilers. In Vintshevski's picture–gallery of London poverty, one therefore finds fewer portraits of Jewish immigrants than might have been expected.

His fame in America increased with the founding of the *Worker's Friend* (London, July 1885), the first newspaper published directly by Jewish organized labor. The *Worker's Friend* was distributed effectively for five years continuously among Jewish workers in America. There were even radical organizations established specifically to support it financially.

Vintshevski's poems in the *Worker's Friend* did not just depict the way
of life of Jewish sweatshop workers, but also roused them to battle against
their exploiters and oppressors. In his poem *To the Worker's Friend* (July
1885), Vintshevski announced that "those who saw and plane and whittle
every day, who draw the cobbler's thread and knead the clay, live poorly
and sadly, and have no house or home"; that "those who plow, sow, and
bake bread are unable to find bread when slack times or illness cast them
into poverty"; that "those who spin the wool and sew the clothing, who
build the houses with sweat and effort, themselves live stuffed into dark
rooms like cattle in stalls." He ended with the prediction that in time
"working would be an honor and going around idle would be shameful."
Vintshevski's voice sounded even more powerfully in his battle-poem
It Stirs (June 1886). There one also hears a Biblical note:

Do you see, children,
how the golden calf quivers and shakes?
It's because it hears now
how the slaughterer's knife is being sharpened for it.
You, the calf, the cattle-idols,
the unclean of Canaan,
he, the working man,
now wants to obliterate!

Vintshevski's battle-poem had no model in prior Jewish literature in Hebrew or Yiddish. It was influenced by the worldwide revolutionary poetry
of the nineteenth century. It was influenced by Shelley, Johns, and Morris
in England; Hugo Poiter and Beranger in France; and Heine, Herweg, and
Frolingrat in Germany. Most important, however, was the influence on
Vintshevski of the worker-masses themselves, their poverty, hope, and
struggles.
And if Vintshevski occasionally wanted to pluck a string from the Jewish past, he did not use the motif of the Jewish exodus from Egypt. The former *Maskil* knew all too well that, according to Jewish tradition, that
liberation did not come through the organization and courage in battle of
enlightened slaves but through external forces. Vintshevski therefore pre-

ferred to recall the freedom struggle of the Maccabees. In his *Marseil-laise* (March 1887), Vintshevski declared to the Jewish workers:

Even in the 'Land of the Hebrews,'
you would have remained slaves of the men with money!
All right, then! Show the world
that you are descended from the Maccabees!

In general, however, Vintshevski's battle-poems were thoroughly inter-national. He was like the social prophets of long ago, a 'folk-prophet.' He addressed his Yiddish poems to the workers of all peoples and all lands. In his poem *A Broom and Sweep* (October 1889), Vintshevski spoke for worldwide struggling labor, which would sweep out, with its mighty broom of revolution, all parasites, and would ready their heirs "to eventually live in the future society as progressive and brotherly people." And at the end of the 80's, Vintshevski came out with his 'prophecy' to all peoples, in the name of the spirit of freedom which was coming "to free the nations from cannons, armies, and spies"; "to teach them to honor work," and "to live in peace and happiness… amid pagans, Christians, and Jews."

Vintshevski's labor-poems and battle-poems in the 80's were written in polished Yiddish, in all sorts of rhythms. They organized and led the Jewish workers in the struggle for a better life, and likewise developed their taste for beauty, rhythm, and sound. His ordinary poems, dramatic poems, satires, parodies, and serials, as well as his translations of the novels of the time, enriched the Yiddish language through new words and usages and provided models for Yiddish literature in America in all its forms. When he later emigrated to America in the first half of the 90's, he was met by broad masses of readers who had developed their ideas and esthetics from his work of the 80's.

Avrom Reyzn (1876-1953) was one of the most famous and beloved of Yiddish poets, and was also a masterly writer of short stories. He was the poet of the defeated and rejected—ordinary, gray, colorless people—but he infused his poems with love and compassion. His deceptively simple (though beautifully crafted) poetry led to his being thought of as a "folk poet."

~

Avrom Reyzn

Our Song

To all of those who take along
to every land our lovely song,

in tones of joy or tones of sorrow,
both short and long, today, tomorrow,

in new or ancient rhythmic form,
of sun or rain or winter storm,

of hum-drum days or holidays,
of life's green times or evil ways,

of new — the city's iron rails —
or old — the village hills and dales,

of lovely brides, with braids or curls,
or poor and quiet little girls,

of battle or forgiving ways,
of ancient or of modern days —
no matter!

As long as songs ring out aloud
to make us Jews feel tall and proud.

Yiddish

Yiddish, O sweet language mine —
where'er I am, for you I pine.
'Midst strangers here and there,
you are my home-strength anywhere.

Where'er I lay my weary bones,
I hear your sounds, your homey tones.
Through my window, where'er I be,
the sounds come drifting in to me.

And not just tone, but also word
from distant times can still be heard.
Where'er I am and hear the sound,
I feel my brothers all around.

And not just words, but also book —
Yiddish books how sweet they look!
For Perets, Mendele, and more
my Yiddish land to me restore.

I never feel astray, alone
when I can hear the Yiddish tone.
With books and journals all in tow,
I feel at home where'er I go.

A Man

Into the house there comes a man—
he's weary, bent with care,
and at the doorstep stops quite still
and casts his eyes 'round everywhere.

No hint of human feeling
is present on his face.
He puts his hand out silently
and begs for alms and grace.

It is a man, the world's great crown,
the highest, brightest one,
but see how lowly he can be,
how common—uglier there's none.

The smallest worm upon the ground
finds food — he needs no aid —
but a man, the crown, must beg kind folk
to have his hunger pangs allayed.

I Envy Them

I envy them, my brothers dear
and sisters there beyond the sea.
I feel like a withered leaf
that's torn off from the tree.

I'd wander there along with them
in loneliness and fear and want,
and share their tears along with them,
though fear of death would haunt.

I envy them their suffering,
would count myself twice blessed
to share the sorrows plaguing them
that never let them rest.

Into that group of wanderers
I'd join and share their fears.

We'd send our prayers to Heaven's halls
and wipe away our tears.

The children who would follow there
I'd teach of want and need.
With fear-filled eyes they'd learn to feel
the terror of the foeman's deed.

I'd lead them through the fields and leas,
through swamps and bogs of loam.
I'd stroke their pale and youthful cheeks
and comfort: "Soon we'll be back home."

When night would fall and bring more fear —
too late to wander more that day —
I'd pad for them with all my clothes
a bed on stacks of hay.

With kisses I would warm their hearts —
to sleep I'd rock them with my tears,
so dreams of joy might come to them
and take away their fears.

The Prayer

We hear the distant thunder
and lightning blinds our eyes.
O God please spare poor people
beneath your threat'ning skies.

They labor long in meadows,
so far away from home,
and have no dry protection,
no cover, trees, or dome.

Their wagons now are trav'ling
on roads with heavy loads.
The inns are still much farther
along the soggy roads.

In market stand with baskets,
with apples, greens , and bread,
they stand outside in downpour,
and cannot shield their head.

And all of those who wander,
who have no place to hide,
protect them, God, from weather —
to havens be their guide.

From Home

There was so very little there —
why does so much remain?
What keeps your essence still alive
to yearn, remember, love again?

A single house stood on a hill,
another stood bent over there.
From whence did all the beauty come
that softly hovered everywhere?

The mighty castles you forget —
the ones you've seen while wand'ring by.
The least of houses from back home —
its image stays within your eye.

You've crossed the sea in sturdy ships,
forgotten mighty waves and storm.

The little pond within the town,
you still recall exact its form.

Along your road you've seen great trees
and many broken by the wind did see,
but still your mind can conjure up
your Gentile neighbor's little tree.

You've heard so many lovely songs —
the sounds of most are long forgot.
But why though some are gone long since,
the ones from home are not.

I And The World

If things were bad with all the world
and things were good for me alone,
I'd surely then invite the world
to share the comforts of my home.

I'd comfort it, give my caress,
and say: "Don't worry so, dear world."
Until it slowly came around
and stood up straight upon the ground.

If all the world were happy now
and only I were full of pain,
I'd come to it and make demand:
"Now you must make me whole again."

But things are bad for both of us:
The world's in pain and I too now.
The world has no one who can help,
nor is there one to show me how.

Ordinary Jewish Girls

I walk the noisy, narrow streets —
the time is six o'clock at night,
and rows of careworn Jewish girls
pass by now, fading like the light.

O Jewish girls, you sweatshop girls,
your faces still show secretly
the charm of former Jewish towns,
a glow that ev'ryone can see.

You walk along the stony streets —
the sky is bleakly overcast.
But still your clothes aromas breathe
of village days from times long past.

And if I deeply look at you,
I see much more, oh so much more:
the crowns of bygone centuries
still shine beneath the yokes you bore.

For all of you are princesses—
your pedigree is in your face.
How you've been enslaved now!
Who will bring you back to God's sweet grace?

A Little Negro Boy

A little Negro boy, with skin like soot,
was playing near my house, out back.
My heart got sad and frightened then:
My God! Your creature looks so black!

But suddenly the black child laughed
while rolling, playing on the ground.
My God, I thought, what's wrong with me?
I've rarely heard such lovely sound.

Then I recalled my brother's laughs
when he was small and near to me.
The mem'ry of those lovely sounds
now made the black child dear to me

When I Kindle The *Khanike* Light

My stars have long since gone away
and dark night has replaced the day.
But night recedes, the world grows bright
when I kindle the *khanike* light.

My strength and pride are gone, you see;
the wild foe laughs and mocks at me.
But now revives my ancient might
when I kindle the *khanike* light.

My poems have no words to say
of strength and valor gone away,
but they resound throughout the night
when I kindle the *khanike* light.

My eye is dimmed by an ancient tear;
it's almost blinded now, I fear.
But see how it reflects so bright
when I kindle the *khanike* light.

Yehoyesh (pen name of Yehoyesh-Shloyme Blumgartn) (1872-1927) was a contemporary of the "proletarian poets" but wrote in an entirely different vein: wordly, intellectual, emotional, and lyrical. He is most renowned for his magnificent Yiddish translation of the Hebrew Bible (the *Tanakh*.)

~

Yehoyesh

A Song for the Sabbath Day

A song for the Sabbath day:
how it pours through my heart,
joyful and full of holiday spirit,
a chorus of sweet sounds.
A song for the Sabbath day.

A song for the Sabbath day:
the song derives from no man.
Only white angels
sang it in Paradise
on the first High Sabbath
after the Great Creation of the world.
And the sun and stars —
all of them sang along
a song for the Sabbath day.

Yes, the sun and the stars
(which hadn't yet seen
any tears on our little world)
sang radiantly:
a song for the Sabbath day.

And from the Birds of Paradise,
a fountain of trills
shot into the choir —
they twittered:
a song for the Sabbath day.

And the flowers of Paradise
rocked back and forth bashfully
and sang along
in their colorful, aromatic
flower-tongue
     a song for the Sabbath day.

And the great, gigantic trees —
they lent their giant ears.
They bent over gravely
and whispered rustling sounds:
     a song for the Sabbath day.

Then, on His Throne of Glory,
with a divinely lovely smile,
the Creator sang along
     a song for the Sabbath day.

1892

Folk-Motif

O mother darling, mother dear,
untie the beads from 'round my throat.
The Kaiser[9] soon will travel here —
I'll help him with his coat.

O daughter mine, my dearest one,
don't let your heart oppress.
Let not the Kaiser fancy you —
you'll wear no beads to dress.

O mother darling, mother dear,
please comb my hair an ugly way,

[9] Here the reference is to the RussianTsar, not the German Kaiser.

or else the Kaiser soon will send
to have me come away.

O daughter mine, my dearest one,
I hope no plans he's made.
Let not the Kaiser fancy you –
just tie your hair in braid.

O mother darling, mother dear,
please hurry smudge my face.
The Kaiser soon will travel here
to take me to his kingly place.

O daughter mine, my dearest one,
you must not be so rash.
Let not the Kaiser fancy you —
I'll black your face with ash.

O mother darling, mother dear,
I'm weeping bitter tears.
The Kaiser soon will travel here —
no such event in all my years.

O daughter mine, my dearest one,
now fly like arrows from a bow.
I fear that he will fancy you —
no peace will you then know.

1913

A Kiss For Mother

A mother's playing with her child,
and father's filled with joy.
A thread is weaving silently,
'round mother, dad, and boy.

Says father to his darling child:
"To mother give a kiss."
The boy does so and laughs with glee —
all three in joyous bliss.

Says mother to her loving child:
"Give daddy twenty more."
He gleefully kisses daddy —
they're happy to the core.

A silent thread is weaving now
around the loving three.
The parents feel like bride and groom,
the way they used to be.

1914

Marjorie

Back, throat, and arms,
naked;
for modesty,
two shawls on her shoulders;
her maiden's bosom
half uncovered,
the lower half
bursting out of its blue tulle wrap;
slender, jaunty hips

playing peek-a-boo
with loose, transparent folds;
black locks of hair
brushed back from her forehead.
A child's face,
and three-quarters of that child's face
consists of eyes,
big eyes
that question, laugh, and joke,
and sing a potpourri
from prairie-lands and tall trees,
from a thousand miles of cornfields
and summer on the Mississippi
and stags in the mountains
and the like —
from skyscrapers
and limousines
and white nights on Herald Square.
All together,
a warm
and trembling
nimble knot of snakes —
a tall
and white
and shimmering bird —
a foaming,
laughing,
bright Niagara.

Sholem Ash (1880-1957) was one of the great novelists in Yiddish or any other language. He was extremely popular among the Jewish readership till he began writing his "Christian" novels, starting with *The Nazarene*. These were deeply unpopular among the Jews, and Ash was virtually "excommunicated" during the latter part of his life.

~

Sholem Ash

Jewish Eyes
(In memory of the Jewish children of Poland)

For weeks and weeks, Rivke Rabinovitsh, the wife of a well-known Zionist activist and Hebrew teacher in Warsaw, had hidden her five-year old daughter, Mirele, with her in the barracks of the concentration camp in Germany to which she had been dragged to work. Her husband had long since been taken away from her while they were still in Warsaw, as had her parents and her eight-year-old son. She didn't know their whereabouts, though she nourished the hope that they were alive somewhere in a concentration camp, just as all the other women there with her in the concentration camp believed or convinced themselves that they believed.

Mrs. Rabinovitsh was in the prime of life, in her thirties, a healthy, strong woman with an energetic face that was far from ugly. Her beautiful, black, sparkling eyes, like two ripe cherries filled with eye-fluids, filled her charming, smoothly sculpted eye-sockets beneath the arcs of her black eyebrows. At that time, the Germans had needed strong workers' hands to clean, wash, and repair the dresses, shirts, and other clothing that they had removed from the men, women, and children they had sent to their deaths, in order to distribute the clothing to the German populace. That was why they had spared Mrs. Rabinovitsh's life and had sent her to the concentration camp, to make use of her ability to work before they sent her also to where her husband and son and all her relatives were — to death.

Mrs. Rabinovitsh had undertaken from the very first minute something that was hard to believe possible under the conditions in which she found herself — to rescue her little girl from the hands of the destroyers and take her along to the concentration camp to which they were sending all the other women. She had previously succeeded in accomplishing what no other Jewish mother in Warsaw had accomplished, namely to hide her lit-

88

tle girl from the eyes of the Germans during the whole time she was in the Warsaw ghetto. She simply placed the child in a hiding-place in an attic, where she secretly fed her. The child lived there behind the large chest in the attic for weeks and months, and never saw the light of day. She got so used to her hiding-place that it seemed to her that the dark corner in which she lay hidden behind the chest was her natural existence, and she no longer cried when her mother came to her as she had in the beginning. All the fear and the danger in which they found themselves were transmitted to the child, young as she was. She understood her situation and cooperated with her mother in hiding from the torturers.

After Mrs. Rabinovitsh had the great good fortune to be selected for work and not for death, like the other women, she decided to take the child with her to the concentration camp. Mirele, who had already had a year's experience in conspiracy, was so well trained that she helped her mother with her plan. Her mother simply pressed Mirele to her body under her shirtwaist and coat. In that way, she smuggled the child into the freight-wagon into which they had stuffed her and the other women, and later into the barracks of the concentration camp in Germany to which they had dragged her.

About eighty or ninety women, all Jewish, were packed together in the barracks, driven there from various countries. The number varied — women came and women left. Sometimes they brought in a dozen new ones, but there was never room for even half of them. They lay on wooden benches covered with a bit of hay. They were squeezed together, one next to another. Most of them were mothers who had been robbed of their children, some of whom had been killed before their eyes. They tried with all their might to suppress the hysteria that seized them when they remembered their children, because whenever they manifested the least hysteria or loss of control they were taken away and sent to a different camp, from which no one ever returned. So the women themselves helped one another to suppress any outcry that might erupt from them when the longing for their murdered children re-awoke in them — each demanded calm and endurance from the others.

"You have to see, do, and outwait everything — outwait it and survive it," they encouraged one another.

And they did outwait and survive, bit their lips and their tongues, and choked back the outcries that erupted from them at night in bed.

That was the time of crisis, when the maternal feelings would awake in one of them and she would begin to shriek: "Dovidl, my Dovidl — where are you?"

The other women would throw themselves on her, press her head down to the straw bed, and stuff her fist in her mouth so she would bite her own flesh and quiet down, because danger lurked for everyone.

When Mrs. Rabinovitsh brought her own child quietly into the barracks, it seemed to the other women that a miracle had occurred — no, that the heavens themselves had opened and a child had come back to them from Paradise to be a solace for them and a reminder of their own children. Mirele was not only Mrs. Rabinovitsh's child — she became everyone's child. Mirele's flesh and blood became their own. It seemed to them as if God had taken all the children they had lost and kneaded them together into the one small body of Mirele, and had given her the eyes of all Jewish children and sent her to them in their pain and suffering. They were not jealous of Mrs. Rabinovitsh — they never considered Mirele the child of just one woman. The maternal instinct in them, which had almost died, found new nourishment. All of them considered themselves Mirele's mothers, and through her they all began to think of themselves again as mothers.

And Mirele let them love her. She was the most typical child, as if all children had fused into one little body. She was too small and too thin for her age. The year of hiding in a dark attic without light or food had shrunken her. She was a miniature child — at five years of age she looked like three: thin little body; thin little arms and legs; a small, narrow, scrunched-up face; thin neck like the neck of a dove before it becomes covered with feathers. But on the other hand, she had eyes — all of the child's vital force, which had run out of her little bones, had lodged in her little eyes. Actually they weren't little eyes — they were big eyes, strange, weird, not of this world, ensconced in two little pits beneath her high fore-head. Her whole short, shrunken face lived, moved, and breathed with Mirele's gaze; the face had been created as a frame for her eyes. The eyes themselves consisted of roundish pools of water that sometimes seemed like whole oceans. Sometimes the eye-waters were still, like a still lake be-neath the moonlight, but sometimes the water-pools became rebellious. At such times, they took on the color of green jade, like that of towering waves in a stormy ocean. Sometimes the water-pools sparkled with the fiery light of *khashmal,* the heavenly burning of the sun; at other times the water-pools were extinguished as if Night had covered them with shadowing wings. Two pupils swam in the watery pools. It's hard to say what color the pupils were — they changed color like a rainbow. Sometimes they were inky black, at other times they were coppery brown, and at still other times they were transformed into transparent blue sapphires. It depended on how Mirele played with them.

And Mirele was able to play with her eyes. She could express with them the full range of human emotion, from the highest level of unearthly exaltation to the desperate outcry of animal helplessness. When she turned her eye-pools to one side and from beneath her heartbreakingly pale corneas her pupils looked forward with black desperation, it seemed as if the world were coming to an end. The pity that those eyes aroused was incalculable; they had the power to radiate such a gaze that it slipped into your heart like a ray of light and there aroused your most intimate feelings. They cast you into such ecstasy that all human emotion — pity, sorrow, anger, violence, love, and outcries of hate — mixed together in you and, despite you, mixed you with the world. On still other occasions, when she played with her eyes and the pupils swam forward from behind their forest hiding-place, from beneath her eyelids into the middle of the water-pools, it seemed to you as if an inconceivable joy had turned on like a light in your heart, and you were happy not to know the why and wherefore, and you didn't want to know.

Needless to say, all the women watched over Mirele, hid her away from any evil eyes during the day, when they left the barracks. When they came back in the evening, their first concern was — Mirele. They shared their meager rations with her. They hugged her. The mothers fell all over her, poured out their repressed love onto the girl's head, and kissed her little fingers. Each of them wanted to comb and braid her hair. Each of them, of course, was dying for Mirele to lie next to her in bed at night, at least for a little while.

Among the women was a young woman, Khane Zilbertsvayg, whom the prisoners called "the little cow". She was indeed like a little cow. She was young, barely eighteen or nineteen years old, a khasidic girl from Galicia, from a wealthy family. The Germans had taken everything from her: they had killed her husband and her father-in -law, had taken away her first-born child, and had exiled her to a work-camp. The woman, however, was herself only a child. She didn't understand what was going on around her, and didn't try to understand; she lived as if she were in a world of chaos. She did her work because they told her to — she knew she had to. But no sooner did she come back to the barracks than she threw herself onto her bed, burrowed her young, blond head into the straw, sucked on her own fingers, and played with her own breasts. She still believed that a miracle would happen, and just as everything had been destroyed all at once, so everything would again come back to life and she would get back her seven-week-old child, so she continued to keep her milk flowing, though the women around her told her that she could expect nothing and would do better to let her milk-flow dry up, because she might otherwise make herself sick, God forbid.

Since Mirele had arrived in the barracks with her mother, the Galician woman had simply attached herself to the child; she had simply stolen Mirele from her mother. She begged Rivke Rabinovitsh, with tears in her eyes, with heart-rending words, to let Mirele lie with her at night, said that she would take care of her and watch over her. The mother, who had lost her control over the child since she had come to the camp, acquiesced in the request of the Galician woman, out of pity.

But no sooner did the young mother feel the child's body next to her than she began stuffing her swollen breasts into Mirele's face.

"I beg you, Mirele, suck a little."

Mirele, who was already a child with understanding, five years old, was embarrassed — every child considers itself more grown up than it is — and felt insulted that the women was trying to treat her like a little child.

"Get away from me — I'm a big girl already," the child defended herself.

"It'll do you good, Mirele. You don't know — breast milk is so sweet and tasty. Try some I beg you."

"Mommy will scold me. Mommy won't let me suck a woman's breast."

"Mommy will be very happy. After all, you don't have any milk here, and a child your age needs milk and sugar. It'll do you good, Mirele — try some."

In that way she gradually convinced Mirele to comply with her request, and just for fun she took the woman's breast into her mouth.

Food was scarce in the concentration camp. The child hadn't seen a drop of milk for many months. She was happy for a little fat. And though she didn't like her first taste of breast milk, and spat it out, soon the liquid itself and the sweet taste it left in her mouth got her excited and she tried it again. The second time, the breast milk tasted good to her.

When the women later found out what the "little cow" was doing with the child, and when her mother tried to take Mirele away from her, the women agreed among themselves:

"Let her do it, by all means — it's better that way. Breast milk puts marrow into your bones. It'll do the child good — she has such thin little limbs."

So Rivke Rabinovitsh acquiesced, as long as it was good for the child, and allowed the child to suck the young woman's breast every evening.

The fact that Mirele was suckling from one of them made the child even more a partner of all the imprisoned women. Now they all took care of her. During they day, when they were at work, they had to hide her from an evil eye. Though one or another of the Jewish women always remained behind in the barracks to clean up and keep the barracks in order, it was possible that one of the female guards, or even Fraulein Gertruda herself might come in for an inspection and find the child, so the women searched out a hiding-place for Mirele under the wooden floor-boards, where they kept her hidden all day. Mirele, who was already used to conspiracies from her Warsaw ghetto days, accepted it as a natural thing that it had to be that way. Only when the women, after having eaten standing with their plates at the field-kitchen, came back from work and turned out the lights did the play between mothers and child begin. Each of the women was eager, if she couldn't comb the child's hair, at least to caress it, touch it, and recall by that touch the childish bodies of her own children.

The women still continued to work thus, day and night, at sorting dresses, underwear, and overcoats that had been removed from the victims before they had been shoved, naked, into the crematoria. More than once, a woman sorting the clothing had convinced herself that she recognized a familiar garment that might have belonged to someone in her family. But a person can get used to anything — there's no limit to a person's ability to adapt. The will to live is so strong that he or she can overcome all difficulties. And the will to live, the will to survive and endure, had already killed any desire in these women for anything that was not relevant to their own survival. The survival instinct, like a thirsty mushroom, had sucked into itself all feelings and emotions, and had allowed no instinct to be expressed other than what was directly necessary for the maintenance of their own lives. So, like old grave-diggers, they had already gotten used to death. They sorted the clothes that were still warm from the bodies from which they had been removed, and they cleaned off the blood-stains that the wounds had left on them and washed from the shirts the sweat of terror with which the fear of death had soaked the linen, and they mechanically laid out the stacks of clothing — shirts, overcoats, children's blouses, and shirts — without a groan, without a tear, so as not to arouse the anger of the German guards who had issued an order to remove from the sorting detail, immediately and on the spot, any women who showed signs of hysteria or rattled nerves, and send her to the division where they operated the gas chambers and crematoria.

Once, when the women were standing next to the tables and picking up individual pieces of clothing from the top of the packs of clothing that were piled up there, a child's jacket that a women picked up was still attached to a doll that had gotten hooked on a button of the jacket. Such a thing happened frequently, finding a doll among the children's clothing. That was very dangerous, because the women would be unable to control themselves and one or another would cry out reflexively, which always ended up with her death. For that reason, the women used to throw away the dolls, push them away from themselves so they wouldn't come in contact with them. This time the woman who found the doll hid it quickly under her robe, brought it to the barracks, and later, when they took Mirele out of her hiding-place under the wooden floor-boards, gave the doll to the child.

All the women liked to tie dolls for Mirele out of various scraps from dresses, and they gave them to the child to take into her hiding-place under the floorboards so she would have something to play with. Making dolls for Mirele became something the women were eager to do. They found in that a certain satisfaction that they couldn't explain. And each of the women pushed her little doll, which she had made secretly and often at the risk of her life, into Mirele's hands. But the doll that the woman had brought for Mirele, hidden under her robe, was a real one, from the time when there were children in the world and people made dolls for them that they could play with freely and openly. The doll had real live hair that could be braided, and big eyes, almost like Mirele's, that could be moved by pressing a button. The child was happy with the doll and the women were too. Each of them wanted to hold the doll in her hand and play with it for a while. The Galician woman, the "little cow," pressed the doll to her breast and bathed it with tears. They had to pull the doll out of her hands because they were afraid she would burst out crying.

Just as Mirele had, the doll brought new life into the barracks. The women sewed clothes for it and made little blouses, tassels, bonnets, and shawls. They dressed the doll in a different outfit every day, and they played with it.

The two female guards, who often came into the barracks to inspect it, noticed doll-clothing on the women's beds and often an untied doll, and several times they grabbed the women by the hand when they were sewing little dresses for the doll out of scraps of material. The guards didn't undertake to do anything themselves, but they informed headquarters that the Jewish women must be hiding something in the barracks.

One evening, when the women had already come back to the barracks to go to sleep and were already getting undressed, the chief guard of the women's division of the concentration camp, Fraulein Gertruda, a troop leader in the "Hitler's girls," came into the barracks.

Fraulein Gertruda wore her blond braids in a broad bun on top of her large round head, like "Gretchen."[10] She wore a khaki skirt down to her ankles, a pair of elegant, shiny boots on her shapely legs, and a light, low-cut blouse from which her naked fleshy arms protruded. In one hand she held a whip. Along with its stag-horn handle, the whip had a thick, long tail made of braided oxhide. Next to her stood two big, dark-brown German police-dogs, and behind her were two tall Gestapo men in black uniforms, wearing shiny S.S. knives with black steel hilts and red, white, and black enameled swastikas.

The women stood next to their beds, breathless and petrified.

---

[10] The archetype of a German girl—heroine of Goethe's *Faust*

For a long time, Fraulein Gertruda said nothing, just looked piercingly at the women. With her cold, sharp, blue eyes, like those of a threatening timber wolf, she looked them over with a penetrating gaze and slowly shifted her steely gaze from one woman to another. After a long silence that seemed to last for an eternity — and it was so silent that one could hear the shadow of the Angel of Death, which was now in the barracks, moving along the walls — she raised her other naked arm and exhibited the doll that had been found, which she held in her hand.

"Who does this belong to?" she asked without anger, but drilling her eyes into one woman after another.

The deathly pale women said nothing. You could just hear their hearts beating and see their chests rising and falling.

"Answer me!" Frau Gertruda exclaimed, with a harsh shriek that was reminiscent of the roar of a great cat, and she brought down her long ox-tail whip with a whistling 'Crack!' onto the heads and breasts of the women.

The barks of the dogs accompanied the 'cracks' like an echo.

"It belongs to all of us, dear Fraulein. The women like to play with dolls, in their children's memory," an elderly woman who no longer had anything to fear dared to answer.

"So! They like to play with dolls for their children's sake." the Fraulein said. "We shall see."

She took the doll and held it under the noses of the dogs. When the dogs had sniffed around the doll, she ordered them with a gesture:

"Find her!"

Howling and barking, the dogs dug under the wooden floorboards. In a little while one could hear the heart-rending shriek of a child , and soon the dogs dragged Mirele out from under the floor-boards by her feet.

Perhaps the child was more afraid of the people she saw than she was of the feral dogs, but when they dragged her out she stopped shrieking, even stopped crying. She was quiet, but her eyes flashed with an unearthly light.

Mirele's gaze fell upon the eyes of Fraulein Gertruda, and it was as if some unknown, previously unfelt sensation animated Gertruda. Mirele's pitch-black pupils moved down to the horizons of her large, watery eye-pools, and from beneath the thinned-out, emaciated corneas they shone out with a moist, heartbreaking, pleading look. The pupils changed color with the speed of a waterfall as she gazed: now they took on the hue of a pitch-black abyss and now their borders quickly changed and manifested an orange glow, then a violet glow, and then turned to a deep blue like two large, otherworldly, water-clear sapphires.

"What eyes!" Fraulein Gertruda couldn't restrain herself and exclaimed to the two S.S. men who were standing behind her.

Her face even changed for a second — creases appeared in her smooth, white, creamed cheeks, near the corners of her mouth. Even her cool, feline, steely-sharp blue eyes shone with light. The flash of light in Fraulein Gertruda's eyes, together with the creases around her mouth, ignited a ray of hope in the women's hearts.

"Real sapphires! I've never seen anything like them," exclaimed one of the Gestapo men.

"Ach, what ear-rings you could make out of them," the second one said.

"What?"

"Jews' eyes, of course."

"How?"

"If one can petrify animals eyes, it must be possible to do the same with human eyes."

"Jews' eyes."

"It's a thought."

The entire conversation between Fraulein Gertruda and the S.S. men lasted only a minute. They conducted it quietly, as if the women couldn't hear them. Suddenly Fraulein Gertruda shook herself, grabbed the girl that the dogs had dragged out by the feet, and turned the child's head toward her.

"A knife!" she called out to the S.S. men.

And immediately the blade of a knife that one of the S.S. men had drawn from its sheath, on which the words "Blood and Honor" were engraved, glinted in the air like a sacrificial knife.

"Cut with a lot of flesh," one of the S.S. men, who was holding the child's hand and turned her on her back, advised in a loud, indifferent tone.

A shriek like the roar of an animal was heard from the women. Immediately, however, they choked back their outcry. Several of the women threw Mirele's mother onto a shelf and stopped up her mouth with their fists.

* * *

In Weimar, in the famous city that is connected with the name of the famous German poet Goethe, in the large new city hall that bore the name of the second national poet, Schiller-Hall, an evening reception was given for the S.S. General von Wagner. The general had come to the city to inspect the famous concentration camp, Buchenwald, which belonged to the city, and after he had found the camp in excellent order, the city fathers, led by the mayor, mounted the festive occasion as an expression of thanks that their city had the honor of housing such a famous concentration camp, which brought fear to all of Europe with its famous gas-chambers, crematoria, and death-factories.

Into the blindingly bright great hall, where the distinguished men of the city and their wives had already gathered around the general, came the chief guard of the women's division of the camp, Fraulein Gertruda. This time she wasn't wearing boots and military clothes. Since the evening was a civilian one and was supposed to have a cozy Germanic character, almost a family affair since the city leaders had brought along their wives and daughters and a dance was supposed to follow the reception, the Fraulein came dressed as "Gretchen," emphasizing thereby that the city belonged to Goethe.

She wore a loose medieval robe of red wool, with a sash over the hips and a square cut-out in her narrow caftan. From the cut-out projected a creamed, white, fat neck that carried her roundish, doughy, naked face. The two cold, steely-blue eyes in her face never moved — they were like dead stone eyes set within naked borders without eyebrows. But what most emphasized her Gretchen-character were her two heavy blond braids. This time the braids were not wrapped in a bun on top of her blond hair, but hung like the two heavy weights in a grandfather's-clock, all the way down her full, well-padded back, and, as if by command, down to her knees. The braids, with their heaviness and their thickly woven texture, were more reminiscent of the tail of a whip, the symbol and mark of her occupation, than of girlish pigtails.

Though her eyes sat motionless and frozen beneath her eyebrowless forehead and didn't sparkle at all, in contrast the large ear-rings that she wore hanging on chains from her earlobes sparkled with human understanding from the first entry of the Fraulein into the hall. The ear-rings in her small, delicate ears drew everyone's gaze. They consisted of two large stones in the form of human eyes, set in white gold frames, and they dangled on two long golden chains from the ears.

It must be admitted that the specialist who had undertaken to petrify Mirele's eyes for Fraulein Gertruda's ear-rings had done his work to perfection. He had brought out all the characteristics of Mirele's eyes and all the magic of her gaze. Just as in life, Mirele's eyes possessed large, sparkling water-pools, but the 'master' had succeeded in retaining in the water-pools all of the delicate tissue of the thin, delicate blood-vessels that were coursing on Mirele's eyes while the Fraulein was carrying out her 'operation' on them. By means of the blood vessels, he had also succeeded in a masterly way in bringing out the mother-of-pearl shiny color that the tear drops had in the watery pools, such that it seemed that, as in life, Mirele's pupils were constantly bathing in rivers of tears. In the pupils themselves, the master had succeeded in installing and maintaining the three different color elements they had contained: a sky-blue border surrounded the pupils, the pupils themselves had a beer-brown color, and in the beer-brown background was a round black point. In that black point lay the power of Mirele's eyes. The point was only the size of a pinhead, but an entire unknown and unimaginable universe was drowned in that pinhead. It was as if an ocean of humanity maintained itself in that pinhead. It possessed a sensitivity that reacted to the slightest noise or movement. It seemed as if the black point were constantly moving in the pupil, changing its position as it was touched by the gazes and the rays of light that fell upon it. It also possessed a magical attraction that forced every gaze to come to rest on it, and hardly did your gaze fall into the spark than it was imprisoned there and you had to follow it. Even more — it emitted secret rays that stole into people's hearts and somehow warmed them, demanding something....

And it was indeed the black points in the pupils of Fraulein Gertruda's ear-rings that attracted the gaze of everyone in the 'respectable' and distinguished assemblage that filled Schiller Hall. Wherever she went, the black points of light shone out from the unknown stones in Gertruda's ear-rings and awakened and excited everyone's curiosity. It was as if little Mirele had come back to life and had shrunk and taken up residence in the pinheads in her pupils. The tiny, black, sparkling pinheads smiled to everyone with a child's carefree, happy smile; greeted everyone; warmed everyone; and both smiled and cried, warmed and demanded in the same gaze. It was as if hundreds of thousands of children's lives had placed their last trembling under the knife of the Angel of Death into that black eyedrop. And wherever the Fraulein went, wherever she turned, child's tears sparkled in her ears and riveted everyone's eyes upon her. A child's weeping song rang out from the ear-rings, sung in a childishly mischievous tone:

Daddy killed me,
mommy cooked me,
my little brothers and sisters
gnawed on my little bones.

In the hall it was quiet. People got out of Fraulein Gertruda's way, avoided her. Groups gathered in the corners, whispered secrets into one another's ears, and followed Fraulein Gertruda's steps with their eyes.

The tall S.S. general stood at the front of the hall, surrounded by his coterie and accompanied by the city fathers, the mayor, the local Nazi 'elite,' a few professors from a nearby university town, writers, musicians, and scientists. And the group, with characteristic Germanic respect, kept at an appropriate distance but looked with enthusiasm and happy faces at the image of their divinity —Nazi power. The general conducted himself modestly, smiled charmingly, and permitted himself to be admired. Finally he noticed that something had happened in the hall. He couldn't fail to notice the silence that had developed upon Fraulein Gertruda's entrance, the gazes that were drawn to her ear-rings from all corners, and the whispering among the people. Finally he saw the Gretchen with the long braids and the large ear-rings in her ears, whose steps everyone followed with their gaze.

"Who is that?" he asked his entourage.

"That is Fraulein Gertruda, a troop-leader of the 'Hitler girls,' and chief guard of the women's division of Buchenwald."

"Yes, I've visited her division. She keeps it in outstanding order. What's going on with her? Is it her Gretchen-costume that attracts so much attention?"

"No, it's her ear-rings," they answered him.

His entourage was silent, out of respect.

Finally Gertruda's turn came to bow to the great man.

"What sort of stones are those in your ear-rings, which elicit so much attention?" the general asked the Fraulein.

"Those are Jews' eyes in my ear-rings" she answered.

"Jews' eyes?" the general asked again. "How interesting! May I look at them more closely?"

After giving a military salute, clicking her heels, and standing at attention in front of him, the Fraulein bent her ears down for his inspection. The great man graciously looked at Mirele's eyes through his monocle.

"All the characteristics of an eye, even the little blood vessels woven in," the general couldn't help but wonder.

"Not badly made," remarked a professor, a famous surgeon who was also scrutinizing the Fraulein's ear-rings. "It has kept the network of eye-nerves intact," he said, rendering his expert opinion as a German specialist. "Who made it? It required a thorough knowledge of ophthalmology to be able to petrify a human eye."

"We have in our city a master craftsman in that field. He has always shown great artistry in petrifying the eyes of animals. This is his first attempt with human eyes, and he has succeeded," said Fraulein Gertruda.

"Yes he has," agreed another member of the entourage. "I wouldn't be surprised if in time there would develop a new industry of petrifying human eyes into precious stones. Why not? They would stand competition with the finest sapphires," said a pudgy department -store owner among the other distinguished city fathers.

Throughout the entire time when the S.S. general was gazing with interest at the Fraulein's ears and the discussion about Mirele's eyes was going on, the little girl was lying in the tiny black mid-point of her pupils and laughing with childish laughter that warmed the general's heart and mood with her childishly mischievous joyfulness. Suddenly, the light in the black point changed. It became clouded as if a storm were gathering there. The black point, as it had in life, hid behind the edge of the brown field of the pupil, and looked out from there with fear and piteous pleading, as if it were pleading for Mirele's life. Also the white water-pools of the eyes changed: the thin tissues of the blood vessels became thicker, engorged with blood, and the entire white water-pools became fluid as if the petrification of the eye-substance had dissolved and been turned back into little lakes of tears into which the pupils dipped themselves and broke one's heart with the piteous gazes they aroused.

"Just see how the colors have changed," said General von Wagner, intensely scrutinizing the change of light in the stones.

No sooner had he said those words than something happened. Panic began to rule the hall. Those who were standing nearest the door began unceremoniously but hurriedly to leave the hall. People began to act impatient; they forgot all about the general. Women started to get hysterical. One could hear voices calling out names. A man from the general's entourage turned to an elderly woman and exclaimed in fear:

"Mother, come with me!"

The general turned pale, as did the members of his entourage. He stood petrified for a second and looked at them. Before he realized what was happening, the sound of alarm sirens was heard. Right after that the air was pierced by a sound from the distance like hundreds of thunderclaps combined.

"The American bombers, damn it! Turn the lights out!" he heard an alarmed outcry.

It immediately became pitch-dark in the hall. In the darkness, chairs and tables were overturned and arms and legs flailed. In an instant, the entire Schiller-Hall, with all the leaders of the city and the Nazi elite, became transformed into an insane asylum in which the residents, filled with the fear of God, were running around and fighting with one another to get out. Among those who were seeking protection form the American bombers was also the S.S. general, as well as Fraulein Gertruda, with Mirele's eyes in her ears.

*   *   *

For a whole year, Mirele's eyes lay in Fraulein Gertruda's jewel-box. She put them on only for certain occasions, such as official meetings with high Nazi officials. People didn't dance in Germany at that time, so Fraulein Gertruda had no opportunity to wear Mirele's eyes in her ears at 'light-hearted' events, but she had worn them recently for a charitable purpose, at an event for 'winter assistance' at which all the city fathers were assembled.

People were already used to the sensation that the appearance of Mirele's eyes as ear-rings created. The eyes no longer created a stir or even drew any attention — they were taken for granted.

Aristocratic ladies invited Fraulein Gertruda into their circles in order to look closely at Mirele's eyes. Fraulein Gertruda accepted this with no little pride. The ladies admired the masterly craftsmanship of the pieces of jewelry, praised the mounting, and asked for the goldsmith's name.

On several occasions, Fraulein Gertruda wore Mirele's eyes to private social events to which she had been invited for coffee and cake, what they call an 'at home' in Germany. And in the atmosphere of true German gemutlichkeit that can be found in German homes, they admired the Fraulein's ear-rings and praised her for her original idea. There were young women from high society who begged Fraulein Gertruda to let them try on the ear-rings to see how well Mirele's eyes would suit their faces, and the Fraulein was glad to oblige.

Fraulein Gertruda was popular in the high society of Weimar because of her true Germanic character, and was considered a model of a woman of the pure Aryan type. And at all the social events that Fraulein Gertruda attended wearing her ear-rings, Mirele played a supporting role. With childish naivete, she smiled down from the Fraulein's ears to the ladies and girls, rejoiced together with them, listened to their chattering, and nodded her head. No, she wasn't sad at all — sometimes, from her place in the tiny point in the pupil, she sang a little song to herself with a mischievous smile:

Daddy killed me,
mommy cooked me,
my little brothers and sisters
gnawed on my little bones.

So things went till the American army overran Germany. When the army took Weimar and Buchenwald, among the other things they took from the head guard of the women's section of the concentration camp, Fraulein Gertruda, such as a mattress stuffed with human hair, on which she slept, and a lampshade made of human skin, by which she read, they also found Mirele's eyes, petrified and set in a setting of white gold as ear-rings.

"But those are only Jews' eyes," the Fraulein explained wonderingly, not understanding the stir her ear-rings created among the American soldiers.

Mirele's eye were too alive to be held as witnesses at the trial. They were given to the Jewish chaplain who had accompanied the American army of liberation. The Jewish chaplain brought Mirele's eyes to the Jewish cemetery. Together with the remains of Torah volumes they found in German homes, where they had been transformed into household articles, he laid them in the grave of a Jewish soldier from the Bronx felled by a German bullet during the taking of the city.

The chaplain, as he was standing next to the grave of the Jewish soldier and saying Kaddish, thought about Mirele's eyes and gave a military command to the soldier from the Bronx:

"Take them there for those who need them!"

Meanwhile, in Paradise, in Mother Rokhl's temple, to which Mirele had come after she died when they took out her eyes, she was wandering around, a blind little angel among the saints that were there with Mother Rokhl in her temple. When Mirele arrived in Heaven, the chief angel had decided that she would remain blind for the time being, till her eyes came back to heaven, for Mirele's eyes were of a high grade, suited to the child.

Meanwhile, Mirele was as happy as could be. All the saints in Mother Rokhl's temple paid attention to the blind little angel, for aside from the fact that Mirele was blind, she was also a little orphan, because all the children there whose mothers are still among the living in this world are considered orphans, as is true in reverse of the children here. So the saints made dolls and toys for Mirele from pure Ark-curtains and Torah covers. But here they didn't have to hide her from the killers all day — here she was free. A different saint each day took Mirele by the hand and led her to the "green pastures beside the still waters," as is sung in the Psalms.

Sometimes she was led by a prophetess, sometime by Hannah of the seven sons, or Sarah Bas-Toyvim, or some other holy woman, of whom so many had recently come to the temple, to Mother Rokhl. She even encountered several mothers whom she had known from the barracks in the concentration camp, but they no longer had time for her because they now had their own children, who had been given back to them here. Even the "little cow," the Galician woman who had nursed her when she was with her in the camp, had gotten back her own child, whom she was constantly nursing. Mirele's mother had not yet arrived in Paradise like the other mothers, so Mirele was referred to the Holy Mothers and to the saints, who devoted themselves to the blind little angel.

When the Jewish soldier from the Bronx executed the chaplain's command and brought Mirele's eyes to the correct address to which they had been directed, a flaming angel, aflame with colorful wings, quickly flew up and, on a golden matzo-platter that came from King Solomon's table and was covered with a challah-cloth that came from a holy rabbi's table, brought Mirele's eyes into Mother Rokhl's temple.

When Mirele's eyes arrived in Mother Rokhl's temple, there was great joy among the saints. But when they wanted to put her eyes back into the excavated eye-sockets in her face, she wouldn't let them.

"I've seen so much evil through them! I don't want to see any more," the child said.

And when they tried to convince her: "Silly child, these are your own beautiful eyes," the child replied: "I'm better off without them. I see whatever I want to — I see my daddy, I see my mommy, I see my little brother. With my eyes, I saw only darkness and horror. No, I want to remain as I am."

Then Mother Rokhl, wrapped in her black veil with the Sabbath stars on it and with the Crown of Sorrow on her head, took Mirele by one hand (in her other hand the blind child held her eyes in a tefillin-bag that a mother had sewn for her Bar-Mitzva-boy when he was no longer alive) and led her before the Throne of Glory.

And Mirele laid down her eyes at the feet of the Almighty. And God commanded that they set Mirele's eyes into the Throne of Glory, and there they sparkle with a clear light for all the Jewish children's eyes that have been extinguished.

H. Royznblat (1878-1956) was a pioneering lyricist. His earliest poems were simplistic and sentimental, but his later ones were more profound, celebrating his optimistic faith in life, his love of the American countryside, and his concern for individual joys and sorrows.

~

H. Royzenblat

So Much Sorrow

So much sorrow in the dark brown eyes of the hard-working horse!
He cannot, it seems, bear it in his blood and bones,
so he drags the heavy burden after him, loaded on the big wagon
that screeches, groans, and digs into the earth with its wheels.

So much servility in his body, in his bone-weary steps;
so much repressed suffering in his chin, in his trembling lip;
so much stubbornness in his straining neck, in his intermittent rattling—
it seems to me that he drags behind him all the loneliness and poverty of
the city.

At night, in his desolate stall, his bowels rumble
as he stands and mindlessly rechews the hay with his sick gums.
Behind him, in his sleep, the weariness weeps and melts into the pile of
    dung
that tomorrow will fertilize the plowed, black, newly sown earth.

So much dark patience in the stiff back of the hard-working horse;
so much sorrow and self-sacrifice in every cut, scrape, and welt
that the cruel whip has inscribed and carved into his hide—
it seems to me that he carries within him all the misfortune of the silent
    world.

The Song of the Small Letter

A table, candle, curl of smoke—
a verse on paper white is writ.
Conjure up a lovely world
and then believe in it.

The rich man hoards his gold and coins,
the poor man scrimps and saves, I've heard.
And I—I find my greatest joy
quite often in the smallest word.

I hear the wind sing in the woods,
the rain that pelts the grass so tall.
The loveliest song I've ever heard
comes from a modest letter small.

Quite often just a vowel-sign
no bigger than a tiny mite
conceals within a syllable
a brilliant, lovely rainbow light.

A table, candle, curl of smoke—
a verse on paper white is writ.
Conjure up a lovely world
and then believe in it.

Fradl Shtok (1890-1930) was one of a group of major female Yiddish poets (together with Tsilye Drapkin, Ana Margolin, Kadya Molodovsky, Rokhl Korn, and others) who burst upon the Yiddish poetry scene in the first two decades of the 20th century. They brought an emotionality, lyricism, eroticism, and feminine sensibility that were a distinctively new factor in Yiddish literature.

~

Fradl Shtok

Serenade

Please ope your eyes,
you dearest man,
and come with me away.
The silent night
of silver-wine
composes us a lay.

Don't rest your head
on dreamland's lap,
for my lap waits for you.
The night is blue,
come out with me
and let us yearn, we two

And if the night
in its blue cloak
from forest valley now depart,
and softly weep with tears of dew
from fragrant crystal heart,
then tear my heart
out of my breast
and wash it in the dew,
and with your lips
suck out of me
a quiet "oy" for you.

1910

On the Ocean Shore

What's fluttering so whitely there?
What shines there — can you see?
A sail, a sail upon a ship
that's coming from across the sea!

The merchandise was gotten there
in foreign, distant Eastern lands.
The ship comes fully laden here:
with bars of gold and silver strands
with milky pearls and emeralds,
exotic spice and golden lode,
with fiddles and with purple wine
and strings of beads quite in the mode,

which wealthy people here have bought
from Eastern lands with traders' marts
where young, indentured slavey-boys
are hitched to fragile rickshaw carts

to take for quiet carefree rides
princesses who oft seek surcease
when sounding harps have wakened them
from sleep and dreams of peace.

What's fluttering so whitely there?
What shines there — can you see?
A sail, a sail upon a ship
that's coming from across the sea!

A Contemporary Motif

Why is the lamp in the house flickering?
Why is the wind wailing?
Someone has been hanged
in the middle of this night.

A tall and narrow tree
somewhere along the road —
cold limbs are rocking back and forth
from the branches.

And a crow is croaking
from far away in the night.
From somewhere, the wind
has brought along a star.

A face is shining piously
out of the dark night.
The star above is pale
and becomes extinguished.

Avrom Koralnik (1883-1937) was an essayist of enormous reputation. Leyeles, no mean essayist himself, referred to Koralnik as the essayist in Yiddish. He was educated in four European universities and received a PhD in philosophy at the age of 25. He was a longtime staff writer for *Der Tog,* specializing in essays on literary and philosophical topics. Though the essays were sometimes profound, they were often light and playful, with an elegant, ironical style.

~

Avrom Koralnik

The 'Square Script'

I don't know—it may be that I'm mistaken. It's possible that it's just something I'm used to, but it seems to me that of all the scripts, all the signs that represent sounds, words, and thoughts, the Yiddish script is one of the easiest and clearest. I am still extremely doubtful whether the Latin script, which serves in the entire world today as an example of clarity and simplicity, is really better, easier, or more beautiful than the Yiddish.

Whoever has had occasion in his life to occupy himself with languages and alphabets will have to confess that outside of the Latin and Graeco-Slavic scripts there is not a single one that is as 'modern' as the Yiddish. Modern—that is, sparing with signs and still able to express all the nuances of sound; modern—that is, not cluttered , not melodic, but spare in form and dignified.

For example, pick up Taylor's book about alphabets, leaf through it, look at the various scripts that are collected there, and you'll be simply amazed at how uneconomical people are, how difficult they make their road to understanding the written word. I'm not even talking about such an alphabet as the Chinese, which is actually a dictionary; one has to spend almost a lifetime to learn how to read a Chinese book or newspaper. But even the easier, simpler ones are so complicated that one has to strain his eyes and his memory till he is more or less secure in the language. Take Arabic, for example. It is a language that is spoken by tens of millions of people and a script that is used by the entire Muslim world, that is, by a few hundred million people. How difficult, how full of curlicues, how inaccessible the written word is! You will find scholars who know Arabic very well and understand the Koran, but still can't read every Arabic handwriting. And the same with other, even European, scripts. For example, Armenian, Georgian, and Gaelic—all languages that are reviving and being renewed, and that are trying to enter the cultural mainstream.

Nevertheless, I have seldom seen an Armenian, a Georgian, or an Arab who complains about his script and language, or who avoids it, treats it with contempt, or is ashamed of it.

I have known many Armenians—nationalists, leaders of revolutionary parties. Externally, they were completely assimilated, Russianly assimilated. They had Russian names, they spoke Russian with absolutely no accent, and they took a place in Russian society. But they remained Armenians. Whether they lived in Crimea or in the Caucasus, in Odessa or Moscow, they all had one single goal and one demand: the revival of Armenia. And in whatever culture they lived, they had a deep bond to their own curious, ancient, small-town culture—the Armenian culture.

Each of them considered it necessary to understand his folk-language and to take part—insofar as he was able to—in the furtherance of his culture. And you can be sure that when Armenian lawyers, doctors, and merchants came together to discuss matters about Armenia and the future of their distant, mountainous land, they spoke Armenian among themselves. They were proud of the bit of Armenian culture that had been created 'in exile' in the Meritarist monastery in Venice or around the Patriarch Etshmiazin or in Constantinople.

And my Armenian friends could never understand why Jews, when they are with one another—Jewish nationalists, fiery Zionists, etc—speak all the current languages except their folk-language, or why they are so little interested in the creations of Yiddish culture

I haven't known how to answer them, because they wouldn't be able to understand the true answer that I could give them; they would think it was a joke or a libel. If they only knew the extent of Jewish self-contempt! If the world knew more of our 'secrets,' it would have ceased to pay any attention to us long ago! And the greatest secret of the Jew is that he wants to get away from himself, as far as they let him—that he has contempt for everything that gets created in the bosom of the Jewish people, that even his nationalism and drive to the future are no more than pale shadows of what they were, an echo from the depths that is getting fainter and fainter. If only they knew what we know!

Every time I meet with Zionists, leaders or followers, the masses or those who stand more or less in the vanguard, I am struck with wonder. I see before me people who talk Zion from early morning to late at night, people who give of their time and money and their entire being for the creation of a Jewish future, people who stand, it seems, on the other side of the walls and have no relationship to the cultures around them and are practically strangers in the lands where they live, so strong and all-encompassing is their Jewish interest. Nevertheless, these same people are absolutely foreign to the most profound things that Jewry has produced —to Yiddish culture, to the ancient road to those who are and are becoming.

I know Zionist leaders who have stayed in the movement for twenty-five or thirty years and haven't even taken the time to learn to read Yiddish—or Hebrew! They haven't the slightest concept of what the Jewish people has created.

At one of the Zionist conferences, at a committee meeting that was supposed to work out a program for a reception for Bialik, some Jew from a city near New York, a longtime Zionist, a distinguished 'activist', stood up and began his speech—of course, in a horrible, ungrammatical, Litvak-accented English— and this is what he said:

"I don't know who this gentleman 'Byalik' is; I've never read his poetry. But our cantor has put music to one of his poems, so I understand that he must be 'all right' " And he therefore proposed that they should greet Bialik with Torah scrolls, that children dressed in blue and white, carrying flowers, should sing *Hatikvah*, etc.

And that speech didn't even disturb the 'harmony.' A few of the Zionists smiled. One or two whispered a protest, but most of the group agreed. And that's the way things go: there is Zionism and 'Byalik', and there is a Yiddish movement and a Yiddish culture—what has one got to do with the other?

"Well what do you want—why are you wondering? He doesn't know any Hebrew and he can't read Yiddish! And does he know English? It's just plain ignorance."

No, it's not just plain ignorance. It's something more, something deeper. Look at the others—the lawyers, doctors, and rabbis. They certainly are not ignoramuses. They know English well, they may have Shakespeare at their fingertips, and they read modern English literature. Some of them know German well and are proud of it. They are what you call cultured people. And nevertheless, nevertheless...!

I recall an encounter. One evening I met one of the most famous Zionist activists—not a leader, because he was always in the opposition, but he had been in the opposition so long that he was himself already part of Zionist history. He had spent his whole life constantly speaking, thinking, planning, and writing about Zionism. He had no other interests in life. He was, so to speak, an 'arch-Jew.'

"What's new in the Jewish world," the historic Zionist asked me. At first I didn't understand his question. I thought he wanted to get into a discussion about the deepest questions of Jewish life. He was, after all, an old-time, history-making, famous Zionist! So I began, as one does, in the middle. But I noticed right away that I was talking to myself, that the old-time Zionist didn't understand what I was talking about. It suddenly became clear to me that he really didn't know what was going on in the Jewish world, how the Jewish world lived and spoke.

"Do you mean to say," I asked in wonderment (we were speaking, of course, in one of the European 'cultural languages'), "do you mean to say that you don't read the Jewish press at all?"

"No," he answered.

"Why not, if I may ask?"

"Because I can't read the 'square script."

And suddenly the whole man was revealed to me, the 'activist' with no understanding, the eternal Zionist. I suddenly understood all his comical traits and the source of his out-of-thin-air plans. He had lived for thirty years in an abstract world, a sort of airless void with no content, no reality, no people, and no cultural environment. A cold world, without people—a world that called itself Jewish but had no relationship whatsoever with Jewry and Jews.

For thirty years he had constantly met with Jews. He had sat with them at conferences, had heard Jewish jokes, Jewish songs, and Jewish lectures. For thirty long years he had seen, with his own eyes, the 'square script,' and it hadn't for even one moment aroused a desire to know what those symbols meant.

Can you picture an Arab or an Armenian or a Chinese who is only 'theoretical?' Can you imagine an Armenian or Georgian politician who doesn't even want to understand the language of his people, to have the possibility of reading what is written by and for his people?

But with us that is possible. Not only possible but advantageous. The less the relationship, the greater the say and the greater the right to closeness and leadership.

"What kind of relationship do you have to Jewry? Why do you care about Palestine? What is Hecuba to you[11]? Really only a colonization plan, a Utopia—just like that? Why do you bother with the whole matter?"

The historic Zionist looked at me with wonderment in his eyes. It seems that no one, till now, had ever asked him such a question, and he had certainly not asked it of himself.

"Do you think that the whole wisdom and totality of Jewry lies in the square script?" he asked.

"No, certainly not. But when a Jew who wants to be a Zionist, who constantly talks and lectures about Zion, has so little respect for Jewish thought and the Jewish word that he doesn't want to speak or understand the folk-language, or looks down his nose at everything that the living Jewish reality creates, or considers the whole Jewish culture a 'square' that doesn't suit him and his concept of form—if that is his relationship to the foundation of the structure, then what kind of interest can he have in its walls?"

We parted dissatisfied, estranged, and wondering about each other, the historic Zionist and I. A granite wall had been erected between the two of us—the 'square script.' The letters contain the secret of a magical force. There is in them not only tears and weeping but also smiles and irony and the deep emotions of the Jewish people.

Perhaps that is really one of the reasons that so many 'historic Zionists' stay so far away and estranged from the Jewish people. Between them and it stands the square script, the *mekhitse*[12] of word and symbol, stronger than a *mekhitse* of wood and stone.

[11] "Who is he to Hecuba and Hecuba to him?" A quote from Hamlet, referring to his wonderment that an actor can sound as if he really cares about the person he is portraying, when in fact the person means nothing to him.
[12] The partition between men and women in an Orthodox synagogue—figuratively, any separation or barrier

Yoysef Rolnik (1879-1955) was a precursor and mentor to *Di Yunge*. He wrote soft, sweet, lyrical poems, often just a few stanzas that fixed with great clarity on a single thought or mood. The brevity and imagery of these poems are sometimes reminiscent of the much later poetry of Reyzl Zhikhlinski.

⌇

Yoysef Rolnik

As If Before My Eyes

Let me smell again the odor of the earth
and hear the quiet slapping of the water,

feel the dark coolness of a midsummer barn,
hear the nocturnal call of a meadow fire.

Let me sense and imagine
the tangy taste of half-ripe fruit.

Let the sound of the scythe remind me
of the cheery dampness of the nocturnal dew.

Carry to me on the wings of the wind
the faraway, dry, scraping sound of a wagon,

the sighing of stalks being reaped —
help me, God, to remember the language of the countryside.

From Our Love No Offspring Remains

From our love no offspring,
no memory remains,
except a small book of poems,
yellowed and torn.

When you are already a mother,
you'll remember my poems
and rock your children
to sleep with them.

And when, some day, your grandson
returns from *kheyder*
constantly repeating them,
childishly, in a monotone,

you'll add to them the words
that weren't expressed —
after all, you know better than the book
what should be written there.

Dovid Ignatov (1885-1954) was the acknowledged leader and sparkplug of *Di Yunge*, a group of Yiddish writers who emerged during the first decade of the 20th century as rebels against the "social poetry" of the older generation of Yiddish writers, especially the "proletarian poets"; they emphasized expressing personal feelings, free of community "obligations." Ignatov wrote principally prose, particularly novels, and was the editor of several of *Di Yunge's* magazines and anthologies.

~

Dovid Ignatov

Literature and *Writings*

Some time ago in 1908-1909, we founded a group called *Literature*. Very quickly, a group of novice writers joined. With our numbers and noisiness, our group, *Literature*, became practically a movement, a literature movement on the Jewish scene. Among us were some who later gave up writing, such as the good Mikhl Kaplan, or only started and then stopped, such as Shmuel Fox (now Dr. Fox), and some who later became journalists, such as Yankl Kirshenboym, and even editors, such as Dr. Margoshes. There were also, of course, 'kibitzers,' as a sort of special fraction.

Once we had accumulated a little money (from a few concerts that we arranged at 151 Clinton Street), we decided to put out an anthology called *Literature.* The plan was that I should be the editor or a member of the editorial board. I, however, believed that the editor should be 'a man with a beard,' a beard in the symbolic sense. After long arguments, my proposal was accepted, namely that among us Entin was 'the one with the beard' and that he and two others should constitute the editorial board. The other two were Khaymovitsh and Slonim.

I believed we had chosen a very good editorial board, and that the volume that was to be issued would bubble with novelty and youth and would "virtually surprise the world," and that through the volume we would actually wash away some of the kibitzer/wiseguy plague. From my friends, I extracted and selected the best they had and brought it to the editorial board, to Entin.

I considered and still consider Mani Leyb one of the finest poets that our literature has ever produced, and the series of his poems that I submitted practically sang out from my own blood, so dear to me were his every word and line. One day, however, Slonim came to me, led me out of Sholem's Café, and went with me to the Hester Street park, saying he had to discuss something with me. When we sat down on a park bench, he confided to me that he was simply astounded by Mani Leyb's poems — that the evening before, they had laughed at his poems. "How can a man write such foolish lines as:

Dove-silent blue evening hours
scatter my silent blue supper scattereder.
Now glow hotter and redder
my red roses, my wounds.

Slonim may have been the first in our poetry who made use of modern images and special new rhythms of line and suddenness of picture and word. For that time, such lines as the above cited ones should have been, especially for Slonim, a real joy and encouragement.

My argument for Slonim as one of the editors was based on his modernity. He would, that is, help to ensure that the volume *Literature* would breathe freshness. And here Slonim had not only recited the few lines by Mani Leyb with cynical laughter, but had started laughing again:

"What does "dove-silent evening hours" mean, and what if doves are not silent in the evening? Doves coo in the evening, after all, so how can one say "dove-silent"? And what does "scattereder" mean? One can say "scatter", but how can one say "scattereder"? And how can a poet compare red roses with wounds? That is so unesthetic! That's modernism?! Now take your story *A Winter Night*-- it's modern, but it's full of talent. One might complain a bit about the end: perhaps you don't need it at all or perhaps you might change it a bit, but nevertheless it is full of talent and rhythm. But your friend Mani Leyb's poems — they are simply ludicrous!"

Slonim then laughed in such a cocksure and self-satisfied way that arguing with him would have made no sense. In addition, I was simply at a loss for words — I was choking with rage.

"Where are Mani Leyb's poems?" I asked stiffly.

"Here are all of them," Slonim said to me, laughing and smiling, handing me the poems and adding in a consoling, fatherly manner:

"He'll become a poet again, but he should burn these poems. As his friend, you should see to it that he burns them."

I then went up to Entin's office with Slonim to get the manuscript of my story, using the excuse that I wanted to make a change.

"Perhaps I should throw out the ending," I said.

I knew I was lying, and I couldn't look Entin straight in the eye as I was saying it.

Entin later cursed me out for playing a cheap trick to get back my manuscript and because all the others then came and took back their manuscripts too. He said that I was conducting a strike against the book, and in his anger he called me: "Traitor!"

Entin was nevertheless 'the man with the beard' to me, the man with significant accomplishments, the man who, through lectures and sometimes through the printed word, had awakened our consciousness to what was new and modern in Yiddish literature. I, whom they considered a troublemaker, could not raise my voice against him. As far as talking it out with him man to man, my embarrassment interfered and I couldn't find the necessary words. How long ago was it that I used to save up the few pennies I had in order to pay to hear one of Entin's lectures to Jewish youth about how from the days of Shakespeare to the time of Ibsen and Maeterlinck young talents have had to fight against the backward critics and wordsmiths of their generations? To me Entin was my rabbi, teacher, mentor, and friend, and here Entin had said such words to me! And for what?!

All of this made me so sick that I picked myself up and ran away and hired out as a farmhand to a Christian farmer somewhere in the mountains of Vermont.

When I came back later on, the first issue of *Literature* had already appeared, and instead of the hoped-for book that would tell of a new, young, American stream of literature in America, the book was filled with a long article by Moyshe Katz, entitled *The Search for God and the Search for Self*, a piece of work by Moiseyev, and other such long, drawn-out articles. And above all, and worst of all, was a pallid, horribly empty series of poems by Yitskhok Rayz.[13] God in Heaven! Yitskhok Rayz, the kibitzer, they had allowed to spread himself out this broadly in the volume *Literature*, which was attempting to demonstrate that kibitzing was distinct from literature! And as if that weren't enough, they told me as soon as I came into Sholem's

---

[13] Better known by his pen-name, Moyshe Nadir

Café that at a meeting of our *Literature* group on the previous Sunday, Yitskhok Rayz had been selected as the editor of the second volume in place of Entin, who had resigned. I felt a chill in my heart, and I said coldly and with certainty:

"He won't be the editor."

"What do you mean 'He won't be the editor'? They've already selected him."

"He won't be the editor."

" I mean what are you saying, Ignatov?"

"Just what you hear," I repeated sharply.

This story quickly spread around in our circles.

Moyshe-Leyb Halpern had a very special taste for responsibility. Though very few people knew about it, he waited for me in the restaurant the following day and fixed his big blue eyes on me:

"Is what I've heard true?"

"Yes."

"But Ignatov, you wouldn't do such a thing — it would be a crime! How do you insult a person so?"

"You're the one who has committed the crime and done the insulting here. How do you allow a kibitzer to be selected as the editor of a *Literature* volume?"

"But Ignatov — it's already a done deal. And besides — you weren't in New York. We all know your opinion that an editor should be a 'a man with a beard,' and you see what came of that!"

"That's true, but Yitskhok Rayz must not be the editor."

"But you yourself don't want the job."

"If you need me, I'll be willing."

"But Ignatov, I want you to know that I've seen with my own eyes that Rayz has already sent out announcements and invitations to contribute to Warsaw, Lemberg, and Cracow. What would he look like — it would be a terrible slap in the face! We mustn't do that to a comrade"

"A slap in Yitskhok Rayz's face," I answered, "is a slap in the face of one man. Letting him become the editor of the *Literature* anthology is a slap in the face of all of us, and that will not happen."

In invoking Yitskhok Rayz's notification of and invitation to European writers, Halpern was using a very poor argument. He was inadvertently pouring oil on the fire of my anger. I had always gone around thinking that we here in America had to free ourselves from the hegemony of European Yiddish literature—let them over there look to us and not we to them. And here, suddenly we were extending invitations to 'them', i.e., asking 'them' to come and help prettify our volume. That completely undermined its value, its stature. That's all we needed!

Halpern was torn here between two duties as it were — his duty to his comrade Yitskhok Rayz and his duty to be responsive to my complaints.

"Insulting a comrade like that is not gentlemanly. Even if you're right, you mustn't do that, Ignatov!"

"Halpern," I answered him sharply, "this Sunday there's a meeting of our group. You can vote against me there."

"No, Ignatov," the kind, gentlemanly Halpern answered me. "Voting against you is something I won't do, but I'll fight against taking a new vote. That must not be allowed. It's not ethical. One doesn't insult a person that way. One mustn't!"

A little later, Yitskhok Rayz came in. He was tall and slender, but his face was practically black with excitement. He wanted to talk to me privately. The two of us left Sholem's Café and walked into the narrow little corridor that led to the Palais photographic studio upstairs from the café.

"Ignatov," Rayz said to me, upset and standing right next to me, "I've heard — but you really wouldn't do such a thing to me?! After all, I was elected unanimously. I've already written to Europe"

His face got even darker— I'll never be able to forget the darkness of his face. But I was seized by a wild passion. I laid on him not only my eyes, but also, I think the fingers of my hands, and answered with a burning fury:

"You won't be the editor of this volume of *Literature* even if I have to choke you with my own hands."

Yes, a lot of fanaticism and a lot of hot blood went into the struggle to establish our group, *Di Yunge.*

At the meeting, I became chairman (I think only because I declared myself chairman.) I immediately declared that this was a special meeting of our group and that the agenda was — new elections for the editor of the second volume of *Literature.*

I think Moyshe-Leyb Halpern was the youngest one among us. His hair was smoothly combed and his suit was freshly pressed. He was tall and had big hands, big blue eyes, and a red freckle-face with milk-white teeth and full lips. He stood up like a young lion springing up, and with careful, measured steps began to make the necessary parliamentary motions about the illegality of the meeting. When that didn't help, he took the floor. His teeth, which always shared the hearty, kindly Halpern smile with his beautifully formed, full lips, were not smiling then. A deep seriousness didn't allow it. It was the way I once upon a time saw Dajinsky speak before the deputies of the Austrian parliament. Halpern's big, freckled hands, which always elegantly accented his beautiful smile were the measure of his excited seriousness. From time to time, he grabbed the broad leather belt around his waist with one hand and straightened the glasses on his nose with the other hand. All of that seemed to emphasize his image. He began by saying that he had to declare here that if a new vote took place, God forbid, he himself would vote for Ignatov, but that we mustn't permit a new vote. Our sense of personal dignity must not permit a new vote. Didn't we vote last week? Are we children or adults? By insulting an elected comrade, we will insult ourselves. And we want to bring dignity to literature, after all. We want to elevate the Yiddish word, the Yiddish person who is the bearer of our literature. We must set an example of gentility, of gentlemanliness, if we want to make the necessary impression on the world around us. And so on and so on. He meant all of that with complete seriousness, but he wasn't at complete peace with himself. There was a dramatic, and I would say tragic, tinge to his speech, because he couldn't help emphasizing that he had respect for Ignatov's motives. And that, together with his declaration that if it came to a new vote he himself would vote for Ignatov, resulted in Yitskhok Rayz's being left with almost no votes.

In addition to me, our dear friend Y.Y. Shvarts was also elected to the editorial board. Shvarts and a few other comrades wanted very much to put both our names on the title page as editors of the second volume, the way the editors of the first volume had. However, I still felt that an editor has to be 'a man with a beard,' and we left it that we would settle for writing on the last empty page of the volume: "The current volume is appearing under the supervision of a new editorial board."

For the sake of making a point, the second volume of *Literature* opened
with Mani Leyb's rejected series of poems (which were supposed to be
burned, you understand), and the first one, indeed, was the very strongly
mocked poem:

Dove-silent blue evening hours....

New writers were presented for the first time in the volume: Yoysef
Opatoshu, with a story entitled *On the Other Side of the Bridge*, Avrom
Moyshe Dilon, with his first two poems, and Y.L. Kahan, with his article
about Yiddish folk-songs.

Kahan was a modest and reticent person. He seemed to want to hide
from himself. In addition, he was busy from morning to night with his jewelry business. But I found out that after lunch he used to go upstairs to a
room above the store to take a nap. So I took it upon myself to wake him
from his nap day after day till I got the major piece from him, even though
it wasn't completely finished. The volume also included a long and excellent series of poems by B. Lapin. Yoysef Rolnik , who was waiting to
see his poem published — patiently, quietly and wisely, just as in one of his
poems a peasant on the shore of a river waits for a rapidly swimming fish
that he pulls out of the clear stream just at the right moment and then sells
(*For A Jew's Sabbath*—see *Der Oshets*)— had his classic poem *To the
Table, To the Table—Who Will Go With Me?* published. Included too, of
course, was my *A Winter Night: An American Story*, and two other stories
about American life.

Because of my insistence on emphasizing what was American in us, I
informed everyone who had a desire to be included in the volume that if he
would submit a piece on an American theme he was sixty percent certain
to be included. That promise, to the extent I was able to carry it out in that
issue, didn't do any extra favor for the in any case beautiful and important
volume. Furthermore, I was too strict an editor: for example, B. Botvinik
and Herman Gold, who agreed to the changes I demanded, remained very
dissatisfied afterwards.

The really great dissatisfaction, however, revealed itself at the meeting
after the volume appeared. About twenty writers were represented in the
volume, but the group *Literature* comprised about 70 members, and at the

following meeting almost all of the members who hadn't been published took the floor. The criticisms by the dissatisfied took very strange forms, and it looked as if they would never end. So one fine Sunday I decided that I wasn't going to go to meetings any more. When I didn't come for a few Sundays, the whole game stopped, and in that way the group *Literature* petered out with time.

The second volume remained unsold, just like the first one. We had no place to keep the books, so Meisel, the protector and guardian of better Yiddish books, agreed to keep them for us. I'm inclined to believe that of the thousand copies we printed of each of the two volumes, he must still have about eight hundred.

* * *

After that, two full years passed. The 'friends' of our movement eventually had full opportunity to demonstrate that it had been, generally speaking, a tempest in a teacup. And there were even also some who found it necessary to reassure people that *Di Yunge* had not, God forbid, deliberately withdrawn from the battlefield in order to regroup, gather new ammunition, and then, with renewed strength, mount a new attack with better prospects for victory. Oh, no! Such a thing might happen with other groups, but not with us. In our case it was not more than a feeble attempt by pretentious people, just an echo from an empty place. We Jews, it seems, are destined for nothing better, etc.

Among ourselves, we had no inkling at all that we were strategists, but strategy was working among us by itself. Those were two years of external ceasefire and deep internal bitterness, but also years of selection and preparation. Then, one morning, I opened my eyes on the cot in my little room on Washington Avenue, and the minute I opened them I almost seemed to hear: "Anthologies — we're going to publish anthologies." I realized that a decision had been made here, almost unconsciously, as it were, and that it was a decision that had to be carried out. It had to! And it had to be done without an official group, and there had to be only a couple of contributors. The much decried, much mocked collection *Literature* had had too many people involved in it. We had to revitalize and rehabilitate *Di Yunge*, and we had to do it by bringing together just a few people.

And I decided in my own mind that the first volume should consist of writings by only four people, and who the first four should be.

All the stifled dreams about a new Yiddish literature that would arise before our eyes and would, like a bright stream, enter world literature, had fallen apart for me. So later that day I dropped in on Mani Leyb, who lived far away from me, somewhere in Brooklyn:

"Mani Leyb — we're going to publish anthologies!"

"Well, Ignatov! When?" Mani Leyb cried out, astonished, and asked: "When are you calling a meeting?"

"No meetings!" I answered decisively.

"Really, Ignatov?! Entirely without meetings? And what will they be called? *Literature?*"

"What they'll be called, I don't know yet, but certainly not *Literature*. There'll be time enough to think of a name. Have you finished the third ballad?"

In those days, I went around demanding that other poets start to write longer pieces. I wanted to see in Yiddish a novel in verse, like *Eugene Onegin*, historical works like *Mazepa*, or *Boris Goudonov*, or a work like *Gorie To Uma* (Troubles From Wisdom). In the case of Mani Leyb, I had gotten him to start writing a novel about a Jewish shop-girl, but he had only made a beginning. I was more successful with him when I drew his attention to ballads and folk-tales. I myself was then working on a series of stories that a grandmother was telling to children sitting around her near the fire of the stove, weaving her life for them through the folk customs and beliefs, through the rise and fall of the fires in the stove. That example helped me a lot here. My words, it seems, resonated for Mani Leyb, and he started to write his *Little Wreaths of Flowers*, which were supposed to be three ballads. Mani Leyb still fought with me quite a bit about why I was so demanding, and wrote only two ballads and part of the third. My eyes used to light up with each new line, each image, each emotion and nuance of emotion. It seemed to me that I was watching the virtually magical birth of a folk quality that had lain hidden in its purity for generations and had now, in the form of stories, started to sing of joy, of Fate, and of sorrow, with a kindly, healthy, playful smile about everything.

The last of the these ballads promised to be the most important, but the moment I asked Mani Leyb whether he had finished the third ballad yet, he, in order to avoid answering, asked me a question:

"Does Zisho Landoy know about the proposed anthologies yet?"

"No, Mani Leyb, you are the first to hear it from me. Landoy will be the second to hear it, but not till this evening. He's working now, painting the ceilings of a house somewhere, or putting wallpaper on its walls."

"He's a great poet, Landoy."

* * *

Despite all the noise made by the movement around us, we didn't have any readers, though quite large audiences used to come to our literary evenings and they used to receive the writers who appeared with warm applause. There were various reasons for that: admittance was only 10 cents and the anthology volume cost 25 cents. But it might also have meant that looking at writers, and even listening to them, is a lot easier than reading them.

I had decided that the new anthology should be called *Writings*. That name, like all new names, didn't please anyone. Even Yitskhok Rayz, who carried a burning grudge against me, wanted to help me nevertheless, and several times he accosted me and followed me in the streets and complained:

"What does *Writings* mean? One refers to Perets' writings, Mendele's writings, Sholem Aleichem's writings, Kobrin's writings, but an anthology can't be called just *Writings*. An anthology has to have a name, and *Writings* is not a name."

And he would add in a mocking tone:

"You know what? Just call it *Manuscripts*."

Our good friend Max N. Meisel, to whom I turned to buy the anthology *Writings* even before it appeared, also explained to me that *Writings* was no name for an anthology, and when he heard that its price would be 60 cents, he looked at me and said:

"You know — they say about your writing that it's crazy. Well — I don't know about that. Perhaps it's talent. But 60 cents for an anthology of works by unknown writers — that is insanity! That much I know. Listen, my child! We couldn't sell your anthology volumes, which cost only 25 cents!"

"But I'm only going to print 300 copies of the book."

"That, too, is insanity. If that's what you're going to do, then why print it at all? Isn't it better to print more copies and make the price cheaper? After all, you have to try to attract readers."

"I've decided that there are no readers, for the time being, and that we publish the books out of an inner need and not because of external demand, and that has to emphasized openly. It is necessary to make that point clear. I have written a declaration on the last page of the volume: *"The present book of writings is being published in a very limited number of copies. That, of course will make it possible, on some other occasion, to 'curse us out' as aristocrats who don't care at all about the readers. But the present volume appears in such a limited number of copies because we have learned a lesson from the weak sales of the previous volumes."*

Right after the anthology appeared, I was especially strongly mocked in *Di Tsukunft*. First of all, they said, my story in the volume used the word 'and' too often, and secondly, how do you publish and declare publicly that you have no readers? Wasn't that foolishness? And the one who wrote that was my subsequent long-time dear comrade Borukh Vladeck.

But the volume just happened to start selling very well, even though the price was raised to a whole dollar. People were to be found who started to think: "A dollar for a book in Yiddish? That's for me! Such an impression did it make. And after that we published the 'Special Edition' in another 200 copies.

*   *   *

Moyshe-Leyb Halpern was not represented in the first volume of *Writings*, because I had decided that only those would be in the first volume who hadn't published during the whole period of the so-called ceasefire, either because no one wanted them anywhere or because they didn't want to publish for new people. Halpern however, had published from time to time during that period. (Halpern was never angry at me because of that; he was, as I have already mentioned, a man with a great feeling of responsibility, though not everyone knew he had it.)

*   *   *

Ayzland was a very quiet, fine fellow. He used to come to our gatherings and used to meet us at the Klings' house and on the hill in Claremont Park, or on Sundays at my place in the room on Washington Avenue, which he used to call his *khasidizm-shul*. But it never occurred to me to count him as one of *Di Yunge*. The couple of poems he had published (I think in the Zionist weekly *Dos Folk*) were pallid and flat— well intentioned but airless. That he had pretentions to be published in the anthology *Writings,* and in the first volume yet, was quite unexpected, and I didn't want to hear of it. But something accidentally came to his aid: I wanted to have an article about *Di Yunge*, but there was no publicist among us at that time, and I decided that even a stranger could write about literature (in this case, *Di Yunge*) in our book, as long as he wrote what should be written. I began to run around looking for critics among the older writers, but none of them, even those who had half promised me, wanted to do it. It turned out that my belief in *Di Yunge* had had a good effect only on the young writers. The older ones were simply afraid of being discredited if they started writing about us as if we were 'real' writers. A couple of them offered us poems, stories, or just some little article. That only increased my desperation, because though I had real respect for some of them, I didn't need the pieces they proposed to send in for the planned volume, and the fact that they didn't understand that upset me.

Then Ayzland came to me:

"That you don't want to publish my poems — well, perhaps you're right. But you're running around looking for an article about *Di Yunge* — why would you want to give people about whom you have a low opinion a chance to refuse you? Why shouldn't you give me the opportunity?"

And so, after some more brief discussions, it was decided.

"OK—write it. As long as it's what we need, I'll print it."

So Ayzland wrote a lengthy article entitled *Di Yunge*. Despite the paeans of praise about all of us, I decided to print only the first half, the part about our young poets. The piece was not in the tone or tempo of the other pieces in the book, but still it said what we wanted it to say.

The first anthology volume, as already mentioned, was treated humorously in Ayzland's article, which spoke of the boys of *Di Yunge* as if about 'real writers'. It was severely mocked by Avrom Reyzn. Reyzn, whose magazine, *The New Land*, had recently started appearing, took the liberty, speaking almost entirely about our contributors, of writing that "some fellow named Ayzland writes there about the poets and gives the impression of children playing house."

All of us took that as a terrible insult:

"What does he mean by writing "some fellow named Ayzland"!"

On Opatoshu's motion, it was decided in my room that we would declare a strike against Reyzn's *New Land* because of the insult he had hurled at 'our' Ayzland. Ayzland's honor had suddenly become everyone's honor.

For the second volume of *Writings*, Ayzland's piece about the prose writers still didn't satisfy me, though of course he praised all of us and all of us wanted praise about ourselves printed. When the comrades pressed the point strongly, I proposed that if it was so important to them, I would publish the piece for their sakes, but I would remove the part where it talked about me and eliminate every place where he mentioned my name. That seemed to sober the comrades, and after that they said nothing more to me about the piece.

The second volume of *Writings* (1913) was published without the participation of Ayzland, but Ayzland never forsook us. He remained *khasidically* loyal, and as before, religiously observed his Sundays in my little room.

Before the third volume came out, Ayzland came one day and read me the following lines:

It's noon. Around us, all is quiet.
Only a single machine
is humming like a bee, somewhere in a corner.
A girl is eating, cracking the shell of an egg,
and one or two others are sipping tea
in a warm and cozy mood.
Nearby someone is munching onions and bread —
and there are pale girls painted red.

And in the window I sit alone,
my legs crossed and my hands in my lap,
and look out — just look out.

That quiet, fine way of observing the very simple things in the simple, gray life around us, that way of describing the simplicity of an ordinary gray day of a worker in a New York shop — all of that was so different, so much quieter, deeper, and truer than the screaming poems of Rozenfeld and Bovshover of those days. It was also so different in tone and color from the poems of Rolnik, Landoy, Halpern, and Mani Leyb. I and my comrades felt that a new tone had now been presented, a tone of factualness, a tone that brought in the half-shadowed, half-quiet, important everyday. This introduced a larger scope and strongly influenced the other poets of our group. Though I remained cold to Ayzland's later poems after that, I find it thoroughly important to emphasize that his series of poems that were published in the third volume of *Writings*, in the year 1913, were a very great accomplishment. They helped to illuminate, in a new and different way, the life around us, our own poor shops, our own poor houses. They posed for us a new and sobering demand. The refined Zisho Landoy was the first to answer the call, and that, together with his unique, bizarre unexpectedness and deep religiosity, affected that very important Yiddish poet in a quite different way.

* * *

Yes, we are living in a bitter, severely oppressive time. It's difficult to write jubilee articles, difficult to have celebrations in such a time. The light from the Betar conflagration, set by the Romans, shines more powerfully today than ever before. But celebrations, even in bitter time, make their own light. With that light, I have tried to cite the accomplishments of our early days, in which our jubilee honorees participated. I have also mentioned several comrades who are still alive and will live among us for a long time yet, though tombstones have already been standing on their graves for a long time.

Brooklyn Heights, NY, July 1944

(From the book *Torn-Out Pages*)

Ruvn Ayzland (1884-1955) was one of the three most prominent poets of *Di Yunge* (the others were Mani Leyb and Zisho Landoy.) His poems, which encased some- times strong emotions in a few words and chiseled lines, exuded a soft and gentle spirit.

~

Ruvn Ayzland

We Are Both Old

We are both old—
two old folks, with soft, clouded eyes
sitting by the window.
A lovely day, the sky just slightly overcast
with thin white clouds.
She says: "Hey old man, it's getting cold—
shut the window and put your warm robe on."
I sit and quietly smoke my pipe and read a page
and think: how eternally foolish women are.

The clock chimes,
and she, she turns around and looks
with long glances at the clock-face
to see how late it is,
though the clock sounds the hours clearly.

So late already—how the day flies!
A shrug of narrow shoulders and her hands fall to her lap.
And suddenly I'm cold. I poke my head outside
and see the thin white clouds turning red,
and I know that night is already lurking somewhere.

Still-Lifes

1

Bread and cheese and honey on the simple table—
goldenly the tea calls attention to itself
in two thin glasses,
and greenly cool and fresh
the water jug, bedecked with dew, beckons.
On a window-sill, a woman's handkerchief,
and beside it a small, wise hand
on a slender songbook
covered in wine-colored silk.

2

Like cool, full breasts with hidden fire,
heavy grapes lie next to
brown, masculinely long pears.
Womanly wanton, with tender redness,
two apples hug a cold, wise, shiny orange.
Two bananas stare like dull golems.
Avidly, like a girl after a first kiss,
a red cherry tears itself from a twig.

To Zisho Landoy

There is still a brightness that calls,
a tree that blooms, a road that leads somewhere,
and the joy of going.

There is still a book, a newspaper at hand,
a chair, a sofa, and a bed,
and the joy of resting.

And when the palmetto gleams in steel-green
and the vine climbs the white and pearl-grey walls;
and when the red roofs glow and the hibiscus flames
between dark pines and the green palmetto—
the heart blooms.

But when the enemy catches you unawares
and treads with heavy elephant feet on your chest
(the oleander in front of the window stills smells of sweet almonds,
And the bougainvilleas still caress with the cool violet red),
suddenly your tongue becomes like parchment and your eye like glass,
and all your limbs cry out, stiff and cold with fear:

"So soon?"

Twenty-Five Years Later

This Spring marks twenty-five years since the publication of the third
volume of *Shriftn* (Writings). That was an important date in Yiddish literature, because with those three volumes there began and ended the era of
the poetic movement that gave new direction to all of Yiddish literature, a
movement known to this day by the general, not very informative name *Di
Yunge* (The Young Ones). In the Gentile world, those three volumes would
now be considered rare finds, sought by professional collectors and considered treasures by book dealers and individual bibliophiles alike. Not by
us. Not long ago, I saw one of the volumes lying on a bargain table out in
front of a store, priced at all of fifteen cents. True, the bargain didn't remain
there for long—a taker quickly appeared. I am not sure, however, that there
would have been takers if the price had been not fifteen cents but, say, a few
dollars, or even just one dollar.

My doubts stem from a sad experience: several years ago, when the
twenty-fifth anniversary of one of our most famous poets was being celebrated here in New York, his closest colleagues published a selection of
his finest poems in a handsome deluxe edition, beautifully printed on the
finest paper and bound in morocco. The entire run was only thirty-seven

copies. In the Gentile world, such a book would have cost hundreds, and hundreds of people would have raced to buy it. But we priced this rare book at a mere ten dollars, and though it was advertised far and wide and almost two thousand people attended the anniversary celebration and the newspapers reported about both the event and the unusual book that the poet's colleagues had presented to him as an anniversary present, not a single person in all of America or anywhere else in the world wrote in and ordered a copy.

Non-Jews would celebrate the twenty-fifth anniversary of *Shriftn* not, God help us, with committees and a commotion in the newspapers and community halls, like the ones we constantly create for this or that 'great,' but with memoirs, critiques, and analyses; with revised editions, assessments, and reassessments; with a worshipful approach or the reverse— caustic irony; with explanations of the good things, the positive things that *Di Yunge* had contributed to Yiddish literature or the reverse— the bad things and the harmful things. But we let the date pass silently. No one writes a word, no one celebrates, no one even goes off into nostalgic raptures about the 'good old days,' and no one mocks them either. Only with a cultureless society is such a thing conceivable. Perhaps that's why we talk so much about culture: "If there isn't any brandy, let's at least talk about brandy!" So beloved is our Yiddish culture that no less than two big umbrella organizations fight over which shall have the honor of dealing with it, just as *khasidim*, in the old days, used to fight over who should have the honor of dealing with a great man's corpse. An apt metaphor.

For me personally, the book on the table elicited sentimental feelings, for though the first three volumes of *Shriftn* covered an important period in the history of Yiddish poetry, the appearance of the third and final volume was a not inconsequential milestone in my own life. In that volume was published my series of poems *Fun Ale Teg* (Of All The Days), which, in its time, barely made the grade. Much more important to me, however, that was where I found myself, for the first time, as a poet with an outspoken personal voice and style and a poetic approach of his own. I am not embarrassed to say that my heart skipped a beat when I spotted the oblong book with its thick, leather-colored cover with the long green inscription snaking over it lengthwise and the two thin little green trees on the crest of a small hill in the center. I went over to it the way one approaches a former lover that one meets suddenly after not having seen her for many years and having forgotten about her: with a bit of the old warmth and a mixture of curiosity and fear, because the eye, willy-nilly, is mercilessly objective — it sees a streak of gray in the hair and a row of wrinkles on the face, in addition to the numerous fundamental flaws that were always there and you knew they were there but you consciously overlooked them. How would those poems strike me today, twenty-five years after publication ? Would they be dated or still have the freshness of long ago ? What about the fundamental flaws of which I was aware even then but pretended not to see? In those poems, as noted above, I had found my path as a poet — was I still on it or had I long since gone on to other paths and byways?

And what about the whole volume, which had caused such a stir in the Yiddish literary world at that time? How would the poems of the others and the cadence of their prose sound to my ears now? To what extent had my path paralleled theirs, and where had the paths diverged? What had happened to them in the course of those twenty-five years ? How many of them were still close to me and to what degree were we estranged? And if estranged, what had led to it? What had happened to Yiddish literature in general during those twenty-five years? How many new people had appeared on the scene and how many of them had brought individual voices?

These and many other questions ran through my mind as I stood at the bargain table and leafed through the volume. But instead of an answer, there came wafting up to me from its pages sunlight and greenery, romantic hours spent in parks and on long walks through Bronx streets still under construction, talk and smoke over tiny tables in cellar restaurants smelling of mildew and amid the cozy walls of a bachelor's cramped room, pain and longing, sorrow and joy, long-vanished faces, voices, laughter, the sighs and tears of women who loved and were loved, the sharp words of colleagues who had been rendered sleepless by poisoned days and nights, poems and lines from poems by those same colleagues that made one drunk as if from wine and echoed in the ears for weeks, the springs and summers and winters when we were young and hopeful and vivacious and argumentative and sure that there was only one artistic truth and that we were its only prophets. Alas, alas! Could twenty-five years really have passed since then?!

Ten people had contributed to that volume, of whom three had since passed on. Another three had never truly belonged to the group. Of the remaining four, only two remained close—we seldom met the other two. Those who had died were Moyshe-Leyb Halpern, Avrom-Moyshe Dilon, and Zisho Landoy. Remaining were Mani Leyb, Dovid Ignatov, Ayzik Raboy, and myself. Mani Leyb and I were still as close as we had been then; both of us were estranged from Ignatov, and Raboy had distanced himself from us. He began working for the *Frayhayt* at a time when the party line was to separate oneself, and he obeyed religously, obeyed to the extent of openly proclaiming that he refuted all his previous writings—and he meant it, for in the pieces he began to publish in the *Frayhayt* there was no longer even a trace of the Raboy who was so dear to us since his first mature efforts began to appear in *Shriftn* and whom we had gotten to know personally at Ignatov's bachelor's studio on Washington Avenue, where we used to gather every Sunday.

When we saw him for the first time, everything about him looked big and dark and healthy. His movements were slow and broad, redolent of the small town and strange to us urban dwellers. His dark face lit up with a smile full of big, healthy, beautifully horse-like teeth when we were introduced, and he extended a big, healthy workman's hand. From the very first, he radiated an earnest simplicity and freshness to which we were not at all accustomed. In contrast to the rest of us, at our first meeting he spoke not about literature but about the farm somewhere in Connecticut where he still lived at the time. Things weren't going well for him there, and sooner or later he would have left it anyway, but, if I'm not mistaken, that first Sunday afternoon at Ignatov's studio hastened his leaving it.

In those days, we were all full of literary ideas and plans, like ripe fruits full of juice, and when we met, the 'skins' would burst and the ideas would flow out in our conversation. The long hours every Sunday at Ignatov's, from afternoon till late in the night, were so rich in ideas, so exciting and mutually stimulating, that for three days afterward we were still savoring the inspiration we received there and for the next three days we lived in joyous anticipation of the next get- together. Quite often it was truly a pleasure to spend a Sunday there. So you can imagine that after such a Sunday spent in the warm company of friends (for which he had yearned even before he met them) Raboy would not be able to stay on his lonely farm very long. Soon thereafter he moved to the city and, of course, became a regular like the rest of us.

I don't know whether it was his going to work in the same shop as Ignatov that made him feel he had too much of Ignatov during the week to want to spend Sundays with him in addition, or whether he didn't feel comfortable amid so much talk of literature, but just like the characters in his stories and novels, he himself was not very talkative. Theoretical discussions left him cold. So he used to think a lot and say very little. Talking, for him (I'm speaking of those days, when we all contributed to *Shriftn*), was not the explanation of a thought but the whole of the thought. Often, when a conversation was growing heated over some kind of theoretical matter, he would suddenly break in to relate an episode. At the start, it would seem to us that the story had nothing to do with the matter we had been discussing, but as we listened (and we had to listen, because what he told us always aroused our interest), we would realize that somehow his story really did relate to that matter .

From Raboy's stories and novels of those days, you would get the joyous feeling that you were reading the work of a man who had perhaps never read a book in his life and felt that there had been no stories before he wrote and that literature itself had begun with him. His remarks were raw and clumsy, but not without charm, and even weight. But the later Raboy renounced the old one even before he started working for the *Frayhayt,* though he himself may not have been aware of it. The change was already noticeable in his *A Jew Came to America.* Way down deep, however, he retained the same honesty he had had before, and now and then it won out over the fallacies he had allowed to seduce him. Even after his public split from his old self and from everything and everyone that linked him to it, he still couldn't escape his essential self—Raboy remained Raboy.

Our estrangement from Ignatov had begun much earlier, as long ago as the completion of the third volume of *Shriftn*, but the final split came somewhat later. In our hearts, we still have a feeling of warmth and closeness to him and Raboy, and they probably feel the same about us—I often yearn for them. When I hear Ignatov's voice on the telephone (I haven't heard Raboy's voice for years), my heart reaches out to him, but the moment I meet him, I feel that though his health and the well-being of his family concern me, talking with him about that which concerns a writer the most— writing—is something I cannot do. In the course of these twenty-five years, a distance has grown between us that is greater than the distance of time—

we speak two different languages, so different that we no longer understand each other. Did we ever understand each other? Yes and no.

All three volumes of *Shriftn* contained important and valuable things, and not just for their time. In each of the volumes, there was one item that outshone all the others: In the first volume, it was Yoysef Opatoshu's *The Romance of a Horse-Thief*; in the second, it was the same author's *Morris And His Son Phillip*; and in the third, it was Mani Leyb's *Yingl Tsingl Khvat* (The Fearless Boy). These evaluations refer to the opinions of the reviewers and the broad audience of readers, but within the narrow circle of poets, we were far from agreeing with them. The 'connoisseurs,' as Opatoshu angrily labeled them, felt that the sole merit of the first volume lay in Mani Leyb's and Zisho Landoy's poems, Moyshe-Leyb Halpern's poem *In a Strange Land*, and Ignatov's *The Strong Man*. The rest, they felt, might just as well not have been printed. In the second volume, the inner circle found Isaac Raboy's fragment *The Lighthouse*, Mani Leyb's and Zisho Landoy's poems, and parts of Ignatov's *In Keslgrub* (In The Whirlpool) worthwhile. From the third volume, however, they found it hard to single out any one piece, for just about everything pleased all of them—-except that which had been a hit with the general public, Mani Leyb's *Yingl Tsingl Khvat*, which instantly became a classic. That poem made Zisho Landoy physically sick, and when he couldn't stand something, especially from a person close to him and for whom he felt affection, he could lash out so violently that the target would 'see stars.' In Landoy's eyes, Mani Leyb had fallen from his poetic heights with *Yingl Tsingl Khvat*. I agreed. Mani Leyb's lyrical poems had always captured us with their vividness, fine nuances, delicate feel, and the musical quality of the lines, which were almost always loaded with hidden energy, and here he had suddenly come out with a rhymed tale in which clumsy trochees chased each other in a sing-song pattern, with affected childishness! That was then, but when I read his children's tale now, I recognize how unfair our judgment was. With all of its flaws—and it has quite a few—and aside from the fact that it has been made to appear banal by hundreds of imitations, *Yingl Tsingl Khvat* was and remains a masterpiece, with its purity, its fine and quiet humor, its flowing diction and deft rhymes, and, most importantly, its innumerable images, scenes, and situations that are presented so lightly and playfully, often with just a stroke or two. It will always have a place of honor, and not only in our children's literature.

In our eyes, at that time, Mani Leyb's short lyric poem *Shtiler, Shtiler* (Stiller, Stiller), with which the third volume of *Shriftn* opens, stood on a much higher artistic level than *Yingl Tsingl Khvat*. Now, however, I see that we were wrong about that, too. True, that short lyrical poem has four wonderful stanzas, but it also has excessive padding: a passage that repeats itself like a refrain no less than three times, when we could have done without it altogether.

It occurs to me that that poem impressed us, the esthetes, the proponents of 'art for art's sake,' not so much because of its artistic value as because in it our moral outlook on life had been poetically expressed for the first time. Incidentally, that outlook probably seems reactionary in the current turbulent and revolutionary time. On our way to artistic truths, we came to realizations that could only lead to a particular moral outlook on life. One of those realizations was that no man can raise himself to true art so long as he tries to exceed the strengths that are etched into his character and blood. In order not to exceed them, the first and most important thing is to try to understand them. The path to such understanding must lead to humility—when one recognizes the limits of his own abilities, he also senses the greater forces outside himself that he will never be able to reach, let alone overcome. What one cannot reach, he ceases to want. Perhaps only a child wants pie in the sky. In other words, in order to achieve completness in whatever one may undertake, he must not exceed the limits of his own abilities—he must give up the rest. No sooner does one come to such an understanding than he must accept it as a guideline not only in art but also in life. When we of *Di Yunge* set esthetic goals for ourselves, we also accepted ethical responsibilities, through which the goals were to be achieved. One of them was resignation. Mani Leyb was the first to make poetic use of the resignation-motif, in the previously-mentioned poem. *Shtiler, Shtiler* is a poem about the hope for the Messiah that has lived in us for thousands of years and for the sake of which we have renounced the dearest things and have endured the most difficult things in life (incidentally, Mani Leyb was the first modern poet in America to deal with the Messiah-motif.) The hope is that the Messiah will come, if not today, then tomorrow, and if not tomorrow, then the day after, and

From his pure and shining face,
his robe so white and clear,
his joy will come upon us here
and we will gain his holy grace.

But what if he doesn't come, if the entire hope of millenia is only a deception, a swindle, a mockery of our dark fate? The grief will be great and deep, but the stubborn will to endure will be greater still.

If it's true we've been deceived
and mocked about our bitter plight,
and through the long and lonely night
in vain have we believed,

we'll feel ourselves a broken folk
and bend down to the floor.
We'll sit so still and speak no more—
just stiller, stiller, quiet smoke.

Resignation rises to the level of heroism. This, I believe, impressed us more than anything at the time, and we therefore overlooked or pretended not to see that in Mani Leyb's poem, the Messiah will arrive on nothing other than the clichéd "white horse" and will wear nothing other than "a clear white robe." We also overlooked the fact that the key word "shtil" (still), which should set the tone of the poem, is repeated so many times that it virtually begins to scream.

In my younger years, when I read a poem once or twice it stayed in my memory. As time has passed, everything has been erased, but the tone and flavor of the poem have remained. I can even recall whether the sun was shining or it was raining, and what aromas were hanging in the air. When I heard a poem recited, the reader's voice and tone, the faces and voices of those around, and indeed the whole atmosphere stayed in my memory. When I recently reread the five poems that Zisho Landoy published in the third volume of *Shriftn*, he rose up before me just as he was in life: thin and blond, with large blue eyes and very full, sensitive lips that always twitched when he recited. His voice, like Halpern's, would become completely different when he was reciting than when he was speaking. Halpern simply hypnotized you with his slow, long, rolling reading style, and if I hadn't known that he had many followers and admirers on the other side of the ocean, where they had never heard him, I would have said that he owed a large part of his success as a poet to the way he recited. Landoy, in contrast, was unable to mesmerize a large audience with his recitation, but anyone who heard him recite one-on-one never forgot it. His voice would go into a kind of falsetto, which should have been unpleasant, one would think, and yet it had great power. And what he could make of a poem with his recitation! With just one placement of stress, he could kill a poem forever, or, conversely, bring out the most important and beautiful part of it, planting it permanently in the heart of the listener. This was as true with other poets' works as with his own. Interestingly, when reciting others' poems he could occasionally disappoint, but with his own—never! When I read the above-mentioned five poems these days, I see that those that I didn't like then, I still don't like today, and those that captured me then have lost none of their appeal for me over the years.

Those of his poems that made a splash then were: *Negerins* (Negresses), *Dinstik* (Tuesday), and *In Der Yugnt* (In Youth), a poem adapted from a Biblical theme. He was reproached for striking the pose of a young tough simply for shock value, and it was indeed true that he sought to shock, but that in no way diminished the beauty of the portrait he painted in *Negerins,* the indifference he described in *Dinstik,* or the lovely form he gave to a naïve, ancient Jewish view of the difference between men and women in *In Der Yugnt.*

Ignatov had also been accused of seeking to shock the reader by declaring his love of snakes in his introduction to *Phoebe,* but this was not true. He wanted to perplex rather than shock the reader with this very strange declaration. True, in essence it was supposed to be no more than a symbol, so to speak, an indication, a hint that the story he was setting out to tell was about a girl who was a snake that poisoned with flirtation instead of venom. At the same time, however, he used the opportunity to demonstrate his fearlessness, his uniqueness, and his differentness. All humans fear snakes? Everyone is disgusted by them? Then I shall show them that not only do I not fear them, not only do they not disgust me, but I can sit down and consider them so dispassionately that I can see how beautiful they are, and come to love them for their beauty. That will to show off and make a point of his originality (quite often in a not-very-clever way) kept Ignatov from becoming the fine artist he could have become. This character trait of his led to our not always understanding each other, even at the time when we were very close. It manifested itself not only in his writings but also in his editing of *Shriftn*. The volumes he published had to be the most beautiful, even in regard to appearance, and he spent massive amounts of money and energy toward that end. Naturally, none of us could be opposed to that. And though Landoy looked askance at Ignatov's 'little pictures' even then, his disapproval was directed not at the outward appearance of the books but at the drawings with which Ignatov had decorated them from the beginning.

I have already noted elsewhere that Landoy felt that we of *Di Yunge* should concern ourselves in our publications solely with the art of words. All other arts, in his opinion, had to be excluded, because in our appreciation for other arts, insofar as we had any, we were no more than dilettantes. To give up space in our publications to visual arts or music, for example, would therefore be pretentious, in his opinion. Mani Leyb and I both agreed and disagreed with him. We both could have done very well without the pictures in the volumes, but their presence didn't bother us either. On the other hand, however, all three of us were strongly opposed to the 'weight' and 'importance' that Ignatov wanted to give *Shriftn* by including the works of older, eminent writers. We did not want an established celebrity to 'decorate' and give more 'weight and importance' to our journal—we needed to achieve our own importance through our own creations. By placing ourselves in the shadow of a celebrity, we would certainly never achieve it.

That trait of his, wanting to add something to what he already has, has done Ignatov much harm. He is surely one of our finest talents—none of us has yet written prose as wonderful as his. If he would content himself with the great gift he has been given, he would achieve much, but the trouble is that he doesn't content himself with it—he always needs something more. Even that might not be a problem, but the fact that the 'something more' doesn't come from himself but is arbitrarily selected, and is mostly very inconsequential, and the fact that the 'something more' is so often and so strongly stressed, makes him look ridiculous and makes him overlook the fact that in the end it is all only trivial and superfluous material that could have been excised from the publication like so many unnecessary tumescences. Tumescences are never a sign that the organism as a whole is unfit, merely that the particular area is unfit. Ignatov's short introduction to *Phoebe* caused people to overlook the immense merits of that work, one of the most beautiful and successful novels we have in Yiddish. There is little in our literature that is comparable to his language, tone, and rhythm, his mode of introducing characters, the moods that grow from the encounters, the conversations and silences, and the dramatic atmosphere that hangs over it all. As in *Phoebe*, so in his other past works: there is enormous talent everywhere, but there is also a great deal that is superfluous and overly intellectual, hiding what is good and central.

Over the course of the years, Raboy's *Herr Goldenbarg* has become somewhat dated, as have all our pieces from that time, but the magic and charm of his simplicity have remained. There are contrivances in his work, too, but they don't bother anyone—at worst they elicit a smile, but never derisive laughter. Even the contrivances have their charm, that special Raboyesque charm whose source one can never determine. When you read about the joy that begins to grow in the young farmhand when the Jewish farmer, Herr Goldenbarg, brings his sister's girl, Dvoyre, to the farm in the Far West, you sense here and there a superfluous word, or even a contrived line, but taken as a whole, the joy spills over to the reader, just as in a fine poem.

Like his hero, Raboy himself is no great talker. When he wishes to 'say' something, he may not find the right word, but he almost always correctly senses the proper tone and manner of the character whose feelings he has conceived. Very few writers have feelings that are as awake as Raboy's, especially that Raboy with whom we were so delighted in our youth.

From *Fun Undzer Friling*

Yoyel Slonim (1884-1944), another prominent figure in *Di Yunge*, wrote principally essays, though he sometimes wrote poetry about such things as peacocks and nightingales.

~

Yoyel Slonim

Yiddish In America

Though I was reared in America,
I spoke only Yiddish at home.
I devoured Yiddish novels with my eyes
and dreamed only of becoming a poet.

My mother often sat bent over a prayer-book —
the gas lamp in her room glowed weakly.
I'd see on her face the light of the Divine Spirit
and a sort of holiness in her hands.

My father, restless, would walk around and sing
Berditshever[14] tunes, prayerful and soft,
and I used to look at him in wonderment
while wondrous goodness penetrated my heart from above.

I so loved the simple people,
the boys with real, true speech,
and when our rabbi blessed us from the lectern
my heart used to fill with pure joy.

I was alert to folksongs and *khasidic* tunes
through the noise of the sweatshop and my deepest poverty.
I dreamed of flaming rhythms and magical sounds
in Yiddish, the mother-tongue of my soul.

---

[14] From the town of Berditshev, a stronghold of *khasidizm*

145

And Yiddish poets, those from Russia or Poland,
from Lithuania and Galicia and from all the world,
came enveloped in a certain radiance,
with deeply wounded hearts

They went through darkness to the light,
hunched-over in shops, without anger or regret,
composed bright songs on Yiddish,
and built a magical castle here in America

And at the Hudson river and the lakeshores,
multi-colored Yiddish songs flamed up
with love for America, on untrodden roads
toward freedom, intoxicated by folk-themes.

And I — I went along, rain or shine,
through rocky roads or roads of grass,
toward the dream with everyone,
and felt happy—I am a Yiddish poet

2.

I meet a man and he greets me in Yiddish;
my heart grows warm with joy.
I'm back on the East Side —
real Yiddish speech caresses me.

And here's a little *shul*. Men are glowing over the Talmud—
Jews, inflamed, old and gray.
And here's a *khasidic shtibl*[15]— enthusiasm.
We stare and take pleasure.

And here's the clubhouse of the Bund,[16]

---

[15] A small synagogue
[16] The Jewish Labor Bund

and a red banner flutters in the window.
The sounds of "We swear, we swear,"[17]
fly out like stars being sown.

And here's the Zionist clubhouse, *Hatikvah*[18] —
they dream special dreams there,
and there echoes: "In the land of the cedar" —
they soar through mirages and miracles.

And next to the Alliance[19] — students, discussions,
debates, and everything with flame.
And Shakespeare, Spinoza, and Hegel and Goethe,
and Plato, Socrates, and the Rambam.[20]

And young colleagues, like dear brothers —
our heart is a magnet.
We speak about skits, about poems,
about how good it is to be a poet!

And farther — sad tones wail from a piano.
I am rooted to the spot.
'What does all this mean'[21] lulls me to sleep
in my quiet mood.

I don't know why,
I could never explain the secret to myself:
why I love folksongs till it hurts
and Talmudic melodies to the point of tears.

---

[17] Words from *Di Shvue* (The Oath), the Bundist anthem
[18] The title of the Zionist anthem
[19] The Educational Alliance, a nonprofit Jewish educational institution on the Lower East Side
[20] Maimonides, a famous medieval Jewish scholar and theologian
[21] A Talmudic saying

Is it because the light of our grandparents
is magically hidden in them,
or because I saw in them
phantasmic faces of martyrs?

Or is it because my father used to sing
the most beautiful melodies after *kiddush*,[22]
or because I imbibed my love for Yiddish
with my mother's milk?

I only know that wherever Fate may take me,
to whatever lands I go,
the light of Yiddish will shine eternally in my heart
like the light from the menorah.[23]

[22] Blessing of wine
[23] The eight-branched candelabrum lit on *khanike*

Zisho Landoy (1889-1937) was one of the most talented of the poets in *Di Yunge*. He was an exponent of "pure" poetry, free of social themes and excessive rhetoric, and he celebrated the joys of everyday existence.

∿

Zisho Landoy

I'm The Man Of Song

I strolled through the city
and saw nothing at all,
as if before my eyes
there stood a blank wall.

No such wall was there, though—
the street was completely free.
Just houses, streets, and people
that I'd chosen not to see.

It wasn't some deep sorrow
that blotted out my sun.
A spring inside my heart
had simply overrun.

And what I understood then,
what I then perceived,
was for my understanding
alone by Fate conceived.

My blood, a deep and flowing stream,
a river flowing free,
is one with generations
before and after me.

I've something more to tell you,
but telling would be wrong,

149

for you are men of action
and I'm the man of song.

Until

Until our hour shall come,
we'll have joy and not succumb.

Let our eyes stray where they may —
life will blind with its array.

Children who can barely walk
master that and learn to talk.

Day breaks, sun shines, clouds fly by,
then night comes, blots out the sky.

And amidst your raven hair
sprouts a gray one, oddly fair.

Through the course of every pace,
wonder, wonder at His grace.

For Our Destroyed Jewish Life

For the Jewish life we had, now destroyed,
I fall and pray before you, God.
I weep for our mother Vilna,
for Kolomeya and for Brod,

for Warsaw, Kovno, Kalish, and Lemberg,
for cities large and small ones too,
for all the enemy has destroyed
and the destruction to ensue,

for every dirty Jewish alley,
for every store I cry and mourn,
for every bar, pawnshop, and inn,
for every measure falsely sworn,

for every Jewish bordello
among the homes of Gentile folk,
for everything that once was ours
that's gone and vanished in the smoke.

Clean and bright is all that's Jewish—
that impoverished life shall rise again!
Rock to sleep with quiet words
the saddened souls of men.

Ana Margolin (1887-1952) wrote beautiful, emotional, sensuous, lyrical, and distinctively feminine poetry. Though she was the life- companion of Ruvn Ayzland, one of the most important poets in the group *Di Yunge*, and also contributed to *In Zikh*, the journal of the Introspectivist group, she is not generally considered to have been an actual member of either group.

≈

Ana Margolin

Mother Earth

Mother Earth, much trodden, sunwashed —
dark slave and mistress
am I, my beloved.
From me, the lowly and sad,
you grow like a mighty tree-trunk,
and I, like the eternal stars and the flaming sun,
circle in long, blind silence
amid your roots and branches,
and half-awake and half-dozing
I seek high heaven through you.

Full of Night and Weeping

A silence, sudden and deep,
between the two of us,
like a confused letter
announcing parting,
like a sinking ship.

A silence without a look, without a motion,
full of night and weeping
between the two of us,
as if we ourselves
were closing the door
to Paradise.

Avrom Moyshe Dilon (1883-1934) was another of the poets in *Di Yunge*. His poems often expressed great longing.

~

Avrom Moyshe Dilon

Our Song Is Not Of Today

Our song is not of today —
it's for the coming years.
I feel so sad, my dearest friend,
though I choke back all my tears.

Deliberately, with rage,
they raped our yesteryears.
My weary hands are weeping,
though I choke back all my tears.

And where are they taking us today —
have we nothing left to give?
My dearest, closest friend —
can we pardon them, forgive?

They've torn apart all time,
and torn the thread of life.
My dearest, closest friend —
can we forgive their angry strife?

Our song is not of today —
it's for the coming years.
I feel so sad, my dearest friend,
though I choke back all my tears.

Our Word

Our word is not yet dead
though our sky has turned to red
and the sun is setting, setting —
our word is not yet dead.

If it's dying here and there,
our word will bloom somewhere,
will rise up in some other place —
our word will bloom somewhere.

And meanwhile drive away your fear
and the black devil right here,
lurking on our shores
in heavy darkness and in fear.

Our word is not yet dead —
sing and weep here now instead.
Weep and sing over our bread —
our word is not yet dead.

Dovid Eynhorn (1886-1973) differed from most of his contemporaries and other Yiddish poets in that his poems were suffused with traditionalistic and religious themes. He also frequently wrote on Holocaust themes.

~

Dovid Eynhorn

We'll Stay in *Shul*

We'll stay in *shul*.
When the last person's steps have disappeared
and the wind has extinguished the Eternal Light,
we'll light the Light again, my child.
It must not go out,
we must not forget
to light a candle to the spirit of my people.
We'll stay in *shul*.

The three daily prayers
we'll pray alone.
When the Sabbath bride comes,
don't cry, my child.
We must not be sad—
she has remained for us .
our only old friend.
We'll stay in *shul*.

The *shul* needs no crowds of thousands—
individuals have always guarded its beauty.
It will, like a mother, hug us and bless us
till the eternal night comes, my child.
After we're gone, the birds will sing
and the wind will mourn us at midnight.
In the evening, in the shine of the dying sunlight,
a dry blade of grass will whisper the closing prayer.
We'll stay in *shul*.

155

Binyomen Yankev Byalostotski (1893-1962) was a late member of *Di Yunge*. His poems often reflected the realities of urban life in America. In addition to poetry, he wrote many tales and legends. He was also a teacher in Yiddish secular schools.

∾

Binyomin Yankev Byalostotski

The Torah Lad

A song about the beginning — a melody and a youthful voice are heard.
A boy is sitting at his Torah: "In the beginning, God created..." he chants
    the words.

"And it was evening and it was morning" — evening, morning, how good
    it appears.
Farther on came slavery, famine, wandering in the desert years.

Little Torah lad, study. Wonder, wander, sun and sand.
A multitude travels with the Ark and a dream of a land.

Desert-generation— one, none. "God guards your inheritance when you
    die —
you shall only see your dream from a distance- here in a column of clouds
    your grave will lie."

Miracles of ancient times — across deaths you spring.
LittleTorah lad — of miracles you sing.

Leafing through the pages—many, then one more.
A ship is traveling on the Red Sea, to the Eilat shore.

It carries barrels of oil, the flame of hope it bears
for the children of Israel, my brothers over there.

Fish dance to meet it — the waves dance along.
It seems I see Leviathan, so regal and so strong.

Through the Gulf of Aqaba, the ship sails on its way.
The enemy lurk in the cliffs, like hungry wolves at bay.

Descended from Amalek, with blood–tipped angry spear.
O little Torah lad, shout: "Let us strengthen one another and be strong
    here!"

Here sank Pharaoh's troops, with chariots in tow.
"To the Promised Land — let my people go!"

There David established our border, our door;
played his harp for the Creator: "O Master, we implore!"

There wise King Solomon the flaps of ships unfurled,
to sail them to all the peoples of the world.

There between two mothers' claims judged he:
one was willing to divide the child —false, he judged, was she.

There he learned the language of the birds
and spoke to them, the Torah says, with beautiful, wise words.

There Solomon carried David's banner forth —
ruled from Beersheba to Dan in the North.

Little Torah lad, the ancient, shining deeds review—
deep and clear as the Red Sea, their message ever new.

The Queen of Sheba heard of Solomon's wise glory —
set out to sail her ships to him, an ancient, lovely story.

The flapping, bright red hen flies forth apace
and leads her to our homeland place.

She brings ebony and precious stones as well,
and says to Solomon: "You're very wise, I hear tell —

so say the people in every land I've seen.
I'll ask you riddles — hear and tell me what they mean.

What pours from the earth in a mighty flume,
but can damage a house and consume?"

Answers Solomon: "Oil, like water, flows from the deep —
people from it blessings and joy can reap;

but if you set a match to it, woe unto you!
Your house burns up — its contents too."

Asks the queen: "Do you know other things, Solomon, my dear?
What is brighter than sunlight and purer than a tear?"

Answers he: "The light of wisdom is brighter than the sun, I wot —
the love of my folk, Israel, is purer than any well I've got."

Old riddles. Here's a new one — who knows what it means?
A ship is sailing on the Red Sea, toward Israeli scenes.

Little Torah lad, "The story is finished" is well known,
but for other peoples, not our own.

Our liberator has gone with the setting sun —
Joshua, Nun's son, is now the one.

The beginning and the end now merge — the road stretches ahead,
just as the Biblical prophet's visions have said.

Vilna, Warsaw — destruction and a river of tears;
Jerusalem stands alone — our hope throughout the years.

In the days of your years, with sorrows quite a lot,
a ship is sailing on the Red Sea, sailing to Eilat.

Zalmen Shneyer (1886-1959) was a distinguished historian and essayist about Yiddish literature, as well as a poet and novelist.

~

Zalmen Shneyer

A Song to America

Greetings, Columbus' land! My words today belong to you. You are different from all the other lands I know.

On your gigantic fields, one hears not the gasping of plowers or the song of reapers but the crackling of coal and the whistling of steam. Machines put their iron shoulders beneath the heaviest loads, and your children free themselves more and more form the ancient curse: "In the sweat of your face shall you eat bread."[24]

The cruelty of big children, the instinct of a healthy animal, and the philosophy of the 'superman' ring in your harsh slogan: "Help yourself!" Beneath your hammer, weak people mixed with garbage are forged into metal — lazy people get scalded.

To you, life is a game, death is a game, science is a game—-one football of many colors.

Even your money-makers are not as greedy as in the old world. The dollar rolls stormily, like a silver disk in a great arena, and the fastest one catches it. Wealth, to you, is a game like any other game. Even the exploited people applaud: "Bravo!"

And these children of yours, while playing their games, have made you the granary of the world. In their running around the world, they have showered you with bread and gold. It's not those who sit sourly next to a pot of coffee, not those who pat their own pates, who will appreciate your energy, your good-natural hardness.

And if the Messiah ever comes to you to liberate you from the tumult, to free you for higher goals, he won't come riding on a white donkey but

[24] Paraphrase of God's curse on Adam and Eve when He expelled them from the Garden of Eden

on a steel eagle, an eagle of silvery aluminum driven by hidden light-
waves.

* * *

Don't be so conceited about your skyscrapers, America. A great role in
their erection was played by Shklov, my village, and the modest folk who
grew up there beneath shingled roofs. Many others such villages, too. A
generation ago, you accepted all the oppressed people driven out of impoverished, overpopulated lands — all the downtrodden people like Zundl
and his family, who lived in a little shack on the Dnieper.

People mourned them as if they were dead, all those who emigrated to
you with their last shirts and pillows, America, for you were mysterious
then and they said many terrible things about you a generation ago. They
said that you were so far away across the ocean that no one would be able
to come back again. And they asked no questions about how you got there.

In *kheyder*[25] they said that people were sentenced to death there for the
slightest crime. And this is how one is killed: an iron *shikse*[26] sits on an
iron box and the sentenced person has to kiss her; she then bites his head
off and it falls into the box.[27]

But the greatest horror of all horrors was that one had to work on the
Sabbath in your land. No decent child in his right mind could understand
that at all. Only ignoramuses, coarse people, poor tailors, cobblers, and
generally people who had nothing to lose could commit such a terrible sin,
week in and week out.

When those exiles were bouncing along on the sad little wagons, amid
their poor possessions, to the steamship or the highway on the way to you,
America, they were accompanied by head-shaking and pious sighing by
the high-class people, the way evil men are accompanied to Hell or soldiers to war. Black slaves into slavery! It was as if the older, wiser, craftier
people were driving them out of all corners of town and selling them, like

---

[25] Jewish religious elementary school
[26] An unmarried Gentile woman
[27] A caricature of how a guillotine works

Joseph in Egypt, to serve foreign masters, to desecrate the Sabbath, and to speak English instead of Yiddish—sold as slaves for the sweatshops, sent across the merciless waves in unseaworthy ships.

But the same thing that happened with Joseph and his brothers happened here too: the sold, naked, young man grew up into Joseph, the second to the king, the provider of food to his old father and his 'sinful' brothers in the old country in the years of famine.

And the daughters of that 'Joseph', and his wife, that skinny Litvak[28] girl raised on potatoes in the old country, blossomed as American's guests. Brooklyn and the Bronx were flooded with dark-haired human flowers, all the mothers and daughters of former tailors.

That was the revenge of history itself! What upper-class people frown upon, she smoothes out, sooner or later. If you don't let her, she'll have her way with blood and conflagration.

* * *

Our Noah Pandre fought for his future in his village, with his strong body and his fresh spirit. He fought against the whole surrounding community, against Jews and Gentiles, against debasement and the yoke of strangers' wills. But he always felt like a step-child. Whatever he did, good or bad, was wrong. They shouted him down and confused him. They dragged him off to prison and waved the whip of the law over him.

Till he couldn't stand it any more and, sprayed with the unclean blood of his persecutors, he fled to you, America! Once and for all he paid them back for generations of servility— fear, and insults, and the axle-shafts of his wagon were his weapons. Like the spine of a body, he fled from the village, like a hard bone on which all the weak ones had leaned and thought it was coming to them.

And soon after his disappearance, the whole fabric of the village collapsed. It became dirt-poor, withered. It huddled together in constant fear of pogroms, dreamed, and waited for destruction. The protector had left! The storm-wind had carried him away!

---

[28] A Jew from Lithuania, Latvia, northeastern Poland, or White Russia

He landed on your juicy ground, America, that seed carried from the other side of the ocean. He took root in your ground, struck deep roots, and blossomed with leaves and flowers.

And he still lives somewhere, of course, that Noah Pandre, like an oak with gray hair, and looks with a child's smile at his children and grand-children around him, all of them citizens of this land, safe under the sky.

You'll recognize them, his children, from their gray eyes surrounded by pitch-black eyelashes, the firm clefts in their chins, their broad shoulders and narrow waists, and the goodness that pours from the crinkles around their mouths. You'll recognize them at football-fields, at speakers' plat-form, amid gigantic machines, and on plowed fields. Something has be-come of them—they have certainly not remained in the shadows.

Pandre's blood, when he fled, was too hot to permit his seed to go lost and degenerate quickly. They have certainly blossomed on the American ground like sunflowers above heads of cabbage.

Look for them and you'll find them! If not the children of my Pandre, then the children of yours, for every little village had its Noah Pandre.

My Shklov is only a symbol, a sort of magic mirror into which each per-son looks and sees himself, his youth, his one-time home.

Look for them in America, Pandre's children, and you'll find them!

And write me a greeting from them.

I can only tell you how it happened, and how Pandre had to flee to the land of Columbus.

(From *Noah Pandre*, Volume 5)

Lamed Shapiro (pen name of Leyvik Shapiro) (1878-1948) wrote principally impressionistic short stories. He is sometimes referred to as "the Yiddish Kafka."

~

Lamed Shapiro

Word-Sounds

As soon as I crossed the threshold of the next world, the Welcoming Angel grabbed me by the lapels with a furious rage:

"Evil person! What is your name?"

I forgot my lines and stammered that I was Leyvik, son of Khaye-Blume, who ran around in the autumnal Ukrainian nights on the sidewalks near his house in a small village and dreamed dreams, all of which later came true, but in a completely different way than the boy had imagined.

He rapped me on the head again, and asked:

"Did you concern yourself with religion?"

I answered again, somewhat abashed:

"When I sold herring, I cheated a bit, but when I dealt in words—that was concerning myself with religion."

The eyes of the Welcoming Angel grew somewhat milder. He came down from the threshold, let me through, and said:

"Go on farther, go. They'll decide what to do with you there."

Keep your writing honest! It's a noble profession. But don't trouble other people with that passion of yours. Don't write like a piece-worker—write with enthusiasm or don't write at all.

I don't like the sound of the word "literature." It means "writerliness," but both words are somewhat mechanical, journalistic, and pedagogical, and they lack the breath of life. Perhaps "Torah" would be more suitable? The latter has in it a certain majesty. And literature is, after all, the modern Torah.

* * *

163

Book.

People-of-the-Book, *Tanakh*, Bible.

Hordes, Ten Commandments, Beginning of the Nation.

The times of Ezra the Scribe—the process is finished.

The thread is drawn farther under the aegis of religion. Prayers, prayers of forgiveness, philosophy, till or just before the Renaissance. The beginning of Yiddish literature—a message from Heaven to the earth.

Previously, there had been songs about love and wine, the *Song of Songs* and the miraculous story of Ruth, but love - of God and of fine-quality wine? This was the beginning if Yiddish literature, also religion, but the story has been told too often already.

Yes, the People-of-the-Book, literature—modern Torah, the apparatus of thought. Again at the foot of Mount Sinai, roaring and thundering, death and destruction at celebrations, the golden peacock, my own peacock.

In former years, Yiddish literature constantly occupied itself with bemoaning the Jewish fate, till the subject was exhausted, not because the lot of the Jews had improved, and not even because we came to understand that weeping is not the only way to react to the pressures of the surrounding world, but principally because we finally perceived the individual Jew, who is simply a human being, an individual, who lives his own life within the confines of the closed, rigid life of the Jewish people. That led to the birth of the new poetry, the new literature. That new literature abandoned the 'Diaspora of the Divine Spirit; and even the 'Jewish daughter,' and began to be playful, like this:

An apple for me,
and an apple for you, dear,
and a sweet loving kiss
on the lobe of your ear.

(or something similar.)

It didn't end with that. Today, we are far along on the road of universal literature and poetry. Even the 'problems' that have returned are dealt with in a completely different way.

"My creations are drowning in the sea and you are singing!" Wonderful! But that was said about two thousand years, eight minutes, and seventeen seconds ago, and it still has to be said again and again.

And if that's the case? If that's the case, it means that reciting poetry is relevant.

There's a difference between living from literature and living with literature as if you were breathing oxygen.

I even like religious music. When a person sings it and believes in what he's singing, I'll listen to him, listen carefully. But if he has a grocery-list of songs and poetry—I'd give him ten cents a line to keep quiet. Maybe people will keep quiet if they have nothing to say?!

I have a high regard for the medium in which you work, for the tools with which you operate.

He uses language like a hatchet; he hasn't the slightest inkling that it's a violin.

An artist sometimes becomes pregnant because God slept with him and impregnated him. So can we be angry because a man with a book who is not pregnant is disagreeable? But we must not forget: God slept with him!

It is impossible to translate well into the language of thought. We can hear musical compositions many times, but how rare the books that we can read more than once.

Tsilye Drapkin (1888-1956) was one of the three or four greatest women Yiddish poets. Her poems were deeply personal, often highly emotional, sometimes erotic, and distinctively feminine. She was associated with the *In Zikh* group.

~

Tsilye Drapkin

My Mother

My mother,
twenty-two years old,
a widow left with two small children,
decided modestly
not to become anyone's wife anymore.
Her days and years passed quietly,
as if illuminated by stingy candle-light.

My mother never became anyone's wife,
but all the many days
and years of nocturnal sighs
from her young and loving being,
from her yearning blood,
I, with my child's heart, understood
and absorbed deeply into myself.
And my mother's hidden, burning yearning,
like an underground spring,
has poured freely into me.
Now there spurts from me, openly,
my mother's burning, holy,
deeply hidden desire.

To A Young Poetess

What good is it that your gaze pierces deep into things?
Your heart, your heart is asleep.
And when he came
and you gazed clearly
at him, as at a sun,
what good did it do?
You have to burn, like me,
in Hell, in the fire of love—
long and slowly;
you have to be purified three times
in Hell, like me;
you have to love unwisely and without pride,
love unto death;
then, when you recognize death in love,
then write love-poems!

For A Game

For a game, I paid
with my peace, with my life,
and I don't care.

Does it matter why a flower dies?
From autumn or from a storm-wind?
And you, my storm-wind,
you're a hot, lovely youth,
and at your hands even death is dear.

Moyshe Nadir (pen name of Yitskhok Rayz) (1885-1943) wrote both poetry and prose. His youthful poems were full of *weltschmerz* and are somewhat reminiscent of the young Heinrich Heine, combining lyricism and irony. In the depths of his soul, however, he found life empty and devoid of meaning. He had a long fling with Communism, during which he became bitter and sarcastic toward all his former friends and associates; when he left the Party, he pleaded for forgiveness, but largely in vain, and he died broken-hearted. He was the brother of the playwright Elmer Rice.

Moyshe Nadir

New York

I love you, love you, my New York —
I love you quietly!
I love you more than the one
who lends you servile words from his mouth.

They say your freedom is very great.
I believe in that — you betcha!
It seems to me that I can see your Statue of Liberty
from afar, through the smoke.

They say her face shines
and is lit up in the darkness.
But she wastes her radiance
on islands far from shore.

I have nothing against you! Who am I, after all?
Not a recognized citizen,
but if you want me to see your freedom.
tell it to come closer!

Unless your freedom means a light
that cannot stand any air!
Am I right that you didn't expect
a greenhorn to say that to you?

New York, New York! You're hard and black,
like beggars' coins.

You're tall and large — I'm frightened
by your skyscrapers.

Cities

Moscow clothes itself with bears—
Berlin is full of lindens,
and, through raw and heavy hearts,
gray and heavy melodies.

Vienna, my Vienna — how I remember you:
up to your neck in waltzers!
Above the suicidal Danube swirl
cupolas of blue smoke.

Warsaw, with the dangling ear-ring
of yellow and red lanterns—
the dead lives have decided
on life, laughter, and death.

Paris —lawlessness and freedom
live here as man and wife.
Upon the garbage of lawlessness,
the spirit and body bloom.

New York— giant waterfalls,
frozen in mid-course.
From her Empire-peaks dangles
everything that saddens the earth.

Only you, crown city of my life,
Narayev, place full of valleys—
for fifty years your magic
has not diminished, only increased.

Zurich, London, Lemberg, Moscow —
disappear, you faithless cities!
You promised me palaces,
golden bread, and silken clothes.

You promised me on your oath,
platters of everything good,
but you cashed the dirty checks
with an empty smile.

Extinguish yourselves, you cities of the West—
Babel's crowns, with mixed-up tongues!
A bitter keeper of the accounts
has erased you from the list.

Only Narayev—you, my pure one—
clothed in the golden flax
of my boyhood purity,
you are still the blue crown.

My Uncle Itsik

My uncle Itsik is a tall man with a little beard the color of old copper. He walks straight and proudly. He makes faces at people, like a comedian. He keeps himself very clean and neat, and how he makes a living is unknown. My uncle Itsik has no wife. He once had a wife, they say, and she 'pinched' the bread instead of cutting it with a knife and constantly used to chew raisins — out of her apron. So my Uncle Itsik wrote letters here and letters there. She started coughing heavily and he didn't want to wipe his hand on anything but the same handkerchief with which she washed her hands. He called her Ivanekho (from Khava-Nekho). She was crazy about him and didn't understand what the difference was between 'pinching' bread and cutting it if you ate it up anyway. She even bought herself a 'push-up bra', which was then very much in fashion. She used to go to bed wearing her wig, because Uncle Itsik couldn't stand her cut-off hair.

All this went on for a long time, till one day Uncle Itsik thought things over and stood next to her bed and started – crowing. His wife got very frightened and called people together. So the people came running and asked: "What happened?" Uncle Itsik answered that he didn't know any-thing— he had just come home. So the people left, shrugging their shoul-ders. As soon as they had left my uncle stood next to the bed and again started crowing. She again called people together, and the people asked: "What's the matter?" The woman answered: "He's crowing." So my uncle burst out laughing and said he didn't know what to do with her — she had convinced herself that he was crowing. The people shrugged their shoul-ders and left. My uncle started crowing again and she again called people together, and the people said: "What's going on here?" My uncle answered agreeably: "So you see my problem now!"

The neighbors wrote to her parents and they came and patted her head and reasoned with her. It was nothing, God forbid — it would pass. Mean-while my uncle got a divorce.

Since then, he lives alone in a whitewashed cottage with cambric cur-tains. The cottage is sparkling clean and shows signs of the supervising hands of a woman but who, what, and when no one knows. They say, qui-etly, that Uncle Itsik is having an affair with a Brezhanerke—that is a woman who lives in Brezhan — and, they say, he is having another affair with Mariasha, who lives in their little courtyard, is friendly with the po-lice, raises cats, and wears her own hair.

My uncle himself says nothing. His cottage constantly smells of roasted coffee, some sort of genteel odor of German books, and some other kind of intoxicating aroma: the aroma of something forbidden— of a great sin or a stolen treasure.

My uncle speaks little, but from time to time he asks me whether I have heard of Ephraim Lessing. He gives me a book and orders me to learn *The Bell* by heart, tells me I should brush my teeth with a toothbrush dipped in salt, that when I walk I should thrust out my chest like this, that I should talk like this: not 'kha' but 'ha-kha.'

My uncle hates Jews — with all the love of an 'enlightened' Jew who thinks that the only thing that is lacking for the Jewish people to be like everyone else is to comb their beards and side-curls, thrust out their chests, and say a pure 'kha.'

"Live, my child!" my uncle says to me, "life is not a disaster but a joy. Do you understand? Death is a disaster, may the Devil take it. Human life is too short for such a long death. But you are still too young to understand. Go — you're better off taking a brush and polishing your boots. Don't be a ragamuffin."

I take my polishing-brush, polish my shoes, and spit on the brush so my shoes will shine more.

"What are you doing?" my uncle gets frightened. "You too already have the Jewish habit of spitting? Feh! There are bacteria in spit. All the illnesses in the world come from bacteria."

And my uncle starts explaining to me precisely all about illness, how every illness has its 'little worm' and how one 'little worm' eats up the next 'little worm.' Bitter is only the situation of the last 'little worm,' for there is no one left for it to eat up.

My head spins. The polished boots make me dizzy. I feel the 'little worms' inside me – the last 'little worm' is lurking to attack my young life. What does the little worm have against me? I still want to live and love Sarah.

And I run home and start crying.

From *Under the Sun*

My Uncle's House

In my uncle's house, everything was different from the way things were in our house. There a little bird played in a little cage, and in its lower compartment a white rabbit slept. The floor was covered with thin sand, like some sort of hieroglyphic writing. The marks of the rabbit's paws were like a shaky signature. You could smell freshly roasted coffee-beans and 'Enlightenment.' My uncle's house also smelled of lavender-water and brown women's shoes, and two whalebone strips from a corset lay on a candy-box.

My uncle strode around the house with his long, conical feet, looked into all the German books, sighed, and put them away. It occurred to me that my uncle was carrying on a love-affair, not only as people said with Mariasha, who raised cats, but also with the German books.

Noting how I was following him with my hands under my jacket, up and down, like a shadow, he stopped, stroked his red beard, and sniffed with his thin nostrils to see whether the coffee was boiling yet in the littler samovar. Then, putting two fat cups on the table, he exclaimed:

"A final goal! His father is looking for some final goal for him. Stuff and nonsense! Education with rotten teeth! Have you brushed your teeth today, or haven't you had time?"

I blushed at every word my uncle said. My heart was pounding within me like a clock. When I looked at my uncle, it was as if I were looking at the sun. He was tall and fair. His eyes were blinding. I couldn't find a place for myself. My uncle poured two cups of coffee, put a piece of buttered bread on the table for me and gave me two cubes of sugar, because "too much sugar is not healthy for the teeth and a boy like me mustn't get used to sweet things."

"Life," said my uncle, "is a bitter fruit that is good for your health, while death, may the Devil take it, is an onrushing disaster. Every decent man should be very ashamed to die."

When my uncle spoke of death, he got pale and agitated. He took out a pocket-mirror from his vest-pocket and looked at his tongue, took a powder from a sort of little box and poured it into his mouth so delicately that it was hilarious! He drank it down with a gulp of water and calmed himself:

"There — there is no death!"

My uncle bore within himself secrets that were as far away as the stars — so strange, so bright.

Meanwhile, I opened a German book that was lying on the table.

"When you read German," said my uncle, "take off your hat. Have respect for a book. A book is a strange house—you don't go into someone else's house with your hat on your head. That's a Jewish habit."

My uncle wrung his hands, cracked his knuckles, and then smeared some butter very thinly on a piece of bread. No, he didn't really smear it — he tried to push the butter inside the bread with the butter-knife so it couldn't be seen. Then he sprinkled the piece of bread very delicately with salt, ate it, and quoted from the middle of a Biblical passage: " 'This you shall! This you shall not! This you may!' He pesters me like a teacher, that God of ours! Constantly stands at the edge of heaven and looks out through a crack. One can't hide from Him, one can't buy one's way out with Him. Maybe you know what?"

I was drenched by a flash of fire. A feeling of sinfulness and a feeling of joy in another's misery came over me, mixed with sweet fear of the iron cornstalks with which God whips people in Heaven.

"You can't buy your way out with Him. After all, He gave you life! So let Him not give it! Does He really give it? He only lends it till tomorrow, and takes several hundred percent interest for it. How many children does your father have?"

"You don't know, uncle? We are six children."

"Six children! Six hundred percent interest a day! And you can't buy your way out from Him. If he gives a Torah, He takes out its strength and fools an entire people of shepherds into wearing a yarmulke that weighs as much as ten mountains. 'Will you take it?' He asks. Does one have a choice — one takes it."

My uncle was speaking profound and wise words, as if out of a German book. My head spun, both from the strong, freshly roasted coffee and from my uncle's words. My heart grew lighter, the final goal faded away. The fear of the time when I would become a Bar-Mitsvah and take upon myself the 'yoke of Judaism' disappeared the way a mouse that is quietly scratching at night runs away when one turns on the light. From my uncle's mouth, both honey and bile dripped. Droplets of fire and glowing gold fell on me and small staghorns grew on my head.

"Tell your father," my uncle said to me, wrapping in a silken paper some crushed chalk for brushing my teeth, "tell your father that I send him greetings. He'll know what I mean. Go in good health!"

I took the crushed chalk and started to go outside without my hat. My uncle brought me my hat with a smile:

"Are you swimming? Are you sweating? Are you flickering? Just like your mother! You have no plan in your house, no anything. Hoo-ha ... there's a veil over all of you... drunk, but not from wine. Tell your mother, little Itsik, that if she is indeed already drunk, let her at least drink a little good wine sometimes, and tell her to stop stuffing herself with wine-grapes."

"When do I eat wine-grapes then, uncle?"

"I say it figuratively. When one eats wine–grapes, they ferment in your stomach. Eat buttered bread, Itsikl, and don't think about the 'final goal.' Your grandmother also thought about the 'final goal.' Every Friday she tried on the shroud she prepared a year too early. In the end, the mice ate it. Go in good health, and wrap your shawl around your neck!"

From *Drop of My Life*

My Uncle Goes Away

My uncle was a bit absent-minded today: drank his coffee standing up; passing the window, where there were flowers with velvety leaves, he tore off a piece of a leaf, brought it to his mouth, caught himself, and threw it away.

Then he looked for something in his green trunk with the split convex lid. He found a blue hunter's cap, tried it on, and asked me whether it was handsomer than the cloth hat he was wearing. I felt as if my uncle had caressed my heart with his velvety hand, and I said:

"Uncle, you're handsome all over!"

My uncle smiled with his eyes, in which there were many green and brown dots, remained seated with the blue hunter's cap on his knee, and looked at the window, where a butterfly had spread its wings like a piece of fluttering jewelry. Finally he cracked all his knuckles one by one, and asked me whether I had learned *The Song of Songs*.

I said yes, I had learned it.

"Which *Song of Songs* did you learn?" my uncle asked me, and licked his beautiful, full lips.

"What do you mean, which one? The real *Song of Songs*, King Solomon's *Song of Songs*!"

"We know it's King Solomon's," said my uncle, with a faint tone of mockery in his voice. " I mean who interpreted *Song of Songs* for you?"

"What do you mean, who? The rebbe!"

My uncle put his fingertips to his mouth, again deep in thought, and said:

"Aha!"

After that, he sat me on his bony knee, curled my wispy side-curls, straightened out the black sash around my collar that served as a tie, asked whether I had brushed my teeth that day, and then exclaimed:

"Silly boy — The *Song of Songs* is not what you think."

I got very embarrassed and started stammering and blushing and excusing myself.

My Uncle Itsik patted me on the head and said:

"Well, it's not your fault, it's your rebbe with his Moses and Aaron, and the Jewish people, and the darkness of the Tablets of the Covenant. It chokes me. One can't catch his breath here."

I looked at my uncle, who was feeling his throat as if he were really choking somewhat, I looked around to see whether something wasn't burning, sniffed, and then exclaimed:

"Uncle—maybe it's the samovar?"

My uncle burst out laughing with genteel, child-like laughter, let me down off his knee, said to me that someday I might understand, again cracked his knuckles, and told me to give the birds and the fishes and the rabbits enough to eat. He locked the door, put a leather wallet with papers into his breast-pocket, and confided to me very quietly that I should not believe everything the rebbe said and that everything had a soul, even a Gentile, even a rabbit.

"Remember what I am telling you!" he finished, "everything has a soul, even a dog. And don't forget," he said "to brush your teeth everyday."

My uncle kissed me on the forehead. I gave him a kiss on the hand in return. Then he said to me "your servant!" and I said: "Travel in good health, uncle." I waited impatiently to see whether he would kiss the mezzuzah. He didn't.

I took some small pleasure from the fact that I had such a strong uncle who was not afraid of even God himself, but it nevertheless bothered me that he made a nothing of our God.

Uncle Itsik went away somewhere and left me to take care of his little bird, three little fishes, and the rabbit.

The bird had a little cage. The little fishes had a glass globe in which they swam around, and as for the rabbit, my uncle had told me to let it into the broken broiler of our oven, make a bed for it out of straw or hay, and give it the food he had promised it.

When my mother saw how happy I was with the little bird, the little fishes, and the rabbit, she smiled good-humoredly and said:

"My little darling — he'll break hearts too someday."

And she told me to stop tormenting the little bird, stop holding it in my hands and blowing on it, and 'teaching it to whistle like a little Gentile boy!'

"That's not how you show love," my mother said. "If you love something, you don't torment it."

I let the shaking, trembling creature wriggle out of my hands and wriggle into its cage, but because of great absent-mindedness, I forgot to close the cage door. The little bird flew about and started banging its head on the windows, though the door of the house was open. It was confused by the feeling of freedom, didn't know what to do with itself, banged its head on the windowpanes and the ceiling, and looked for a way out through the hard walls, while the open door smiled and showed that it was so simple.

I ran to get a bit of salt to sprinkle onto the birds tail so I could catch it. I took a handful of salt and threw it into the air.

"What's the matter with you?" asked my grandmother, who had come running in at the noise.

"Why are you throwing salt around? Better to throw your hat around and maybe you'll catch that bird of yours. If not, you'd do better to drive it out the door. I already have a few animals and infants, so do I need to have Itsik's bird too?"

The little bird, in its rush to free itself, was blind to everything but its single desire to get free. It sang in short, single syllables, threw itself against the ceiling, banged its head against the window until it was bloody, and then fell down, with one wing elevated as if it were still flying and the other one broken and drooping.

When my grandmother saw blood, she almost fainted. We had to sprinkle water on her. My mother burst into tears. I did too.

It was like the mourning on the Ninth of Av.

My Uncle Comes Back

My uncle Itsik had gone away somewhere and tarried there for about a year. When he came home, he brought a new satchel made of good brown leather with latches and straps, a new hat with a very broad brim and a narrow ribbon, a new walking-stick with a handle you could remove and use as a cigar-pin, and - - a new wife.

The lady, with a light brown complexion like ivory, was dressed stiffly and lightly and wore a stiff riding-hat and a ruffle with beautiful points high around her neck. She had very long, puffy arms under narrow sleeves that barely allowed a girlish hand with five fingers and polished nails to peek out, and a parasol.

He came riding back in a carriage, unloaded his satchel with all his things, helped the lady step down the shaky steps of the carriage— almost carried her in his arms and looked into her eyes with endless and unlimited love.

It had been drizzling for several days. The village was full of a mud that, when it stayed on your shoes for a long time, stained the leather. Many gentlemen walked around with 'stony' boots.

The young lady opened her lemon-colored parasol, looked for a foot path, didn't know what to do with herself, and smiled good-humoredly at my uncle. She said something in loud German about the rain that was coming down and who knew how long it would keep raining like this. My uncle held his new hat with one hand, raised his eyes toward the very ugly skies, and said:

"I think it may clear up by Wednesday morning."

He took his walking-stick and first pushed it into the mud as a ship captain, for example, would test the depth of the water in which his ship had stopped, then looked at its metal 'foot,' sighed, and said:

"It'll be all right."

The carriage-driver carried the satchels and the cardboard boxes. The young lady carried the lemon-colored parasol and held up the hem of her long dress. My uncle carried the walking-stick, tested the depth of the mud, and smiled down at the young lady under the parasol.

In my uncle's house it was now cold and misty. He had given the flowerpots to his German neighbor to look after. The little canary-cage was covered with a cloth and the little bird was not there. The chimney of the samovar stood shakily in place ready to fall off at the first slam of the door. There was no smell of roasted coffee or forbidden literature of the 'Enlightenment' — only the autumn rain, mud, and desolation.

"Ah, how nice and snug," the lady said, like a saint, and may God forgive her for the lie.

"It'll get to look better," my uncle said. "We'll just make some heat, bring in the little bird and the rabbit, and put up some water in the samovar."

"We have a rabbit too?" The lady was already saying "we."

"Of course!"

"How nice!"

The two of them stood there, one next to the other, and burst out laughing.

"After Rome and Jerusalem!" my uncle said in his genteel voice.

"It's not so bad here," the lady said. "You don't see any dead dogs in the street."

"Wait till things dry out!"

"How nice. Ha-ha!" (The lady was laughing through tears.)

I helped my uncle make some order and tie together the half-disintegrated broom with a piece of string, and I swept the house after I first sprinkled the floor with water from the tin spray-can (that's what my uncle had taught me one had to do so the bacteria wouldn't be carried up into the air.) Meanwhile, my uncle himself lit a wood fire in the fireplace and it got a little warmer. Boredom started hiding its head under the bed. My uncle remembered and said:

"This is my nephew, a fine young man. He's already putting..." My uncle apparently meant to say that I was already putting on tefillin, but he remembered that she probably wouldn't understand what that was, so he turned and finished:

"He's already putting money into the savings bank. A practical young man!"

"How nice!" the lady said, " and the 'nice' she spoke had all seven charms and all thousand flavors of the world.

"You'll call me aunt," the lady said, "right?"

I got embarrassed, turned red, and started blowing on the burning wood.

"Don't fool around with the fire — I'll take care of it myself!" said my uncle, "and don't be embarrassed. Go to your aunt, give her your hand, and say "your servant."

I said "your servant" and gave her my hand and stammered badly:
"Aun— "

Outside, it was raining and it was autumn.

(From *Under the Sun*)

Mani Leyb (pen name of **Mani-Leyb Brahinsky**) **(1883-1953)** was the greatest and most characteristic poet of *Di Yunge*. He is credited with refining and purifying the Yiddish language to make it a suitable vehicle for "real" poetry. The poet and critic Melekh Ravitsh said of him: "Mani Leyb is beauty itself."

~

Mani Leyb

Stiller, Stiller

Stiller, stiller! Don't yell your tale!
Stand there, bent over, dark and pale.
Bent over and full of pain,
be still and hold your breath again.

From the depths of the night,
not heard by anyone,
he'll come a-riding on a steed,
softly to our house of need.

And his pure, sweet face
and clear white robe
will proclaim joy to us
and shed on us their grace.

Just be stiller! Don't yell your tale!
Stand, bent over, dark and pale.
Bent over and full of pain,
be still and hold your breath again.

If they've deceived us again,
and if they've mocked us,
and through the whole long night
we've waited in vain,

then our misfortune we'll forget,
bend down to the hard floor

and be very quiet and still —
even stiller and stiller yet.

Be still! Don't yell your tale.
Stand bent over, dark and pale.
Bent over and full of pain,
be still and hold your breath again.

A Sonnet

Eight short, beautiful lines
say more than a book
if I've found the words
for the beauty I seek.
Black sweat from my hands
sprays, like droplets from the blue,
as if the whole sun were burning
in the smallest drop of dew.

No, you haven't emptied
all the oceans with a water-can,
and the word too lies desiccated
wherever there's beauty.
But beauty doesn't come
of itself, like the rain —
conjure it from your spirit,
like the spark from a flint.

Magic — seven times three —
the word comes at my call
and brings beauty with the wind!
Hooves clatter quickly,
and beauty rides on the word,
saddled and harnessed

with magic at its side —
God's rider from afar.

Dove-Silent

Dove-silent blue evening hours!
Spread farther my evening dream for me!
Now —now burn redder, redder
silent roses, wounds of mine.

Now the tumult in the streets dies away —
footsteps and words echo stiller, softer.
Eyes yearning for eyes look paler —
hands squeezed by hands speak more gently.

Now my golden yearning ignites.
My blood grows hotter, my pupils dilate!
Now — now burn redder, redder
silent roses, wounds of mine.

Great Loneliness

There is in the night
a certain wonderful hour,
the hour of cosmic union,
when all the souls in the world
join together
into one great, living soul.

And that great hour
I've spent more than once
with wide-awake, burning eyes,
lost in the night.

I used to lay my face
on the black earth,
like a cow when it dies,
and over me
the great, distant sky
would tremble with silence.

Stars would twinkle,
and I would listen, listen,
till I heard a lost lament
without tears and without words —
the eternal lament
of everything sentenced
to live in loneliness
on our black earth;
the eternal lament
of my mute blood,
which spends in loneliness
that wonderful hour,
the hour of cosmic union
and great loneliness.

To The Gentile Poet

Heir of Shakespeare, of shepherds and knights—
things are so good for you, Gentile poet!
The world is yours wherever your fat swine may tread—
it gives him pasture and feeds your Muse.

Just sit on your branch like a thrush and twitter,
and an answer will reach you from faraway places:
the riches of the fields, the thoughts of the cities,
the full satisfaction of sated souls.

And here am I, unneeded, a poet among the Jews,
grown like a weed on soil that's not ours,
from forebears who were weary wanderers with dusty beards,
nourished by the dust of holy books and bazaars,
and I — I sing in an alien world
the tears of wanderers in a desert 'neath alien stars.

Rhyme

There are wise men
who laugh at rhyme;
they almost grimace:
"Rhyme? A waste of time!"

Well, those clever men
also say they hate
the pure silver of a spring
murmuring early and late.

That's why those clever men
live so very long
like deaf men in a desert —
without sound or song.

But the people and the children
and the poet —just a fool —
in the simplicity of their hearts
love rhyming, as a rule.

The people — its pure wisdom
is as big as all the world,
and through rhyme and lovely couplets
its beauty is unfurled.

And children, praised be Heaven—
their tongues are still so young,
and rhyme stirs the wellspring
of words from a youthful tongue.

Yiddish

The world is full of language,
for every creature speaks.
Each creature in its own way,
each sound a meaning seeks.
The clouds speak with their thunder,
the sun with fire and flame,
the woods with trees a–rustle,
the ocean's sparkle is its name.
The beast knows only roaring,
the bird knows only song;
the springs just softly whisper
the cornstalks hum along.
The flow'rs speak with perfume
and colors endless, bright;
the tiniest of insects
goes buzzing in the night.
But Man, the crown of all the world,
the wise one, he alone,
speaks every sort of language,
of plains and even stone.
In many different languages,
he speaks to you and me,
and only his ears hear them
and only his eyes see.
Wherever there's a people,
a language is there too.
In England they speak English
as Russians Russian do.

In Spain it's charming Spanish,
Chinese in old Cathay,
Romanian in Romania,
in Turkey, the Turkish way.
And Jews speak Yiddish
all through the great wide world,
wherever in their peaceful way
their banners are unfurled.
And Jews speak Yiddish,
a language lovely, plain.
To understand another Jew
is easy, without pain.

Ayzik Raboy (1882-1944), a writer who was part of the group *Di Yunge*, wrote mostly novels, which often described life in the country, on farms and ranches. His vision was informed by his youthful years in the Bessarabian countryside.

~

Ayzik Raboy

Out West

In the evening, when Mr Goldenbarg stepped out of his house to take a look at the far-off field of newly cut alfalfa, he remarked that it looked as if many white lambs had gathered there to bed down for the night. His stable-hand, too, came out to have a look. The sun was about to set on the other side of the hill west of Goldenbarg's house. The broad flat valley had a reddish glow that was soothing to their overstrained eyes. Everything around was still, far into the distance.

To the east, on a hill, a small silhouette of a horse and rider came into view.

The Goldenbargs sat down on an old, overturned sleigh lying outside the house. Dvoyre was still busy with the housework and kept running in and out of the house. The ground resounded to the gentle, rhythmic sounds of her footsteps. The stable-hand lay sprawled on the grass, propped up on his arm and looking off into the distance.

"Just like white lambs, I'd swear," Mr G repeated, looking at the distant alfalfa field.

"I've cut alfalfa in all kinds of places, but the likes of today's harvest — what a marvel!" said the stable-hand , as if he were concluding a long internal discussion.

Suddenly, everyone's ears perked up:

"I think there's a horseman`approaching," Mr G said.

The clatter of hooves grew nearer. Dvoyre quickly came outside and announced breathlessly:

"A horseman is coming!"

They all stood up, except the stable-hand, and moved around to the front of the house as two horsemen approached and called out in unison:

"Good evening!"

"Johann! Good evening!" Mr G answered, welcoming them. " And whom do I have the honor of meeting?" he asked about the other young man.

"This is a friend of mine. I have to talk to you about a very important matter," Johann said, glancing at Dvoyre, who was standing near the doorway clinging to Mrs G.

"To me? Fine! Come on in," Mr G invited them with a smile.

Johann hopped off his saddle in one leap and asked his friend to join them, but the other fellow, his glance shifting from the horse's head to Dvoyre, who, it seemed to him, was sort of mocking him, chose to remain on his horse. The two women returned to the old sleigh after Mr G had escorted Johann into the house through the open door.

The stable-hand was still lying on the grass. He didn't even ask who had arrived. His world and his vista lay out in the distant brownish darkness of the Western wilderness. Dvoyre leaned up against the sleigh and began to fear that Johann had come to ask for her hand.

Mrs. G was bemused. Just at that moment, she happened to recall the time her long-dead mother had appeared to her one evening while she was sitting all alone on her doorstep and gazing out into the silent, empty wilderness. Her mother had come to her as if she were still alive, with a big shawl over her head, and had quietly sat down beside her and asked her sympathetically:

"Daughter dear, where have you gone, to such a faraway country among strangers?"

Deepening darkness was enveloping the prairie, and soon she heard Mr G's voice from the house:

"Rokhl, Rokhl, come in, come in."

Mrs G got right up and stepped quickly to the door, thinking "It's nothing," but all the while she was remembering the two guns hanging on the wall. She sighed a deep sigh: "If only two children had grown up to use those two guns!"

When Mr G called for his wife to come into the house, it became even clearer to Dvoyre that Johann had indeed come for her, and all the revulsion she felt for Johann clamped her heart.

Outside, the darkness had turned to pitch-blackness — one couldn't even recognize faces. Suddenly, however, a bright white light began to appear from beyond the northern side of the thatched roof — somewhere on the other side of the sky, the Northern Lights had begun to shimmer. Dvoyre forgot everything else, jumped up and down, and shouted happily:

"The Northern Lights, the Northern Lights!"

The stable-hand rose from the grass, jumped to his feet, and stood there gaping at the sky:

"What do they want, those ghosts of faraway icy places? They frighten us with their radiant light — just see how the rays rise into the heavens like flaming pillars, farther and farther upward!"

"Cities must be on fire there," Dvoyre replied, coming very close to him.

"And if there are cities that are burning, they must be Jewish cities," the stable-hand added.

Dvoyre turned to look at him. He stood there, like a column of iron, bathed in the Northern Lights. Suddenly she snuggled up to him and asked:

"Isaac, who are you? Isaac, I don't know you, I don't know who you are. Don't be so secretive — tell me!"

The night was dark and light and still. The stable-hand looked at little Dvoyre, put his big arm around her, and said:

"Dvoyre, I have a lot to tell you, but listen first to this: I want you to know that am going to go to Palestine, and I don't want you to think that anything can stop me. Nothing will make me change my mind. There is where I will build my home — not as a foreigner among strangers. I've already been a foreigner all over the world, and I don't want to be one anymore. I want to go to the home of our forefathers. There, when I struggle and work hard it won't be for the benefit of strangers. Mr G thinks that all his neighbors like him — he doesn't know that Gentiles are quietly malicious.

"Recently, when I took our velvet black stallion to Gladstone for inspection, there were many farmers there from all over the area. The government veterinarian examined all their horses and was courteous to everyone. Nobody minded and nobody said a word. Only when Mr G's horse came along did everyone stare at it, and one man said: "The Jew must have poured the blood of Jesus into that horse, the way he shines." To your face, Gentiles speak in such a friendly way: "Mr G this and Mr G that," and that's the real tragedy! They hide their poisonous hatred behind their backs. And when I tell that to Mr G, he refuses to believe it—he insists that this cannot be possible in America: "The Founding Fathers of this country were all equal," he says. Yes, of course—the original founders of this country were all equal, and they opened the portals equally for the whole world. But now look—all kinds of Gentiles have poured in, and they've brought along in their hearts this hatred for everything that isn't Gentile, a hatred their mothers instilled in them with the milk from their breasts. They arrived here and built themselves churches, and within the churches they made schools for their children and appointed teachers who also were suckled on the same poisonous malice toward everything that isn't Gentile. Mr G is convinced that that is impossible in America, but I see it as plainly as the palm of my hand. The day is coming when the 'kind-hearted' Gentile citizens will suddenly rise up against the Jews, draw the sharp knives concealed under their clothing, and plunge them right into the hearts of the Jews."

Upon hearing his last words, Dvoyre shuddered and dropped to her knees in terror, her arms clutching at his legs. Outside it was still, and the Northern Lights shone before them like tall, bright columns in the night sky. The stable-hand grasped Dvoyre's hand, raised her from her crouching position, and walked with her into the wheat-field, between the mounds of bundled sheaves of wheat, toward the Northern Lights. The remaining stiff wheat stalks crackled beneath their feet. The night grew darker despite the nearby, yet distant, white Northern Lights. They walked on and on, meandering among the rows, and then strolled farther and turned back. Then the stable-hand told his story:

"We were nine brothers, sons of a very pious father. Our mother kept a small store in the village where we lived. Father used to do some selling among the local Gentiles, out in the countryside. When we began to grow up, father leased a piece of land and we planted tobacco on it. The village had a bad reputation in the area, and we brothers had a reputation for courage because we continued to live in that village and were not afraid of the Gentiles.

"One day, a wild fight broke out in a neighboring town, over a herring that a Jew had sold to a Gentile on market-day, and it soon frightened the Jews there so badly that they sent out a secret call for help to us, the "nine strong boys," as we were called. We arrived too late—all the Jewish property was already trashed in the streets and the eyes of the Jewish girls had already been gouged out. We were told that the Gentiles from our town had been the first to start the bloody action. All nine of us swallowed hard, turned back home to our own town, and swore an oath not to keep silent about this.

"When we got home, late in the evening, we found our house burnt down. The entire village was silent and dark. Everyone was fast asleep. Our cattle were lying around with their bellies cut open, and we called for our parents but they didn't answer. So we spread out across the silent, dark village, and we acted as if we had all received the same instruction and had all agreed to it: we set the whole village on fire. The fire jumped from one house to another because the roofs were all covered with straw that was dried out from the March winds. Once the deed was done, we all assembled on the tall mountain opposite the village.

"Rising into the utterly blind sky were swirling, deep red flames—the sky was bright red for miles around. For a while it was quiet except for the crackling of the flames that were sating their appetites throughout the village. Then, as if by some distant magic, church bells started to peal. The town was burning and not a sound could be heard from the huts. The rocks on the mountain began to heat up as we all stood stood beside the deep ravine, on the big cliff that in our boyhood years we called "The Devil's Dagger." For miles around, we could see fields and forests that looked bright , as if they were burning.

"From far away, horses came galloping in, and before long we could see a scattered horde of horsemen on the road in our village. Behind them, wagons came riding. The horses that were hitched to the wagons were galloping so quickly that their hooves barely touched the ground, and the horsemen were flying even faster. Wild, drunken howls came from the throats of the riders and drivers.. As they came closer to the burning village, we immediately realized our error: the Gentile population of our village had all been at a party in some neighboring town—they had finished their job on the Jewish town and had then gone to drink in celebration.

"My eldest brother clapped his hands and jumped off the sharp cliff to the abyss below, and before we even heard the dull thud when he hit rock bottom, the second brother jumped, with a loud cry, "Hah!," and then the third and fourth, singing a mournful dirge. Then the fifth and sixth jumped into the abyss, saying nothing and with their eyes shut and their arms folded on their chests. The seventh and eighth brothers looked out at the burning village and at the nearby crowd of Gentile villagers who had come with their wives and at the young fellows who were riding the speedy horses with white scarves threaded into their manes, and jumped too. When my turn came to jump, our pious father suddenly appeared, draped in white, and grabbed my shoulders. I tried to jump and my heart was pounding, but he held onto me and said:

"Let my line not be wiped out! Flee to a distant foreign land and start building anew. Build a home, and when your wife bears you a child, you must tell him everything while he's still in the cradle. And above all, his mother must also know about it, in advance, so she can transmit it with her milk into the child's very blood. Escape!"

From the novel *Mr Goldenbarg*

Moyshe-Leyb Halpern (1886-1932) was the great rebel of modern Yiddish poetry and one of the greatest Yiddish poets of all time. He was an early associate of *Di Yunge*, but soon went his own way. He brought strong individuality; a powerful, earthy Jewishness; a mixture of anger, humor, and eroticism; and devastating criticism of both the old world and the new. He lived a harsh life, mostly in great poverty, and died suddenly at the early age of 46. His death was widely mourned throughout the Jewish community.

Moyshe-Leyb Halpern

Memento Mori

If Moyshe-Leyb the poet should say
he saw Death amid the waves today,
in a mirror-image sort of way,
in the morning, around ten o'clock, let's say —
would anyone who heard
take Moyshe-Leyb's word ?

And if Moyshe-Leyb should say
he waved to Death from far away,
at the very time that crowds of folks
were swimming joyfully, telling jokes—
would anyone who heard
take Moyshe-Leyb's word ?

And if Moyshe-Leyb should swear to our face
that he was greatly drawn to Death,
the way a bridegroom's drawn with yearning breath
to the window of his betrothed's place—
would anyone who heard
take Moyshe-Leyb's word ?

And if Moyshe-Leyb should describe Death this way:
beautifully colored, not dark or gray
is how he looked amid the waves today,
this morning at ten, let's say—
would anyone who heard
take Moyshe-Leyb's word ?

Our Garden

Such a garden,
where the tree has barely seven little leaves,
and it seems to me that it thinks:
"Who brought me here?"
It's the kind of garden
where, with a magnifying glass,
one can see a bit of grass.
Could that be our garden,
such a garden in the morning sunlight?
Of course it's our garden!
What else—it's not our garden?

Such a watchman, woe is me,
with a stick to beat the dogs —
he wakes up people lying on the grass
and drives them far away.
Such a watchman, such a watchman,
who grabs by the collar
people who've done nothing wrong.
Could that be our watchman,
such a watchman in the morning sunlight?
Of course it's our watchman!
What else—it's not our watchman?

Such a bird,
that forgets its children in the nest,
doesn't look for food for them,
doesn't sing morning-songs with them.
Such a bird, such a bird
that doesn't get up at all
and doesn't try to fly.
Could that be our bird,
such a bird in the morning sunlight?

Of course it's our bird!
What else— it's not our bird?

Zlotshev, My Home

O Zlotshev, home of mine, my city
with your church steeple, your *shul*, and your baths,
with your women sitting in the market
and your men besieging, like dogs,
the peasants who come down from the Sasov maintains
with baskets of eggs —
how Spring awakens in me
my poor bit of yearning for you,
my home, my Zlotshev.

But when I recall, while yearning,
the rich man Rappaport,
as he walked to *shul* with his fat belly,
and Hillel's son Shaia, the religious nut,
who would even have sold the sun and its shine
like a pig in a sack,
its enough to make my yearning for you
fade away like a candle going out,
my home, my Zlotshev.

How does the story of that dandy go?
One evening he kept seeing angels around the sun
until a drunk, a Gentile with an axe,
made such a thrust beneath his tailcoat
that it almost killed him.
The Gentile with the axe
is the reason for my hatred toward my grandfather,
and, because of him,
toward you too,
my home, my Zlotshev.

Your ground is witness that I'm not making this up.
When my grandfather and the police
threw my mother out of the house,
my grandmother stood with feet apart
and smiled, sweet as honey,
like a Gentile girl standing between two soldiers.
Cursed be my hatred
that has reminded me of her and of you,
my home, my Zlotshev.

Like a bunch of naked Jews in the baths
standing around someone scalded,
people stood in a circle, shaking their heads
and stroking their beards
around the thrown-out packs and rags
and things in sacks,
and around the broken piece of bed.
My mother still weeps in me,
my home, my Zlotshev.

But our world is wonderful, after all:
in a horse-and-wagon
I dragged myself off to a train
that flew like a devil across the fields
till it brought me to a ship with steerage
that carried me across the ocean
to downtown New York.
That's the only solace, at least for me—
they won't bury me in you,
my home, my Zlotshev.

Women

There are women whose faces light up with joy
at the first words of their little boy,

and to have beauty don't require
a garden white as snow and red as fire.

They don't need the viol's echoing bass
to feel secure in their own space.

They can stand in a cemetery with heads bowed down
or follow a hay-wagon within their town,

or wash dishes in a kitchen somewhere,
or bend over as they sew a shirt's tear.

There's warmth in every move of theirs,
even for the snoop behind the kitchen stairs.

If their pale, autumn faces they hide inside
and it's raining cats-and-dogs outside,

they have but to look at someone with loving eyes
and the sun for each of them will rise.

H. Leyvik (pen name of Leyvik Halper) (1888-1962) is a central figure in the history of Yiddish literature and in the culture of the Jewish people; some have called him "the greatest Yiddish poet and playwright of our time." He was initially associated with *Di Yunge* but drifted away from them. He was often thought of as "the American Y.L. Perets" because of his ethical sensitivity and moral responsibility. His poems revolve around the themes of guilt and forgiveness, and often have a mystical tone. In addition to brilliant poetry, Leyvik wrote a number of dramas, of which the most famous is *The Golem*.

H. Leyvik

Somewhere Far Away

Somewhere far away, somewhere far away,
lies the forbidden land.
Silvery blue the mountains there,
untrodden yet by any man.
Somewhere deep, somewhere deep,
buried in their earthen height,
treasures great await us there,
treasures hidden from our sight.

Somewhere far away, somewhere far away,
a prisoner lies alone all day.
On his head the shine
of setting sun now fades away.
Somewhere someone wanders 'round,
his legs deep in the snow, and
cannot find the hidden road
that leads to the forbidden land.

Stars

I raise my eyes to the sky full of stars,
and I see stars whispering secrets to stars,
and I see stars approaching stars.

I am small, but smaller still are the stars.

I can barely see them. I seek in the stars
the star that is supposed to be my guide among stars.

My father said "Everyone has a star
in the sky, a guide, and you too have a star."

He added "Every Jew is a star,
for God promised Abraham: like stars
will your people be numerous and great—God's stars."

From childhood to old age—in the paths of the stars
paths and circles marked my star.
It was before me, my dream among stars,
and it will be after me, my truth among stars.

In the early evening, at the appearance of the stars,
a light of tranquility is cast on me by my star.
Later, at midnight, with the sorrow of stars,
a look of judgment reaches me from my star.
Still later, before dawn, at the departure of the stars,
there falls on me a hail of stars
that overwhelms me, till my star
shields me with itself and a voice says "Your star
begs mercy for you from the Master of the stars."

I lie covered up, and I hear my star
transmit my name to the Master of the stars.

New York In Beauty

New York in beauty
rises and sets;
now, in the evening,
we eat our supper.

Salad, bananas,
and tea with cake;
such a wonderful meal
in such slack, hard times.

Father, mother,
and first-born son—
the youngest son too,
with his first blond hair.

I wandered all day
throughout New York,
looked for work,
looked for money to borrow.

Didn't find work,
didn't borrow money;
when evening shadows came,
went home tired, worried.

I came home,
sat down on the steps,
temples pounding
feverish hammer-blows.

Hammers swing
up and down,
glow and forge
my head in their flame.

You, like a wonder,
come to my house,
take my hand,
embrace me and straighten me up.

You open the door for me,
you lead me inside.
You tell me, father,
to be what every man should be:

a husband and father.
I obey, I am,
I grow near, nearer,
to my wife and my blond son.

We sit down at the table —
it has long been set.
It's evening now —
you join us for supper.

A Poem About Myself

I saw whipped bodies,
with blood running from them.
When I later became a writer,
I wrote poems about snow.

People liked my poems,
because they were white as snow,
but they often disgusted me
because I hid the blood with them.

Years passed by like that —
it bothered me a lot.
Became a writer once and for all,
and blood lay waiting 'neath the snow.

So once I took my pen in hand
and brushed aside the snow in place,
and every person felt the fear
as earth threw blood into his face.

The blood was still quite warm,
as if it were shed a moment ago.
An angry clamor then arose:
"Why do you torture us so?"

Angry voices cursed my poems,
poisoned their very steps.
My heart was fairly breaking
for the beaten limbs of my poems.

People with prickly scrapers
waved them up and down,
whipped with angry hatred
the naked bodies of my poems.

My poems cried out loudly,
as things do when in pain,
and lay there on the ground,
but never under snow again.

Mima'amakim

Mima'amakim—
a certain word;
a certain word:
out of the depths.
What do you mean,
out of the depths?
What are you saying to me with
out of the depths?
Why are you chasing me,
why are you persecuting me
since my childhood,
since my *kheyder* days,
since my nights of midnight prayer—
out of the depths?

Mima'amakim—
I call to you
out of the depths;
I plead with you,
I stretch my hand out to you,
out of the depths;
I want you to recognize me,
I want to be close to you,
I want to touch you,
I want to reach you,
I want to rise up to you,
out of the depths.

Mima'amakim—
What sort of sound are you?
What do you carry with you
out of the depths?
What do you possess—
out of the depths?
You say it once—
say it again.
sing it again,
and once again:
mi-
    ma'a-
        ma-
            kim.

Whose outcry is that?
Who is fading away?
Whose song is such—
out of the depths?
You say it once—
say it again,
and once again:

out-
   of-
      the depths.

Forever

The world takes me around with arms long and prickly,
and throws me in pyres that burn all the day.
I burn and I burn but the fires don't consume me—
I pick myself up, stride again on my way.

In fac'tries that I stride through, I fall 'neath the giant wheels;
with courage, I blow up the steam-pipes today.
I lay myself down as a brand-new foundation —
I pick myself up, stride again on my way.

Just see: now I'm a horse, in harness of leather;
my raging young rider is whipping away.
I slice through the ground like a sharp-bladed farm-plow—
I pick myself up, stride again on my way.

I sow all of my poems—I sow them like grain seeds;
they sprout and they grow just like grain-stalks today.
But I still lie here like a twisted old bramble—
I pick myself up, stride again on my way.

I live here in a dungeon, blow open the cell-door;
above me the freed man is joyful today.
He leaves me here bleeding, alone on the stone floor —
I pick myself up, stride again on my way.

My clothes bloodily soaked and dragging my weary limbs,
with purified love I am coming this day.
I come to a house and collapse on the doorstep —
I pick myself up, stride again on my way.

Lay Your Head

Lay your head upon my knee—
it's good to lie there so.
Children go to sleep themselves—
grown-ups must be rocked to go.

Children have their little toys
and play with them at will.
Grown-ups play with just themselves
and must forever play thus still.

Do not fear for I am here—
I will not push you far from me.
You have wept enough this day
at what your grown-up fate will be.

You've done your crying, wailing too;
I'll rock you now—to sleep you go.
Lay your head upon my knee—
it's good to lie there so.

Menakhem Boreysho (1888-1949) was a lyrical poet who peered into his inner soul and expressed what he saw there. His poems were filled with longing for God and for holiness; he considered them inseparable from religion, philosophy, and history.

~

Menakhem Boreysho

There's A Story Going Around

—There's a story going around:
the Jews, they've crowned a king.
—The Jews? A king? And where is his land?
—The land they inhabited in ancient times.
—Their ancient land? But the Turks rule there!
—That's exactly the reason! They are poor, the Turks,
and for a few little pots of Jewish gold
they'll sell the holy mountains and valleys
and throw in an extra gift: half a harem.
—And what say the Christian rulers about that?
—Therein lies the tale: wherever he goes,
that Jewish king, palaces and courts
are open to him with favor and honor.
The rulers have made a certain calculation:
'Who really needs the Jews,
who are always underfoot?
The Turks want them? By all means!'
What do they care where the Jews go,
as long as they get rid of them once and for all.
—That certainly makes sense: once and for all!
And when will this happen?
—They say any minute! The German Kaiser himself had a hand
in making the deal with the Turks, and he himself
will soon visit the land being bargained for
and set the price.

So whoever has his eye
on any Jewish possessions
can get them for a bargain now:
a store, a factory, a house, a mansion—
they'll sell everything cheap now.
—And maybe the whole thing is just a fairy tale?
—Go talk to a fool! A fairy tale?....all the newspapers are full of it!

A Prayer

God of mine!
You are alone,
I am alone,
so we're both alone.
Your loneliness flickers, a sun for the Earth,
but it weighs down my shoulders
and falls like a stone at my feet.

God of mine!
You come from You,
I come from You,
so we both come from You.
You consider eternity as one day—
I live on borrowed time
and await Your call every day.

God of mine!
You are in You,
I am in You,
so we're both in You.
I remain in You with my loneliness and sorrow—
I follow You as a slave does his master.
I go, till you call me to You.

God of mine!
You are for You,
I am for You,
so we're both for You.
Let all that I do be in Your honor—
accept it all as an offering.
God of mine, God of mine—You!

Yoysef Opatoshu (1886-1954) wrote principally novels and short stories. He was the most gifted novelist of the group *Di Yunge* and was a major contributor to its annuals and anthologies. He often described full-blooded, earthy, ignorant-but-crafty thieves and smugglers; his first, and one of his most famous, novels was *The Romance of a Horse-Thief.*

∾

Yoysef Opatoshu

Judaism

Doctor Abulafia, the chief rabbi of the Sephardic congregation *Nevey Shalom*, had been in a bad mood all morning. The 60-year-old Abulafia had always prided himself on following in his father's and grandfather's footsteps. His father and grandfather—rabbis in Amsterdam—were very firm. They never allowed a Christian man or woman to convert to Judaism for the sake of a marriage.

That's the way Rabbi Abulafia did things in New York too. He had been the rabbi of *Nevey Shalom* for thirty years now, and more than one Christian man or woman had come to him to be converted. When nothing else helped, Abulafia, like Shammai, chased the would-be converts away.

It was a Friday evening. The rabbi had finished reciting *Song of Songs*. He put on his Sabbath garments and was ready to go to *shul*. Meanwhile, he went into the rabbinical courtroom and sat down over an open volume of Jewish lore. He was just waiting for his wife to bless the candles.

The Negro maid informed him that Mister Bizhorn wanted to see him. Rabbi Abulafia didn't answer her right away. In a single moment, an entire lifetime passed before his eyes: old Bizhorn, who had built the synagogue, had been dead for two years now; he had left an only son; the son, Henry, who was following in his father's footsteps, was one of the most distinguished members of Abulafia's congregation. But why had he come here now, when they were about to bless the candles? The rabbi hesitated—should he go out to meet him? Just because Henry was rich? He remained seated. Bizhorn opened the door to the courtroom and struck a pose as if he himself were letting someone in. A young girl came in. She was pretty, extremely pretty, with dark eyes and red hair. The rabbi stood up. Bizhorn shook hands with the rabbi with his right hand, and introduced the girl with his left:

"This is our rabbi, Doctor Abulafia, and this is Miss Helen Moore."
Miss Moore looked at the graying rabbi. She pointed to the open book of
Jewish lore and her voice trembled:

"I came to register, Doctor Abulafia. I want to become a Jew." She was
shaking. Abulafia smiled. He turned the pages of the book to the last page
and showed it to her:

"There's no room to register, my child; the book is already completely
filled up."

The rabbi brought out one chair, two. He seated the guests and cocked
an ear as if to say:

"What good things can you tell me?"

It was the usual story. The 25-year-old Bizhorn had fallen in love with
his secretary, a Catholic girl of about twenty. Both of them were happy.
But Henry had promised his father that he wouldn't marry a Christian girl,
and that if he did, he would have her convert to Judaism. Henry had told
her that. Helen had not hesitated for a moment, because everything that
Henry said was holy to her. The two of them had come to the rabbi to have
him convert Helen immediately.

Rabbi Abulafia listened to the two young people and smiled. That was
only on the surface—in his heart, resentment seethed. He was angry at
himself, angry that he was not being straightforward, that he was not telling
the couple that according to Jewish law it is forbidden to be converted for
the sake of a match. If one yearns for the Jewish God, wants with all his
heart to serve Him, then one converts. Love, marriage — that should come
later.

But Abulafia didn't say that. He asked her perfunctorily whether her
parents knew that she was going to convert and agreed to it. They were just
as much in love with Henry as Helen was. The rabbi was silent for a while.
He was still considering what to do. And when his gaze fell upon the radiant face of Bizhorn, who was standing next to the young Christian girl
and trembling, it became clear to him that this time he, Abulafia, the rabbi
of *Nevey Shalom*, would not be able to have his way. The rabbi wiped his
eyes with his hand and assumed a posture and an expression as if he had
passed from our world into another. He turned to Helen:

"You really want to become a student of mine?"

"Yes, rabbi."

"Well, all right then. What's today? Friday? Monday we'll have the first lesson in Judaism."

"How many lessons will I have to take?"

"It depends on you Miss Moore," said the rabbi, steeling himself to be nice to the stranger. "You have to know the essentials of Judaism. You have to go through, with me, if not the entire Bible, then at least the Torah. You have to learn how to pray. Such a 'course' usually lasts three months."

"Three months?" Helen made a face as if she were about to burst into tears.

Bizhorn consoled her, assured his beloved that she would spend only a few weeks with the rabbi. She turned happy again.

The rabbi's Sabbath had been disturbed. Why did he take such pride in following in the footsteps of his father and grandfather, when in reality he was a lowly slave who did whatever the wealthy Bizhorn told him to?

Abulafia took revenge. He saw to it that the lessons with Helen would be a living Hell for the girl. Right away, at the first lesson, the rabbi threw up a mountain of difficulties. When Helen assured him that she would overcome all the difficulties, that she was a 'sport' who drove her own automobile, swam, and went hunting, the rabbi stared at her in astonishment and asked her:

"What has Judaism got to do with sports?"

"It does."

"For example?"

Helen knew how the procedure for communion went — she knew the entire ceremony: they would put up a picture of Jesus, and the convert had to pierce it with one blow.

The rabbi grabbed his head with both hands. His eyes, his lips — everything contorted as if he were in pain. His voice was full of pleading to be believed:

"It's a libel — it's an ugly libel, Helen. That's not what Judaism is. Jews never did that, don't do it now, and will never do it."

That Monday, the rabbi spent a longtime convincing Helen. He spoke from the heart, with such pain that the girl went home with tears in her eyes.

The same thing was repeated at every lesson. The 60-year-old Abulafia took revenge for his willingness to give in, for his weakness in not being sure of himself, for the foolish libels that are trumped up about the Jews.

The rabbi and his lessons were torture for Helen. She had dreamed of joy, and here she got punishment and suffering. As the day of conversion approached, Helen was completely bewildered: so many sins, so many sins — how would she get through it?

Rabbi Abulafia, his two assistants and the sexton, all in Sabbath garments, were in the vestibule of the small ritual bath. On a silver platter were cakes and liquor. Abulafia had prepared papers. Bizhorn paced back and forth nervously, from one corner to another, as if Helen were not converting but going into labor.

From behind the closed door, crisp words could be heard. It was the rabbi's wife and her helpers undressing Helen and preparing her for the immersion. And when Helen, bewildered and embarrassed from standing completely naked in front of perfect strangers, stepped into the cool *mikve*, her hands and legs started to tremble. The rabbi's wife yelled at her:

"Make the blessing! Immerse yourself!"

Helen sat down, tried to immerse herself, and remained in the water up to her chin. She shouted: "Jesus Christ!", turned pale, and immersed herself.

A commotion developed. The rabbi's wife went to the men with a question:

"Such and such happened. What do we do?

Rabbi Abulafia closed his eyes so as not to meet Bizhorn's gaze, and asserted himself:

"Helen will have to study more about Judaism."

President Smith

It was the Sunday before Rosh Hashanah.

The New York-to-Chicago express train raced in like a demon, whistling and gasping. Passengers started tumbling out of the cars. Some moved to the exit and others just stood there. From the last car, Reb Yosl the cantor emerged. He was a tall man with a long black beard that was turning gray at the edges, and he was wearing a rabbi's hat. He had come to pray with his fellow townsmen, the people of Mlave, on the High Holy Days. Reb

Yosl put down the valise he had been holding in his hand and started looking around, looking for the delegation from the *Anshey Mlave* synagogue
that was supposed to be waiting for him. Truthfully, Reb Yosl had hesitated
about traveling to Chicago. As a cantor, he was more of a 'sayer' than a
singer. In addition, he was a *khosid* and devout, and here he had taken such
a long journey. His fellow-townsmen, however, had insisted. They had
sent him a hundred dollars and then another hundred. His wife and children had chimed in" "Go, Yosl; go, daddy." So he went. And now —
where were the people who were supposed to be waiting for him?

The officers of the *Anshey Mlave* synagogue, Berl the tailor and Borukh
the butcher, saw the man with the beard and said to each other:

"That must be him."

"It looks that way."

Borukh the butcher, a big, husky man, walked over to Reb Yosl. He
stretched out his right hand for a *sholem aleichem,* and with his left hand,
he took the valise. Berl the tailor said:

"I recognized you right away, Reb Yosl."

"And I recognized you too," said the cantor, proferring him a warm, soft
hand. "You're Berl, of course. Didn't you once sing in my chorus on the
High Holy Days in Mlave?"

"You remember, Reb Yosl," said Berl the tailor, swelling with pride..

Borukh's car was parked on a dark little side–street. He sat down at the
wheel, and when the cantor and Berl had gotten in and closed the door, he
notified them:

"We are going right to the synagogue."

"To the synagogue?" asked Reb Yosl, wonderingly."

"Your fellow-townsmen are waiting for you."

The car turned and twisted through streets and alleys, went up and down
hills, bounced up and down, and drove on. The cantor didn't know whom
to answer first, Borukh or Berl. Both of them bombarded him with questions, kept asking about relatives, other townsmen who lived in New York.
When it grew quiet for moment, the cantor caught his breath and asked:

"Is your president, Max Smith, from Mlave? Seems to me I knew everyone in Mlave, but I don't remember that name."

Both of the synagogue-officers burst out laughing.

"Of course he's from Mlave," said the butcher, starting to drive the car faster. "As soon as he started to get rich, he changed his name. I'll tell you in a moment who he was in the old country. He's been here for a long time, more than forty years. You certainly knew his father, the red-headed Khatzkl with the parrot."

"Khatzkl the organ-grinder? The fellow with the barrel organ?"

"Oh, oh – Reb Yosl remembers", said Berl the tailor hugging his head with joy. "That's exactly what they called him."

"Our president, Max Smith, is Khatzkl's oldest son," added the butcher. "He's extremely rich, has a shoe-factory, a son who is a doctor, and a son-in-law who is a doctor. But if you ask him who he was in the old country, he pretends to be deaf, dumb, and blind: he doesn't know, he's not from Mlave at all, he comes from a village near Mlave. Such disgraceful behavior— to be ashamed of his father and his father's background. And, you, Reb Yosl, please — if you don't want to throw a monkey-wrench into things, don't mention anything. You don't know him, he doesn't know you — you're strangers to each other. Otherwise, Max is a fine young man. He eats and drinks beautifully, and most important — he always has open pockets. If we have to help a fallen 'brother', Max never refuses.

The two lamps in front of the *shul* were blindingly bright. The cantor didn't remember getting out of the car or entering the synagogue. Familiar faces that he had seen as a boy or a young man smiled to him: "Our Reb Yosl, our cantor." No more New York, no more Chicago. The cantor saw before him the walls of the market-square, the little houses with little roofs of straw and shingles. He saw Warsaw Street and Plotsk Street, the little street on which the *shul* stood. All of Mlave came alive for him, spoke to him, came alive in the several hundred eyes—dark eyes and light eyes— that looked up at the cantor, devoured his every word, swelled with pride, and sang along with him parts of the High Holy Day prayers that Reb Yosl was more 'saying' than singing. And Reb Yosl himself? Every pair of eyes was not only very familiar to him but was attached to a name and a nickname: There's Moyshe the mare, there's Pinkhes the stallion, and there's Wolf the peasant.

Dozens of hands started clapping for Reb Yosl:

"It's our old Reb Yosl!"

"His 'saying' is as sweet as sugar!"

"Good! Good!"

"What do you mean 'good'?! We could kiss every word."

Borukh the butcher elbowed his way through the crowd and made room for the president, who was taller and broader than the tall cantor. The butcher introduced him:

"Brother president, I'd like you to meet the Mlave cantor."

"Who you are I don't know ," said the president, extending his hand to the cantor. "I myself am not from Mlave, but you certainly can pray. It was good, very good. Now we'll go to a restaurant, a kosher one, to have a bite."

His underlings started to mill about around the president, jostling one another, forming a 'bodyguard'.

In the restaurant, there was a long table covered with a tablecloth and the president and his wife were seated at its head. On the president's right sat the cantor; on his left sat Berl the butcher. While they were eating and having a few glasses of whiskey, they talked about Mlave. They mentioned things they had heard from their fathers, grandfathers, and great-grandfathers. Only the president remained silent. He ate a lot, drank quite a bit, and remained silent. About twelve o'clock, his wife said to him:

"It's midnight, Max"

"So?"

"The children are waiting for us."

"Let them wait, the big-shots, my doctors."

"I'm tired."

"Go, then. Who's stopping you? So I won't hear the clever talk I've heard from you all my life!" the president said loudly. "Let that go too — go, go!"

"Max, have you had too much to drink?" Borukh the butcher tried gently to intercede.

"You, Borukh the tailor, shut up!" laughed the president drunkenly. "My children, the doctors, are ashamed of their father, of Max Smith. But you, Borukh, you are the same 'big-shot' as I am. Do you remember, Borukh, how we used to chase Gentile girls together in Mlave?"

The crowd around the table burst into laughter. The president bent over to the cantor and whispered in his ear so everyone could hear:

"Mlave cantor, I can no longer be silent. I'm from Mlave too. I remember you and I remember your father, the old Mlave cantor. You just mentioned the little street where the *shul* was—that's where I was born. You knew my father well. Who in Mlave didn't know Khatzkl the redhead? Khatzkl the organ-grinder, with his parrot. Did you know him, ha?" The president became more personal. "Why are you silent?"

"Of course I knew him," Reb Yosl conceded.

"I want you to know that though my father had a lowly profession he was a decent man who cried all day on *yom kipur*, and I, little Max his rotten son, have been ashamed of my father. From today on, no more! Mlave cantor, no more!"

He turned to his fellow townsmen:

"Do you hear, townsmen? I too was born in Mlave. I'm Khatzkl the redhead's eldest son. My name is Manes, not Max. Why are you all silent, townsmen. Enjoy yourself at my expense. Wine, whisky, whatever you want— at my expense. Hey, where is he, the owner of the restaurant? And you, Reb Yosl—I promise you solemnly that I won't set foot outside the *shul* this *rosh hashone* and *yom kipur*. Do you believe me?"

"I believe you, Manes," said Reb Yosl, not knowing what to say. "For that alone my coming to Chicago for the High Holy Days was worthwhile. For that alone, Manes, we the people of Mlave will succeed, through prayer, in winning a good year."

Yisroel Yankev Shvarts (1885-1971) was a poet who was closely associated with *Di Yunge*. He was particularly interested in translating modern and medieval Hebrew poets into Yiddish; his translation of the poetry of Khayim-Nakhman Bialik is a classic. His poems *Blue Grass* and *Kentucky* were radical departures from the New York-centricity of almost all the American Yiddish poets of his time.

~

Yisroel Yankev Shvarts

I Love The Earth

I love the earth on which I walk —
fresh is the earth here and fruitful and fat.
Girlish earth, so submissive, gentle —
it kisses my steps with its grass and cools,
exhales the savor of apples from its innards.

The breezes fan me and caress my cheek.
I know this earth is not sanctified with blood —
my father lies somewhere else and rests —
but my child is a piece of her earth,
glows in its light and has her good fortune from it.

Kentucky

Seems to me a chain is still clanging somewhere,
a whip whistles through the air,
and a man howls like a dog.

Someone grinds his teeth in pain —
in his gaze, hatred flashes,
and his wound drips warm blood.

But a bright sun shimmers
at trees laden with blossoms,
on the clean, bright street.

Their faces are black as pitch,
and the warm south wind caresses
and carries not a breath of their hatred.

Parting

We've parted from our old home —
a storm wind has blown us here from far away.
Someone has left an old mother somewhere,
and one a father's grave 'mid the grasses.

But each of them has a heavy heart,
and each has choked down silent tears;
with packs on their shoulders, children at their sides,
on strange streets, with memories from afar.

And someone has brought a sack of earth,
an old book stained with his grandfather's tears —
a silent sorrow, an age-old sorrow,
an echo of heavy sighs in his ear.

Ripped off like a branch from the old tree,
we've started to build our new home.
The old trunk is there, its heart cut through —
the great, broad ocean between us.

And like a young sapling that sprouts
from hard, cold rock, without a mother's womb,
and begins to bear tiny, weak branches —
thus did we blossom here.

Years have passed. New life-giving sap
has streamed through the sapling;
the roots have burrowed deep,
and new songs have rung out in its head.

Bronx

After all the incarnations of time and years,
after all the wandering in the great, wide world,
I've tumbled back into the Bronx,
for me still the most beautiful corner,
at the top of the giant city of New York.
The Bronx, with its parks and streams—
grassy, full of flowers, with shade-trees,
with cracks in the rocky granite
through which paths have been cut,
spraying sharp sparks.

My youth flutters here in the streets—
I haven't aged. My eyes look far upward
to refresh themselves with the full freshness
and light of youthful days; my arms are open
to embrace everything around. There was a street here
called Wendover, between the two parks,
Claremont and Crotona—a nest of dreamers
and young visionaries, each one
with his own light and radiance,
in love, enthralled by word and song.

O light of youthful days and moonlit nights
in the hilly Crotona Park of those days—
with the fluttering of girlish eyes
in youthful faces, the faces
of near and dear ones, who lie long since
in the fields of Long Island and New Jersey.
And me, the last, the hand of Fate
has brought back to old Bronx—
where I began—to end there.

Legacy

Generations have wept over me:
"My child—remain a Jew;
may your father's legacy and suffering
be guarded in you heart.

"I was not punished with gold,
but God gave me my spirit.
I carry many generations in me—
He doesn't deny us His grace.

"I am weary, I am old, you are young—
go forth—may God protect you, my child;
may your soul emerge still pure
despite life's temptations and sin.

"Do not forget our course through the world—
be a Jew"..he said no more,
but his gaze shone and glowed
with hope and silent prayer.

In the synagogue, the eternal light burned
with its flickering, sorrowful light—
I bent over with awe and deep reverence—
my face in the Holy Ark's curtain.

A. Lutski (1884-1952) was one of the poets associated with *Di Yunge*. He was hailed for the novelty and picturesqueness of his poetry, which was often about various animals and the inanimate features of Nature: stones, rain, sun, etc. The critic Melekh Ravitsh praised him for combining lyricism, simplicity, and deep emotion.

∼

A. Lutski

How Many Persons Make A People?

How many persons make a people?
One.
Who is the one?
I am.
I—am the people Israel.

That's how every Jew should feel.

How many persons sustain a language?
One.
Who is the one?
I am.
I—sustain the Yiddish language.

That's how every Jew should feel.

How many people need to study Torah?
One.
Who is the one?
I am.

That's how every Jew should feel.

A Poem About Writing

A good writer
writes well.
He knows
connoisseurs read him.

A poor writer
writes poorly.
He says:
What does the reader know?

Just a well written poem
is not enough—
it has to have charm
and meaning.

It should be wise,
it should be clear.

The most important thing
is to be brief, to be sharp—
that's all you need.

A Mother Frog

A mother frog
washes her froglet
with her little paw
in a marsh...

The mother frog
sings in the mud,
a hearty little song,
like a fiddle...

"Little jumper,
little singer,
little bird
of mine.
My life
I'd give
for your pleasure…

"Your mother,
in her grave,
will be proud of you —
you will have long
forgotten
about her.

"For how
could you
remember her?
You'll sing
and jump
much higher
than I.

"I hear
in your croaking
your clear
cries;
to me it means nothing else
but that you're growing up
to be a nightingale."

A human mother,
a frog mother —
a mother is a mother.

A Good Poem

In pure art,
there's everything:
there's truth,
there's a.....

In a good poem,
there's spirit,
there's thought,
there's song.

Clear lines,
each word in its place.
Wherever you look,
there's life.

The masterwork
is quite nearby—
the world can be found
everywhere.

Berish Vaynshteyn (1905-1967) wrote poems that have been described as a tour-de-force of expressionistic poetry about the lower depths of New York. His writing had a rough surface, uncouth syntax, much Galician dialect, and naturalistic American details in surrealistic form.

~

Berish Vaynshteyn

For You, Poetry

For you, poetry,
I've abandoned the morning
and have gone down into the empty night.

The streets are quiet, and the lamps too;
they glow, but they have no reason to.
The paved street is silent—
all the autos have left the city,
leaving the shops behind
to the stars on Bleeker Street.

For you, poetry,
I've abandoned all the glowing signs
and gone down to the waters of the Hudson River,
where the anchors soak, and the ropes;
piles of boxes lie there next to sacks.
Sailors still slept on the deck
in those days

For you, poetry,
I've mixed with streets, with lives,
with moons, with oceans, with songs;
I've squandered my weeks on sorrowful burdens,
on bright truths—
for you, poetry, till the end of days.

On Your Soil, America

On your soil I am fated to sing the song of your land.
I've seen so many people, so many ships in your broad harbors.
From the languages of your peoples I've learned to be in a strange land,
and I've begun to understand that though Rayshe, Galicia, is my home,
my city is New York, my streets Ridge and Pitt,
and you've gotten even more homelike to me since that sad day
when I saw my parents die on your soil, America.

My dear parents—grandchildren of Jewish wanderers from Amsterdam,
ancestors in George Washington's great times
who set sail fearfully over flood-like waters
with their Sabbath-candles, prayer-shawls, and phylacteries from old
    Holland,
and for skinny Lincoln brought the wisdom of the "holy Moses"
to the cotton fields to comfort the weeping of the Negroes.

There are so many sad streets on your soil, America!
Jews go around uncomfortably among your houses,
bent over with sacks of merchandise hanging from their weary shoulders,
and trade in cloth and gold, as in Warsaw and Lodz,
in English, Spanish, Italian, and Yiddish.

On your foggy nights, on the avenues, on the squares,
one can see how lonely people can be on the earth.
Your new moons rise thinner and paler
and pour their sorrow onto faces, onto drunken bodies
when your ground is windy and snowy, America.

Somewhere at a great distance, away in the blue deeps,
ships sail on your shadowy, twisting waterways.
On the hanging bridges of Manhattan, Brooklyn, and Queens,
cattle, in the reflection of the knife, walk to slaughter,
and make even grayer the bit of loneliness of your soil, America.

Nights raise the smoke of cities and reflect from cold roofs.
The blue of the skies gets as sad as the city, the windowpanes.
All along your waters, flaming tugboats steam,
spewing flaming foam, shaking the timbers of the riverbanks.
The harbor lights on the warehouses grow wintry and dim;
watchmen walk sorrowfully around amid your foreign goods.

Evening shores—sad and drunk with fog.
Light-skinned and dirty-brown sailors stand drunkenly in the taverns,
stand at sleepy bars, with bowed heads,
and talk to the empty beer-glasses with dripping mouths.
From ropes and anchors, their hands are hard and nimble,
and can rig masts in the middle of the world, the middle of the ocean.

In November, everything gets rust-colored and yellow.
Boyish fires smoulder from nail-studded boxes, boards, and cans.
God, what longing one sees in Jewish, Negro, and Italian faces.
"East Side, West Side"—everywhere the same windows and the same
      night.
And if a man dies on your big, broad ground, America,
it's as if he had died in many lands at once!

Melekh Ravitsh (1893-1976), together with Perets Markish and Uri Tsvi Grinberg, constituted *Di Khaliastre* (The Gang), a literary group that was a powerful force in Yiddish poetry in Poland during the interwar years. He was also an encyclopedic bibliographer of Yiddish writers and an incisive critic and essayist, particularly in his later years in Montreal. There he also wrote poetry that expressed his sadness and loneliness and probed the mysteries of life and death.

~

Melekh Ravitsh

On The Day Of Judgment

There's not enough blood in my body
to be reincarnated as tears,
tears salted with fire,
to weep out, to the very bottom, the sorrow and shame,
yes, the human shame,
of your old body, your old years,
that the Nazi-German inflicted on you,
in the Belsen crematorium,
old mother of mine.

He stomped on you like a bear,
with heavy boots studded with spikes—
trampled you like a sack full of rags.
And when you were trampled enough,
he drove you with dogs to the gas.

Your silent old outcry
only the old, deaf Mother Earth—
the inanimate one—
heard.
But what more could she do for you
than be the unmarked grave for your bit of ash?

No, there isn't enough blood in my body
to be converted to tears
to weep for your sorrow, old mother.
And there's also no punishment in the world,

not in Heaven and not on Earth,
not now and not in the future, even in Hell,
to measure up to your crime,
German Nazi.

Even if all the crimes of the world,
from East to West and all around the world,
from the beginning of Time to its end
and from one edge of the Universe to the other,
were wiped away by the water of forgiveness,
there would remain hanging in the void
the blackest stain of all the worlds—
your crime, Nazi.

Even if there had never been any crime
anywhere or at any time,
your crime would be the first and will always be the last;
for greater darkness cannot be.
Even if the earth again becomes
the ash of the Universe
and is exposed to the rays of all the stars,
it will never, never again become light.

There is no punishment for your crime—
it's beyond Man and beyond punishment.
Even all four death sentences of the Talmud together—
stone, lead, chains, and sword burning with fire—
would laugh, if they were able to understand and laugh,
that they had to be the instrument
of the punishment for your crime,
Nazi.

There is no iron that can burn out such eyes.
There is no chain that can pull out such a soul.
There is no stone that can smash such bones,.
There is no sword that can cut through such a neck.

And his boot trampled you,
mother of mine,
good among the good
and best among the best,
trampled you,
you and your millions of sisters
and sisters' sisters and brothers' brothers.
You were so good, mother—
you taught me, after all, from Friedrich Schiller's canon,
that "all men are brothers,"
and also, from Goethe's poem,
that men should be noble
and helpful and good.

They trampled you with boots,
like a pile of rags—
stomped on your living body as if on dead clay,
and then drove you with dogs to the gas.
You were accompanied only by the bodyless wind,
your only companion.
It sought you out at the edge of the pyre—
wanted to caress you for the last time,
caress your ancient, long, snow-white hair.
But the Nazi tore out and shaved off your hair in order to stuff mattresses
     with it,
and snored heavily
when he got drunk on pitchers of Jewish blood.

So the wind caressed only your naked skull,
went with you
to the threshold of the gas chamber,
and whispered hastily in your ear:
"An easy death,
good old child of mine!"
and even the wind fled in fear.
But you, mother,

with all your sisters and brothers,
went to your Jewish fate.

There isn't enough blood in my body
to be reincarnated as tears,
tears salted with fire,
to weep out, to the very bottom,
the sorrow that the Nazi German inflicted on you
in the Belsen crematorium,
old mother of mine.

There is no iron that could burn out the Nazi's eyes.
There is no chain that could pull the soul out of his throat.
There is no stone that could smash his bones,.
There is no sword that could cut through his neck.

And there is no beast
that, even after twice ten years,
could eat away from my heart, from my memory,
the pain of remembering you every day,
and could eat away,
together with pieces of my heart,
the image of your last moments
in the Belsen crematorium.

Man will be noble
and helpful and good,
and all men will be brothers,
but first there must disappear from the world,
into the abyss of forgetfulness,
the last, last, last
drop of Nazi-poisoned blood.
And until that hour
there is no forgetting—
none, none!

Y.L. Perets
(fragment)

Though the complete collection of Perets's poems comes to almost three hundred items, though he wrote his plays mostly in poetic form, though he began his literary career with poems and ballads and also ended it with poems, the children's poems, he was not a poet in the truest sense of the word. His language is pure. It is often so full of Hebraisms that it's like a sort of bridge between Yiddish and Hebrew. His language is so rhythmical — not so much melodic — that even his essays, to say nothing of his stories can be rendered in short lines, as if they were poems in prose. If one had to arrange the works of Yitskhok Leybush Perets according to their importance, one would have to place his folk-tales in the first rank, then his plays, then his realistic tales, then his symbolic tales, and only at the end, his poems. And this despite the fact that among the poems are several masterly ballads and several lyrical pearls, and most important, several social poems of great feeling.

*   *   *

As previously mentioned, Perets was a practicing lawyer till the age of 37, and was talented in a profession that demands much clarity and logic. The profession left its characteristic mark on his fiction too: he often uses in it the words "court" and "trial," and very often the word "justice," and even scenes of actual trials, on earth and even more in heaven, are depicted in his works. For example, the heavenly trial scene in one of his folk-tales, *Bontshe Shvayg*, which became world-famous and has been translated into many languages. Even after giving up the legal profession, Perets remained an advocate: for poor, hardworking ordinary people all over the world, as well as for the poor of his own people.

Perets believed in authenticity and forthrightness in life, and he was therefore a great foe of assimilation. He believed in the possibility of peoples living together in harmony, with two or even more than two peoples on one territory, if that's what luck and fate ordained. He was fluent in three languages besides his own Hebrew and Yiddish: Polish, Russian, and German. He was proficient in world literature, and was especially fond of

Polish, Russia, and German literature in the original. He had in front of him, practically before his eyes, the millions of Polish Jews, who were then an integral part of the five million Jews in the Russian Empire. Perets believed in the possibility of national-cultural autonomy for the Jewish masses. He also fought for the idea that all peoples should work for the cause of humanity, the highest goal— each people in its own direct way and we Jews in our Jewish way. A large number of his essays represent one long series of battles against soul-deadening assimilation.

*   *   *

But not only sociocultural matters were the content of Perets's verbal legacy—a large proportion of his essays are also concerned with purely literary themes. Even Perets could not avoid the issues that were so popular at the beginning of the twentieth century: art for art's sake and art for the sake of ideas. As one who was deeply rooted in his eternal tradition as a Jew, Perets believed in the prophetic approach to artistic literature: eternal ethical ideas in eternally lasting — and, therefore in the highest degree beautiful— forms. In one of his essays of that type, he meditated about the differences and meanings of two Yiddish words for poet: *"poet"* and *"dikhter"*. To him a *"poet"* is an artist with words, who can sometimes sacrifice ideas and ethical feelings for the sake of art and beauty. *"Dikhter"* is a more exalted concept: to be a *"dikhter"*, according to Perets, means to be a prophet. Perets also concerned himself a great deal with criticism and mores in the newly developing Yiddish literature. He perceived that Yiddish literature was world literature in miniature, and should therefore not limit itself to themes about the *shtetl* It should not be a stagnant pool when Jewish life was a world-stream that encompassed the entire world in time and space, although— as often happens with preachers—Perets himself remained thematically limited in time and space to the *shtetl* and to his century. His leading, authoritative, inspirational words, however, influenced younger poets by what he had accomplished in literature, written with his own hands. Here, for the sake of example, we will mention one name: Sholem Ash. In 1900, that name made its initial appearance in Yiddish literature, with Perets' blessing, and only a few years later in world literature in dozens of languages.

*   *   *

The works of Y.L. Perets — especially his folk-tales, which, by the way, always have a very interesting and often even intriguing subject— became more and more the foundation of modern humanistic Jewish pedagogy. The children and young people themselves decided that. Official pedagogy confirms only the fact that, more than any other writer, children love to study the stories of Perets both in Yiddish and in Hebrew. Perets has a classical place of honor in both national literatures of the Jews. Perets tells stories and educates. He is not a preacher, a castigator and demander— he is a bard, a mime, who goes from village to village, from city to city and, most importantly, from heart to heart. People gather around him not because they have to but because they want to, because they are drawn as by a magic spell. No small part of this is due to his precise, crystal-clear, and distinctive language — rhythmical, picturesque, and resonant. He draws pictures of his heroes with just a few brush-strokes. He describes, at great length and definitively, their activities and their experiences. In that sense, he is like the *Tanakh:* he leaves enough room for the creative fantasy of the reader. That is the secret of the connection that young people have to him. And yet none of his stories is just a story—all of them are linked to the life and the suffering of his people, and the life and suffering of his people are linked to the life and suffering of all humanity throughout the world.

*   *   *

Let us leaf through a few stories:

At the Head of the Dying Man's Bed — A whip-stroke to the face of all hypocrites. True piety resides in the heart and not just on the lips.

The Treasure — True belief is to be found in poor people — in the end, the kingdom of the earth will be theirs.

Reincarnation of a Melody - - Not the form of things but their soul determines whether they will last for eternity.

Downcast Eyes — Not in externals can deep piety and the most exalted modesty be found. Even after his death, the truly virtuous man must fight for truth.

Hear, O Israel — God is with the poor in spirit, but the truly rich in spirit hear the heavenly word and the heavenly melody even in cacophony. God hears the most beautiful song even in the ugliest groan, as long as the groan comes from the depths of the heart, from the deepest belief in Him.

If Not Even Higher — The most psalm-like talk of virtuous service of God is less convincing to people than the simplest, even the coarsest good deeds.

Berl Shnayder — If true piety doesn't receive its reward from God, it must demand it from Him, for only through reward for goodness and piety and Divine righteousness will human righteousness be achieved.

*   *   *

When Perets died, Khayim Nakhmen Bialik, the father of modern Hebrew literature, compared him to the prophet Elijah, and wrote this in a letter to Jacob Dinezon, Perets' lifelong friend: "Perets' death made an impression on me as a sort of 'ascent to heaven.' His creations were like that after all—a horse and chariot of fire. He flew by stormily in his fiery chariot, and lightning flashed ahead of him and behind him. It seems to me that he will show himself again more than once, with good humor. Just like Elijah . . . . he has after all, like that zealot and son of a zealot, not really died."

Shmuel Niger (pen name of Shmuel Charney) (1884-1962), who was the elder brother of Baruch Charney Vladeck, was, by common consent, the finest literary critic in Yiddish literature. His descriptions and evaluations of Yiddish writers are considered definitive.

~

Shmuel Niger

Bilingualism
(fragment)

The extremists on both sides have remained extremists. They still believe that we can and should have a culture in one language, Yiddish or Hebrew. They have remained true to their theories. Those who don't measure everything against abstract ideas, those who take historical reality into account, are different: they respect the experience of the Jewish people as a people more than the slogans of this or that faction. They have always known, and still know now, that bilingualism is a deeply rooted tradition in Jewish literary creativity and in all of Jewish culture since after the biblical period, so they don't want to tear the living literature of the Jewish people to pieces. They don't want to be like the false mother in Solomon's trial, the 'mother' who was prepared to cut the living child in half: "if it is not for me, it will not be for you." They don't want to say: "Joseph Perl's *Discoverer of Secrets* in Hebrew is yours—take it; ours is the *Discoverer of Secrets* that he wrote in Yiddish, which he never published; Yitskhok-Ber Levinson's Hebrew *Mission in Israel* belongs to you—we'll take his Yiddish *Lawless World*; Mendele's *Fathers and Sons* in Yiddish is, for us, no more than a translation from another literature—the Hebrew original belongs to you; our pieces of Mendele are *Fishke, The Mare*, etc; Perets' *The Organ* has value for you Hebraists — for us Yiddishists, only *Monish*, etc. exist. Bialik is ours only with his few Yiddish poems—his folk-poems or *The Dead of the Wilderness* have no relation to our literature."

No, they are opposed to that kind of 'difference'. They want to have a whole and healthy Jewish literature, not a crippled one with two separate halves. Yiddish, for them, did not mean and could not mean the denial of the Hebrew cultural legacy. With their Yiddish, they came not to diminish but to augment our cultural treasures. Their slogan was not "Forget Hebrew!"; they cried "Don't forget Yiddish!"

Their train of thought was like this: There is respect for Hebrew among us, but not for Yiddish; Yiddish too must be respected! At the present time, Yiddish is the language of daily life for the majority of the Jewish people, and if we don't want the people's life to be denigrated, its language must not be denigrated. In and through Yiddish, we create and enjoy what we create: the vehicle for our spiritual pleasure, which is also the tool of our creativity, must be refined and cultivated universally. The growth of our self-awareness, of the worth and the role of the Jewish folk-masses, is taking place before our eyes, and it must be expressed and crystallized in the growth of the self-awareness, self-worth, and creative role of the poets, storytellers, scientists, researchers, and others who use the language of the people.

So it has been with other peoples, and so it must be with us.

Khasidizm, haskole, Zionism, socialism, folkism, the fight for civil and national rights — all the manifestations of awakened and activated people-power have led and must lead to the revival of the versatile enrichment of the people's language, the people's art, and the people's literature. That was inevitable. Yiddishism, about which we are speaking, is the historical expression of that inevitability.

The revival process of Hebrew and Hebrew literature has been and has remained precisely such an inevitable historical process. The same forces, the same movements, that poured a new stream of life into Yiddish could not have achieved their goals and discovered their possibilities were it not for the *khasidizm,* the *maskilim,* the folkists, the socialists, and, of course, the Zionists.

Both Yiddish and Hebrew have been of great use in our life and strivings, our thoughts and memories. Those who accept Jewish history, integral and complete as it is, accept and recognize both of our languages.

Kadye Molodovsky (1894-1975) was one of the greatest women writers of Yiddish poetry. She addressed a broad range of subject matter and had a particular interest in children's poetry. She also wrote about the joys and trials of motherhood. Her later years were years of wandering and privation, of sorrow for the events of the Holocaust, and of nostalgia for her old home. Towards the end of her life, she founded and edited *Sviva*, a distinguished magazine of Yiddish poetry and prose.

~

Kadye Molodovsky

Women's Songs
(fragment)

A.

The women of our family
will come to me at night, in my dreams, and say:
"With virtuous modesty, we have transmitted a pure blood for generations,
brought it to you like a wine
guarded in the kosher cellars of our hearts."
And one will say:
"I have remained a deserted wife
since my cheeks were like two red apples still on the tree,
and I've gnashed my white teeth, waiting,
through many a lonely night."
And I will give the grandmothers the following answer:
"Your sighs, which sounded like whistling whips,
have driven my young life out of the house,
fleeing from your kosher beds.
But you followed me wherever streets are dark,
wherever shadows fall,
and your quiet, choked weeping chases me
like the autumn winds,
and your words are silken threads that bind my brain.
My life is like a page plucked from a book,
with the first line torn off."

B.

I'll come to the man
who brought me my first womanly joy, and say:
"Man —I entrusted my silent looks to another
and laid my head next to his one night.
Now my sorrow is like the stinging of bees
around my heart,
and I have no honey to salve the wounds."
And the man will grab my braid
and I'll drop to my knees,
remaining at the doorstep,
petrified as in Sodom.
I'll raise my hands to my head,
as my mother used to do when blessing the candles,
but my fingers will stick out
like ten enumerated sins.

C.

Sometimes a stone step
is as sweet as a pillow
when I stretch out on its coldness,
when I can't drag my head,
with its dried-out lips,
to the third story.
Then I am a silent, exhausted girl
scraping the ground with frozen limbs,
and I remain lying somewhere
alone in the night on the stone steps.

D.

For poor brides who are servant girls,
Mother Sarah draws sparkling wine
from dark barrels and casks.

To those who are fated to have a full pitcher,
Mother Sarah carries it with both hands,
and for those who are fated to have but a glassful,
she drops a tear into the wine.
And to street-walkers
who are dreaming of white bridal slippers,
Mother Sarah brings pure honey
on small plates
to their tired mouths.

For poor brides from aristocratic families
who are ashamed to show their patched underwear
to their mothers-in-law,
Mother Rebecca brings camels
loaded with white linen.
And when the darkness spreads out before their feet
and all the camels kneel to the ground to rest,
Mother Rebecca measures out ell after ell of linen,
from the fingers of their hands
to their golden armbands.

For those whose eyes are tired
from looking at every neighbor child
and yearning for tiny hands
and a small, soft body
and a cradle to rock,
Mother Rachel brings healing leaves
found on distant mountains,
and comforts them with quiet words:
"God can open your closed womb at any moment."

To those who weep at night on their lonely beds
and have no one to tell their sorrow to,
so that they talk to themselves with parched lips,
to them Mother Leah comes quietly
and covers both eyes with her pale hands.

What If

What if
the fliers return
and say there is no Heaven?
Where will I turn my gaze
if not on high, if not above?

How will I bear the grayness of the rain,
the dust of the stony streets?
How will I save myself from great revulsion?
And who will help me write poems
if there's nothing there above?

But I won't believe the fliers —
I won't believe them...

Because I have seen an angel,
not just once but many times,
and he rescued me
from threatening plagues.
So I won't trust the fliers —
I won't trust them.

And what if
the fliers return
and deny the existence of Paradise,
the home of the righteous?
And how can I be successful
without the righteous?
If I don't hold onto their coat-tails,
how will I cross over the ditches and cracks in the road?
And who will sustain my poor soul
and where will I loose my tears?

But I won't listen to the fliers—
I won't listen to them.

Because I have seen the righteous,
not once but many times—
they were yoked and oppressed,
carrying the weight of the world on their backs.
So I won't look at the fliers,
I won't turn around and look at them.

Those who weave the blueness of heaven
can reach heaven—
They've walked on miracles, as if on steps,
and know the ways of the righteous scholars.

The Evening Sky

The world is in turmoil,
nowhere any pity.
Sorrow seizes on me—
I am lost in my city.

And perhaps, who knows,
perhaps in our wordly life
man has torn himself from man
and the bond is gone, from strife.

The sky has remained intact—
the stars still shine as bright.
In their shine, we still can see
that an eye watches in the night.

Perhaps cruelty will tire
and Man will rest from pain.

We'll hear a song sung somewhere—
the sun will shine again.

That's what the evening sky tells me.
I look up and my mood grows light.
But then comes day, with noise and tumult,
with murder and with bloody fights.

I see children run and spring—
they play and laugh and sing.
There is a world still, it's not a dream—
the children will grow and bring peace.

I stand at night and see the stars—
the light of Heaven, it seems.
I believe the world will be better—
it's not an idle dream.

The Song of Sabbath

With the six kings
of the six days of the week
I have fought till the eve of the Sabbath.
Sunday they took away my sleep,
Monday they spilled out my salt,
and on the third day, my God,
they threw away my bread
and fanned my face with whips;
they seized my flying dove
and slaughtered it.
And so till Friday morning,
and my entire week is over
when my flying dove dies.

In the evening I lit four candles,
and Queen Sabbath came to me.
Her face shone
and the whole world turned into Sabbath.

My spilled salt
sparkled in the salt-shaker,
and my dove, my flying dove,
flapped its wings
and cleared its little throat.

Queen Sabbath blessed my candles—
they burned with a clear flame.
Their shine drew a curtain over the days of the week
and the struggle with the six kings.
The greenness of the mountain
is the greenness of Sabbath;
the silver of the lake
is the silver of Sabbath;
the song of the wind
is the singing of Sabbath;
and the song of my heart
is the eternal Sabbath.

Borukh Rivkin (1883-1945) was a well known and highly regarded essayist and critic of Yiddish literature who had anarchist leanings. He believed in poems as a medium of spiritual elevation, and often read potential meanings into them. He was particularly taken with Moyshe-Leyb Halpern, who, he felt, towered above his contemporaries in terms of sheer genius.

~

Borukh Rivkin

It's Precisely America That Is Making Yiddish Literature Jewish

The goal that has lurked from the beginning in the subconscious of Yiddish literature—to serve the people as a substitute for religion—was, under the pressure of the first World War, forced more and more out of the subconscious and into the consciousness of Yiddish writers in America. Yes, it was precisely in America, with its safe location across the ocean, that Yiddish literature responded with greater self-awareness to the catastrophe that the War brought to hundreds of thousands of Jews, which was the tragic precursor of the catastrophe of the six million. There, it is true, the catastrophe pressed Yiddish literature hard to the ground, but above the folk masses hovered the Jewish folk-consciousness, which wouldn't have let the literature sink into the ground and would in any case sooner or later have revived it from its swoon. There was a danger that the Jewish masses would fall into the obliviousness of indifferent, self-satisfied, soulless survivors, even if they had still had enough Jewish heart to give charity to their unfortunate brothers. So Yiddish literature, almost like a living being, became goal-conscious, aimed toward the heights rather than the depths.

That goal dictated not only that Opatoshu, the idea-engineer, should plan territorial works, but even that Ignatov, the visionary, should sow visions across the continent and include the new homeland in his theory that "the world is a story. " And the same goal was dictated by Raboy, the least of the theoreticians and ideologues: Judaize America, with its Erets-Yisroel-Bessarabia; and by Y.Y. Shvarts: to do for Kentucky what Opatoshu had done for Poland—run through the history of three generations of Jews, who in the third generation had already lost their characteristics, and cover their gray lives, together with the better lives of their neighbors, the Negroes, with Sabbath-Hebrew ark curtains. Also his second great work — rendering into Yiddish the Golden Age of Spain — was dictated by the same goal:

not to leave the Jews of America with naked faces and empty heads face-to-face with the catastrophes that are staring them in the face.

Even the two pioneer poets who continued to have an influence years after the catastrophe of the first World War—Yehoyesh and Avrom Lyesin—were inspired by the same goal: Yehoyesh assumed the burden of Mt. Sinai—his monumental translation of the Bible--and while undergoing such a heroic discipline, he embraced the most tasteful Yiddish words and expressions, and, while carrying such a heavy load, he attained a certain lightness, in order to hold the attention of the youngest of the young with playful poems that expressed God's secrets of love, faith, and Nature—a task he had set for himself with his very first poem, *A Song for the Sabbath*, in fulfillment of the first commandment of Yiddish literature: to pour out the emotion of religion via the new, free creative channel. And Avrom Lyesin—who in his first period found it so difficult to sing out the eternally Jewish for an audience that had never looked into a holy book and had to start from the beginning—in his second period, thinned out by the catastrophe, nevertheless managed, with all the ancient books in his memory but not relying on them, to elicit the eternally Jewish divine creation from the stuff out of which secular poems are made, and transformed the past into the future—Isaiah's *In The End of Days* into the new world order; Rabbi Akiba into Hirsh Lekert; the martyrdom of the Maccabees into Bar Kokhba; the saints of Babylon and the Middle Ages into the martyrdom of the revolutionary Jews of Vilna, Minsk, and Bobruisk; and the spiritual fire of the Bal Shem and the Berditshever Rebbe into pictures of sunset, forest, sea, storm, and night. He read *kabala* into the hints of Nature. He elevated poetic playfulness to prophetic vision.

Besides those two pioneers, there was a logical transition to two younger ones, who, a while later than the initiators, became part of *Di Yunge*, namely H. Leyvik and Moyshe-Leyb Halpern. They were co-discoverers, with Yehoyesh and Lyesin, that verbal artistry is an instrument that puts out immeasurably more than one puts into it. But different from Mani Leyb's *Island*-group, which created an island of instruments for instruments' sake and poems for poems' sake, instrumentation was no hindrance to taking upon themselves the serious life-work of conscious service to the Jewish people. And just as in Opatoshu's "across the ocean" position, those two pioneers, from the outset, transformed a supposed weakness into the greatest virtue of Yiddish literature in America. The weakness— the fact that the tradition of the holy books was lacking and that the populace here did not have the cap of Jewish consciousness on its head—that weakness forced into existence the virtue: that they should begin to establish the eternal Jewish values from the very beginning, out of their own hearts.

The new beginning in Leyvik: without a long list of ancient holy books in his memory, he established the original Jewish process of God-creation using his own image as a Jewish instrument. That was also the case with Ignatov and Raboy: Ignatov put visions into the readers' eyes as magnifying glasses; with Raboy, it was the Israel-like aroma of the Bessarabian soil, which continued to stick to his flesh. Leyvik drew his second image from inside; he had two images, himself and another, secret one. That was a gift he had had since childhood, when he was hidden and felt ashamed in a secluded corner of the Earth. As a result of hardship, the hiddenness, seclusion, shame, and depression intensified tenfold, a hundredfold, as a result of physical blows. He used to draw Paradise out of a crack in the wall, which made the hidden one feel happy and liberated. In his *Siberian Poems*, that warm, happy Paradise sparkles to him from the frosty snows. It pursues the liberated Leyvik across the steppes. It was the sprinkled beauty that smiled from the *Siberian Poems*, entranced everyone, and gave him a place among *Di Yunge*.

The hardships into which the first World War plunged the Jewish masses in Eastern Europe, the ocean of murder that flooded over them—from Leyvik's single crack in the wall there grew an abyss from which he dredged out Paradise for the entire people. What had previously been his private property he made into the common property of the Jews. *Bright Lamps*, a single lit-up house after a murder—from the burned stones, he senses traces of the Messiah, who has just passed by. From the second of his two-pronged personalities, the hidden one, he drew out the Messiah and marked his steps through the Destruction to the Redemption. A quite legitimate act. That's the way it was in ancient times too. The hand of God was first the prophet himself and then the popular image of the Messiah. Picturing something is a creative act that belongs simultaneously to religion and to art. And the image became Leyvik's religio-artistic principal instrument. And with that, he more than confirmed the discovery by *Di Yunge* that art is an instrument that makes real the dream that one carries within him about himself. Leyvik further strengthened his artistic instrument by consolidating his own dream image with the people's two-thousand-year-old ideal: unlike the old-country Messiah dreamers, with their literary, biblical-passage-quoting, externally decorative Messiahs, there was, in the *Redemption Comedy*, a Messiah, "from the beginning," carried during pregnancy, born, reared, brought to his full growth; and let out into the arena — to give a heartily intimate, suffered-through response to the people's cry of pain, to purify the people's dark today in the bright shine of tomorrow.

And in doing so, Leyvik doesn't renege on the oath to which Mani Leyb swore all poets: on the spot where the poet walks, beauty must be created, and from his poems, expectations of wonder must radiate. The beauty that radiates is not from the place but from the work, even in the case of Mani Leyb, and certainly in the case of Leyvik, especially for human creations — in God's image. Then it is a matter of Creation–like beauty. The beauty in this case is a foretaste of Mani Leyb's future harmonic completion. That is the expectation of wonder. All the poems from the series *Letters to a Friend* could be given the title of the painterly poem *How Good*—God's painterly artistic exclamation: "How beautiful my works are!" The image of *The Friend* is the most humanized—the image of God, Leyvik's creative tool.

And to the present day, beauty comes to Leyvik's poems from sensing God in the images of mankind. As in one poem, *Open Skies*: "Open Skies, awakened fields. The path runs past and turns, and he wishes he would encounter a person. Who? Who? You, you!" The "you-you" expands into the expected, desired God-man persona. Every crossroads in the field has remained wrapped in Creation-like beauty. In the poem *Clouds Near the Forest*, the poet stretches his heart out to the sunset. It's the revelation of God in beauty, the fascination of the God-vision, whose intoxicating deliciousness was tasted by Adam, Moses, the Prophets, the Bal-Shem, and all the giant figures of human liberation.

And now Leyvik seeks to draw out of us the liberating beauty of the revelation of God, which has risen over the heroic deaths of the ghetto heroes. Mani Leyb's stubbornness was in vain. The contradiction between poetry for the sake of beauty and poetry for the sake of serving God is no contradiction at all. Stubbornness is hurtful. The strongest inborn talent needs wings in order to be able to fly with the storm-winds to its fullest expression. One must trust in creative art—creativity will find a way; it will create a synthesis between 'goal-less' beauty and the goal to serve. Leyvik is the proof.

Yankev Yitskhok Sigal (1896-1954) was obsessed with Jewish uniqueness, with the shtetl, and with *khasidizm*. He appropriated for himself the role of prophetic visionary of Jewish tradition.

~

Yankev Yitskhok Sigal

New-Old Song

From the white, silver candle-blessing
my wife approaches me,
shuffles in, her soft dress rustling,
from the bedroom as from a dark distance.

Peace to you, wife of mine —
sholem aleichem, my dove.
Your Sabbath abides in praise
in every corner of the house.
Peace to you, wife of mine.

Just come here, wife of mine —
you angel, wife of mine.
Stand at my right side
as I raise the goblet with gold,
the gold that sparkles red,
and I bless you, wife of mine.

Peace to you, wife of mine —
peace to you, my dove.
Your praise and beauty abide,
your light and Sabbath abide,
in every corner of the house.

Sholem aleichem, wife of mine.

The Wisdom of Yiddish

A gang of street urchins
keep coming to me to learn the wisdom of Yiddish.

I say: "Don't open your little books."
I want to look at them from afar,
I want to read them like an open book,
I want to know and recognize them
I speak to them wordlessly:

"Little ones, dear Jewish boys and girls,
I want to study you,
I want to be able to read you,
I want to be able to write and describe you.
I'll become your bigger, older brother.
How shall we do that?

"I'll read you a Sholem Aleichem story
and see whether you can laugh in the true Jewish manner.
If you can laugh with great Jewish joy
at one of Sholem Aleichem's ever-young stories,
I'll need no better proof
that you'll eventually be able to study
the Torah with Rashi's commentary in Yiddish,
and even the Talmud in Yiddish,
and certainly literature in Yiddish.

"I see you're starting to smile and laugh
even before I bring out for you
Sholem Aleichem's *Adventures of Motl, the Cantor's Son,*
so today we'll start to study
the first lovely chapters of Jewish laughter.
With your radiant faces,
with your beautiful, singing eyes,
we'll delve deeply into Sholem Aleichem
and hug one another with great laughter."

Arn Glants-Leyeles (1889-1966), together with Nokhem Borekh Minkov and Yankev Glatshteyn, established the second revolutionary literary group in American Yiddish literature, *In Zikh* (The Introspectivists), starting with the famous 1919 manifesto published in their own magazine, also called *In Zikh*. Leyeles, as he was often called for short, was the principal theoretician of the group. As the name of the movement implies, the *Inzikhists* felt that true poetry had to filter through the psychological prism of the self. They were early champions of free verse, though they did not use it exclusively.

Arn Glants-Leyeles

The Madonna In The Subway

Across from me in the subway sat the madonna.
Her legs were crossed
and she was reading a tabloid.
She read about a cashier who jumped into the river—
her fiance had left her with a swelling belly.

The madonna put lipstick on her mouth
and continued to bite the burning coal of tragedy.
The madonna stroked her snakeskin shoes
and continued to lament
the drowning of the cashier.

My gaze tick-tocked
and the madonna's eyelids heard.
Her two oblong eye-sockets turned
their suede depths and secrets toward me,
and I understood what she was saying,
the words she was speaking only to me
in the subway:

"In Galilee, once upon a time,
the carpenters, shoemakers, and tailors,
the fishermen, moneylenders, and thieves
needed a Savior and a God.
So I opened my virginal loins
and, in a dark hour, received into my womb
the needy seed of one whose name I still don't know—

a soldier, a stranger, an angry man, a slave of the emperor;
a fisherman with hands callused from pulling on his net
or just some vagabond who happened to whisper just then:
'My God!'

"I can only tell you I got with child.
Oh, there are nights when the spirit stabs my guts
like a vulture's beak
and wraps itself around me like a snake.
There are black, open-hearted nights
that sense the demands of virginal loins.
It was the Spirit of God,
because soldiers and fishermen and vagabonds
demanded a Savior, a God."

The madonna powdered her nose
(which was noble and thin)
and spoke further:

"From the distant dazzle
and bright call,
from the obvious sorrow
in my heavy body,
painters and poets dream up
my portraits down through the ages.
From the flowering Spring
in fields and forests,
hands stretch out and pray:
'Grant it to us!'
Eyes plead throughout the years.
In the crush of reality
in the streets and subways,
people still yearn for wonders,
though they no longer believe in His birth.
One day I will cast off the nets
that enfold and fetter me,

and I'll slake your thirst
with my nakedness.
And hear this:
it will be like that great destiny,
then, in Galilee."

The madonna spoke much longer—
longer, more heatedly, and faster.
But I—I couldn't understand any more.
Amid the pious flutter,
the open-hearted moons and suns approached
and I sensed the movement of God's spirit within me,
like a rabbit or a snake or a bird.

To You, Yiddish Poets

Yiddish poets, you closest brothers of mine,
brothers in the same loneliness, under the same yoke,
in the same lostness and catastrophe—
I write these lines to you, this song of songs,
my most intimate voice,
which will, despite everything,
ring out— today, tomorrow, and after that.
Listen to my words through your searching, suffering, and hustling,
in structured and measured octaves.

Structure myself I must, though I love free verse
and with it I've aired out our language and tongue.
But now I'm afraid of free strides and swings—
our reality wails with funereal wails.
Frightened hang the dreams of the faithful—
they dare not spin hopefully, spin youthfully.
If there are no limits to suffering,
painfully create a fence in strictly structured form.

Our song of the Seventh Heaven,
our song of dew and need nourished by every land—
can it not bear fruit anew from every earth?
Oh, we're far from the basics—
our song, yesterday still a blade of grass, a little flower,
has now reached an adulthood that is seldom granted.
If a hand is pushing us down to the lowest depths,
let's sing today the brightest, loudest songs.

Let them, like timidly fluttering doves,
soar above the mountains and valleys of time
to a time that is lazily indifferent, to a wanton time.
Let them knock on a doubter's windowpane
and tell about our wounded belief
and our need and struggle.
Perhaps a window will open somewhere
and the most alienated person will stretch out his arm.

Seward Park

The park is inhabited, full of old people,
bearded Jews and women in pious shawls.
They sit and read racy stories
of love, berries, licorice, and prayer shawls.

They move their lips while reading.
I look at their excitement with complete forgiveness.
Roguish May is bursting out all over,
and the trees above them are greening lovingly.

The cold blossoms warm up a bit—
the Yiddish words blow a more youthful breath.
Their life has passed like chaff and wind,
so let them be refreshed with burning shadows.

I look at the people. I too see many shadows
and all sorts of colors of chaff.
I see knights and warriors standing guard here,
though each has flown away, like a gull to the sky.

This park saw Yehoyesh's cravats
and Rozenfeld's anger and walking-stick daily.
A bench was once Lyesin's resting-place,
and Slonim recited his songs aloud on the steps.

Moyshe-Leyb laughed gratingly at the park
and Moyshe Nadir joked about it cuttingly.
Landoy looked at the very grass with his nose upturned,
and Menakhem's[29] squinty eyes sparkled.

The heads of hopeful youths fevered stormily here,
dreamed up youthful songs in Yiddish,
struggled with the city and the blows of its streets,
struggled against the world, and made no peace with one another.

A May proudly greened with youth then too,
and each of them sang alone and together.
Now old ladies and whispering old men sit here
and swallow tales of yesterday and paper sins.

Ecstasy

Twenty or thirty pigeons in the Broadway square
hop and peck at crumbs
that fall from human hands.

[29] Menakhem Boreysho

In the midst of hunting and pecking, a pigeon stops,
a 'he' by his size, his breadth,
his soft, hanging throat.
He gazes at a 'she.'
He looks.
With tiny little steps, with lightly treading feet,
with squinty, round, brown eyes,
forgetting the crumbs,
he starts to walk after her.

She still keeps pecking with her gray, hard little beak.

He follows her, follows her, follows her—
she turns away, turns away, turns away.
He tries to mount her—
she doesn't let him. She pecks at crumbs.
He persists, follows her, tries again.

She acts indifferent,
Walks away, walks away, he after her,
mounts her.

She seems to try to shake him off,
squints strongly, barely remains
on her thin little red feet
and—surrenders.

More and more submissive. Very, very patient. Remains—
frozen.
Pigeon ecstasy.
A moment of world-and-life creation.

Nokhem Borekh Minkov (1893-1958), another member of the *In Zikh* group, began as a poet but was more influential as an editor, literary critic, scholar, and lecturer. He wrote a definitive 3-volume book titled *Pioneers of Yiddish Poetry in America.*

~

Nokhem Borekh Minkov

Perets In America

With the rise of the group *Di Yunge*, Perets became a problem and a legend. *Di Yunge* were the modern romantics who revolted against the community themes and the troubling photographic realism of American Yiddish literature.

Zisho Landoy's 'bold' utterance against Perets, "the dead Warsaw literary figure," as he called him *(Literature and Life,* November 1915, page 94), should be understood as a result of the then-current 'battle fever' against the earlier Yiddish writers. There was also a desire to 'scandalize' the dignified older writers and to show off for his own 'unbold' comrades. That's one way to get famous—by being a contrarian.

But anyone who takes the trouble to compare Zisho Landoy's poems of that time, his poems in compressed form, with Perets' poems will be surprised by a certain similarity between them In the rhythm of their style, there is indeed a great difference: in Landoy, the rhythm is a slow and gentle one; in Perets, a hurried one. But in their romanticism there is a similarity. Furthermore, in many poems of both poets, one feels the tone of Heine. One can easily compare Landoy's:

> *sorrowful my soul is,*
> *and outside — night and rain.*
> *I will, my soul go out with you,*
> *into that night and rain.*

with Perets':
> *oppressed my heart with sorrow is —*
> *my heart it grieves in me*
> *although he dearly swore to me*
> *that he would marry me.*

or Landoy's

The streets still damp with rain,
and all is foggy, gray.
Gentle, soft winds blow on me,
and I feel calm today.

with Perets':

The moon is shining, stars gleam too—
my eyes are full of tears.
Ah tell me now, dear fate of mine —
can I still hope with all my fears?

So, too, one hears exactly the same tone in Landoy's *In the Darkness Your Eyes Are More Beautiful* as in Perets' *My Eyes Stare At Your Balcony; They See You Not ....*

Artists of new movements often do not perceive their predecessors. They also fail to perceive their own tradition. Leaders of new movements are too young, too inexperienced, too rash, too revolutionary. Years later, however, with the passage of time, one sees clearly the delicate work of the goldsmith of previous generations, the bonds between one generation and the next.

Di Yunge couldn't understand at that time that Perets had to be a major problem for them. We see it now. We know that Perets' works breathed romanticism, symbolism, suggestion, and mood. All of that found an echo in *Di Yunge*. They didn't want to admit it — they wanted to battle like orphans bereft of a literary tradition. In the end, however, they had to realize that Perets was more to them than an object of admiration.

For Moyshe-Leyb Halpern, Perets was:

...A smoldering log
that burns on the steppe at night, in the circle of a Gypsy
tribe;
a mast of a ship that struggles with the wind and sea;
a last tree of an enchanted wandering forest
in which lightning has severed
thousand-year–old giant oaks from their roots. . .

In the same Perets issue of *Literature And Life* (May 1915) in which the above lines are printed, one finds an artcle by Ruvn Ayzland entitled *What Was Perets for Us?* Ayzland tries to demonstrate that Perets was, for the young artist, "a beautiful legend, but still no more than a legend…we have learned nothing directly from him," writes Ayzland. In that, there is and is not some truth, just as the martyr-complex of *Di Yunge*: "We have no grandfather, we have no father, we didn't even have a teacher; we arrived like bastards, grew up as if from refuse" was not entirely right.

We know now that before *Di Yunge* arose, there appeared on the scene the group *Youth*, which evolved from the dominant social-realistic literature at the end of the nineteenth century. That group gradually began to oppose the tyranny of realism and social themes, and it did that in the name of artistic freedom, romanticism, and individual themes.

But Ayzland and almost everyone in the group *Di Yunge* really believed that "they arrived like bastards." In that regard, they were clearly mixing up two problems: their literary environment and their artistic identity. With respect to their literary environment, they were right — Warsaw had Perets, who befriended and included all the young talent, but here, on the rocky ground of the Jewish community in America at that time, as Ayzland wrote and as the writer of the present lines still remembers very well, "people laughed at *Di Yunge*, mocked us, pointed at us with their fingers, and even threw stones at us. And in those moments of uncertainty", writes Ayzland, "in those moments of painful doubt, we yearned for that brilliant legend, for the environment that surrounded the person of Y.L. Perets."

With respect to the environment, the environment of Perets, which was lacking here, all that Ayzland writes is indeed true. But with respect to values, with respect to artistic identity, *Di Yunge* were certainly under Perets' influence. Perhaps there is a bit of truth in Ayzland's words, that "we learned nothing directly from him." Yes, indeed not directly, but indirectly his influence was great. The principal element in Perets' artistry: "I don't portray persons but their reflection in me, and the reflection is rarely similar to the person", that subjective element, that romanticism more precisely, that impressionism, indirectly and unconsciously strongly influenced the artistry of *Di Yunge*. Even more, however—and here indeed directly— Perets influenced those members of *Di Yunge* and those *Inzikhists* (Introspectivists) who touched on life-problems, ideas, and events of the day in their writing. These influences of Perets began to manifest themselves in America with the appearance, or more accurately the maturation, of *Di Yunge*, and had their principal effect with the rise of secular Jewish schools and the art-theater in America, and when the Yiddish-culture movement arose. Through all the modern Yiddish artists, through the culture-consciousness and cultural activities that developed in America, there also shone the symbol — Perets. At first he was an object of admiration, with no influence whatsoever; later, he became a cult, a living source, a cultural force that nourished us and continues to do so to this day.

Yankev Glatshteyn (1896-1971), an early stalwart of the *In Zikh* movement who later moved onto his own unique path, is a strong claimant to the title of greatest of all Yiddish poets. He brought tremendous poetic skill, including masterly use of neologisms, and a complete self-identification with Judaism and the Jewish people. His poems about the Holocaust, three of which are presented here, have been described as a "secular liturgy of mourning for the Jewish people." He was also a fine novelist and a first-rate literary critic.

◇

Yankev Glatshteyn

My Brother Benjamin

Give me not-yet-wept-out words, God.
I haven't the strength to curse,
and I'll use them to mourn
your worlds turned to smoke.

Why did You need
to have my brother Benjamin wander about
all over the world?
Did You make him Your Chosen One
by always neglecting him and omitting him?

He was a tailor, a weaver,
and grubbed out a meager living.
For what? So You could deck out a poor weaver
in concentration-camp clothes
and lead him, without a shroud or a gravedigger,
to the crematorium?
With one hand You gave him joy—
You burdened his road with his one ·
dream of dreams,
his laughing bit of happiness, with the coal-black eyes;
and with the other hand, his heavy-fleshed wife
from a nearby village,
who sought him out and found him,
and busied herself sharing, bite by bite,
poverty.

Why did You need to play this foolish joke?
You loosed a lightning-bolt and created a piece of misfortune.
You were stingy with him about everything.
You kept slapping him, shaming him,
and not recognizing him.
But You preserved his being
because You needed him very badly,
in order to cremate him at the age of forty-four.

Dear Holy Name—
what was the meaning of my brother Benjamin?
For what purpose did You create him
and not give him even a crumb of happiness?
Why did You ravish his whole life?
Did You really want him and his wife to live
to experience the overflowing joy
of leading their only son
to the marriage-embrace of the ovens,
where You cremated all of them?

Good Night, World

Good night, wide world,
big stinking world;
not you but I lock the gate.
With my long black coat
and my fiery yellow patch,
with a proud step
and at my own command,
I go back to the ghetto.
Erase and stamp out all traces of assimilation—
I am wallowing in your garbage.
Praise, praise, praise
O crippled Jewish life;
anathema, world, upon your unclean cultures.

Though everything is devastated,
I cover myself with your dust,
O sad Jewish life.

Pig of a German, hateful Polack,
thieving Rumania, land of swilling and gorging;
flabby Democracy, with your cold-compresses of sympathy.
Good night, electricity-arrogant world—
back to my kerosene, my tallow-candle shadows,
eternal October, tiny stars;
to my crooked streets, humpbacked lanterns,
torn old scrolls and Biblical studies,
Talmud and its difficult passages;
to glorious Yiddish,
to the sacred law, to deep meaning, to duty, to justice.
World, I stride with joy to your quiet lights.

Good night. I contribute to you, O world,
all my would-be saviors.
Take the Jesus-Marxes—choke on their courage;
Devil take you for a drop of our baptized blood.
And though the Messiah tarries,
my anticipation rises day by day.
Green leaves will yet rustle
on our withered tree.
I need no comforting—
I'm going back to my four walls,
back from Wagner's pagan music
to the humming of khasidic melodies.
I kiss you, O disheveled Jewish life—
the joy of coming back weeps within me.

Without Jews

Without Jews there will be no Jewish God.
If, God forbid, we depart from the world,
the light of Your poor house will be extinguished.
Since Abraham recognized You in the cloud,
You've burned on all Jewish faces
and radiated from all Jewish eyes,
and we've formed You in our own image.
In every land, in every city,
a stranger sojourned with us —
the Jewish God.
Every smashed Jewish head
was a shamed, shattered Divine receptacle,
for we were Your radiant vessel,
the living proof of Your tangible miracle.

Now our dead
number in the millions.
The stars around You are going out.
The memory of You grows dim —
Your reign will soon end.
Everything sown and planted by the Jews
has been consumed by fire.
The dews weep on dead grasses.
The Jewish dream and reality have been ravished —
they are dying together.
Whole communities sleep now —
infants, women,
youths, and ancients.
Even Your pillars, Your rocks,
the thirty-six Righteous Ones,
sleep the eternal sleep of the dead.

Who will dream of You,
who will remember?

Who will deny You,
long for You?
Who will come to You across a bridge of yearning,
leave You in order to return?

The night is eternal for a dead people.
Heaven and Earth are erased.
The light in Your poor world is dying.
The flame of the last Jewish hour is guttering.
O Jewish God, soon You will be gone.

Naftoli Gros (1896-1956) was a poet and translator of German literature (Heine, Goethe, and others) into Yiddish. In New York, he edited the children's section of the newspaper *Der Tog*. He also wrote books about Eugene Victor Debs and about Jewish workers in America.

~

Naftoli Gros

The Cemetery On Chatham Square

On Chatham Square, hidden away
in the shadows of the Bowery and East Broadway,
there lies, squeezed between narrow houses,
hidden from human eyes, distant and alien,
the oldest Jewish cemetery in the New World.

The eroded headstones, row on row,
lie stretched out and listen, listen
to the noise of the Square
and the rushing of people and trains all day.
And high above them at night,
the movements of the stars.

They lie stretched out as if they heard,
deep below, the ancient past
when they could look down from the hill
to the valley and see the open bay,
the green water with the sailships,
and dream of that distant time
when the mountains there were open and free
for the wanderers and foreigners
who, just like those down below them,
came, pursued as they were, across the ocean
in order to begin a new life.

Yosl Klezmer

When Yosl Klezmer plays a party,
all dance like waves at sea.
They whoop it up and drink and sing:
hey tiddledy-dum, tiddledy-dee.

His partner plays the fife,
blind Berl strums the bass.
When Yosl plays his fiddle,
even doorsteps dance with grace.

He plays his fiddle with his group,
he helps the jester with his rhyme.
When Yosl Klezmer plays the fiddle,
the guests all dance in time.

But past one hundred twenty,
when it's time for Yosl to go,
he'll stand before the Throne of Glory
alone and humble, we know.

But when they see him, they'll say:
hey tiddledy-dum, tiddledy-dee—
there he is, Yosl Klezmer,
dancing like a wave upon the sea.

Volf Yunin (1908-1984) was a poet, folklorist and educator; much of his poetry was written for use by children in Yiddish *shuln*. He also wrote a Hebrew-Yiddish dictionary.

~

Volf Yunin

Hear How The Grasses Grow

Hear how the grasses grow,
see how the silence turns green.
To whom shall we leave
the tiny wind
that lies in the woods unseen.
Who will rock the wind to sleep
if not I and not you?
Play one of your great tunes for it,
give it a bit of rest,
and I'll rock it to sleep thus:
dear little wind—ay-liu-liu.
Hear how the ocean breathes,
see how the evening turns blue.
Let's be silent together
about the sorrow that seethes,
that flames with crimson flames
when the evening turns blue.
Who will rock the stars
in the new moon-cradle
if your melody grows still.
I'll hang a bridge for you
over the Seven Seas
so come back to me you will.

For The Choir-Master

For the choir-master, a melody by Volf.
So many generations passed
till we helped ourselves.
So many living limbs of the people lost
with no trace of their bones!
And now, at our rebirth,
in the twentieth year of renewal,
we drape our lamentations
in joy, and we sing of our liberation,
a song from our eternal treasuries;
we, the believers in justice,
who embrace generations of ancient values
in the eternal young lives destined for us.

Bend an ear, my people, and listen to the voice
of one of your young sons and celebrators:
Ezekiel has come to the valley of bones,
and with his finger has pointed and commanded: Live again!,
but to those who didn't die
and are living estranged lives now, in our generation,
he has said: take again each estranged year,
start reliving it, you, my estranged brothers!
And let younger prophets,
with their eternal, believing words,
which are linked with our people,
rejoin you solidly to our tribes
and blow a new breath into you!

Eliezer Grinberg (**1896-1977**) was a poet, essayist, and literary critic. He wrote monographs on Moyshe-Leyb Halpern, Yankev Glatshteyn, and H.Leyvik. Together with Irving Howe, he published some of the earliest anthologies of Yiddish poetry and prose in English translation.

~

Eliezer Grinberg

Old-Fashioned Words to the Astronauts

...Despite the esteem in which we hold science,
it is not through science that we will reach our goal.
Let us build a new bridge between science and
the human spirit.
     Chaim Weizmann

O first ones in the history of the world
to climb to the moon;
O daring shatterers of myths and legends,
emissaries to untrodden heavenly planets;
I, like the whole world, am astonished and admire
your Promethean daring!
But here comes to speak to you
not one of the famous heroes,
but a Jew full of fear and suspicion,
thanks to the thousand-year Jewish night
that has taught him
that the sun has never shone brightly
and securely in the Jewish sky,
and it has never been bright with stars—
without danger.

O Promethean astronauts,
first to climb to the moon,
I stand and admire your victory,

but I come to remind you of an ancient Jewish dream:
a wolf will lie down peacefully with a lamb
and swords will be turned into plowshares.
Our planet, Earth,
is still soaked with blood and tears!
What do you bring back?
A victory is not a victory
if it is not a bridge
to righteousness, justice, and peace.

Pardon me, Promethean astronauts,
that unbidden
there has come to the celebration
a Jew who is still laden
with fear and suspicion—
a legacy of the thousand-year Jewish night—
with trembling, old-fashioned words
about the eternal Jewish dream!

A Guest On Second Avenue

Seldom do I come to be your guest these days,
and if not for an old, dilapidated house
that still remains untouched
(like an old souvenir),
I would never recognize the neighborhood here—
that's how much you've changed, Second Avenue.
But the still-remaining traces of the past remind me
what a great treasure we possessed here.

To all your streets, my closest neighbor,
I said good-bye long ago,
and I avoid you whenever I can.
It's painful for me to encounter you now,

for when I tread on your ground
it's just as if I were
treading on graves of my nearest and dearest.

But do we need to recall all our great losses
so our hearts will wail with mourning?
He who has forgotten all that
never remembered it;
he never shared our joy
and is now no partner in our sorrow.
But however great the catastrophe of our sacred sacrifices,
they have no dominion over our imagination and memory —
true wealth never goes lost.
There is a unique holiday
that shines with eternal fire during the week.
That which only the mind understands in space and time
is not always proof;
there is a secret force that cannot be yoked
by the sobriety of common sense —
it is animated by a higher, deeper meaning.

That force has more than once
relieved the anguish of cold numbers;
it has more than once
breathed into the dry bones
a warm, living breath,
raised them high from the valley of death,
and revived them with wings of faith and hope.

Rashel Veprinski (1895-1981) was another of the great women poets in Yiddish. She shared with the others (Rokhl Korn, Kadye Molodovsky, Tsilye Drapkin, Ana Margolin, and others) a distinctive lyricism; emotionality; and identification with female, often intensely sexual, themes that clearly identified her writing as that of a woman.

~

Rashel Veprinski

Snowflakes

First snowflakes fall upon my panes
as if that were their destined place.
I want to seek and find the words,
to hide them in my song.

What will become of hard-sought words,
with difficulty found at last?
Will they later melt just like
the snowflakes on my window-panes?

Perhaps emplaced within my song
a few bright words I've found will live,
not melt like snowflakes on my panes.
Perhaps my song's their destined place.

My God

I clamber up the mountains of Tsvad—
somewhere there, I think, lives God.
I call Him with my Yiddish words,
and He answers me in Yiddish—and why not?
With His Jews there in the ghetto,
He sanctified the Yiddish word—
in bunkers He sang the Yiddish lore.
Its life then hung upon a hair,

but He brought the remnants out of the camps.
There will be a people, so there must be a God.

I clamber up the mountains of Tsvad—
somewhere there, I think, lives God.
I call Him with my Yiddish words,
and He answers me—in Yiddish.
And why not?

Efrayim Oyerbakh (1892-1973) was a poet, essayist, and literary critic who was associated with *Di Yunge*. He spent a number of years living in and fighting for the Jewish settlement in Palestine. In the United States, he was a president of the Yiddish PEN Club.

~

Efrayim Oyerbakh

To Creative Maturity

Yiddish literature in America grew from the immigrant depths. Its pioneers, in the 1880s, had not previously been writers. They did not bring with them the finished pen of a writer such as Menakhem-Mendl Dolitski, to whom Yehude-Leyb Gordon turned over his pen, crowning him as his successor in Hebrew poetry. Our pioneer writers brought with them no artistic legacy beyond the rich folk-treasure that generations of Jewish life had amassed in them. Immigrants they were, into the immigrant maelstrom they fell, and the immigrant fate they shared, with the sweatshop, peddling, cramped living quarters, boarders, and landladies, with immigrant shame, human debasement, and stubborn Jewish striving for human elevation. When the creative springs started erupting from the hidden places in them, the first theme of their writing was — human elevation. If we take as an example the social themes of world literature and compare them with the themes of our pioneer writers, we will see how different they were in their very essence. The social themes in world literature were in great part a protest against economic oppression and an invocation of the pathos of life; the social theme in our pioneer writers did indeed contain protest against economic oppression, but there was in addition the wounded outcry of the downtrodden person and the striving for human elevation. When Moris Rozenfeld, in his social poems, wept about his bitter fate, there was in his weeping the eternal Jewish outcry of the holy people that must not be debased. Not towards economic liberation alone did the pioneer poet strive, but also toward the elevation of humanity, which is so holy in our basic ethics. Unbeknownst to him, the social outcry of the Prophets tore out of him; his fervor was for the downtrodden person, not for the exploited class. Edelshtat and Bovshover, who were less deeply rooted in Judaism than Rozenfeld, also 'sinned' with prophetic fervor, even when they cut their poems to fit the strict patterns of the party program. The storytellers of that time — realistic, almost naturalistic—brought out the shame of the Jewish person even more sharply. Their central theme was how disgraceful it was that Jewish bosses debased Jewish workers. That disgrace was experienced by the Jewish workers in the sweatshops. The Jewish folk-masses came mostly from small towns, where even the poorest artisan considered himself part of the entire community, and sometimes, in a small synagogue, he could even bang on the table and stop the reading of the Torah. Socially, there was a wide gap between the poor and the rich in the small towns, but in the area of Judaism they often approached one another. We should also remember that in the 1880s Jewish wealth in the small towns grew not from Jewish poverty but from that of the village peasants, and the artisan, the porter, the wagon-driver, the poor shopkeeper did not have so direct an economic confrontation with the rich man that he felt that the rich man was sucking his blood, debasing him, taking from him his worth as a Jew. Only in America did the Jewish immigrant see a Jew, a brother of his who had himself been an immigrant like himself just a few years before, make him his slave. And who was the enslaver? Very often the immigrant had known him from the small town, where he was not one of the upper-class Jews, not one of the big shots—rather, a tailor himself, or a cobbler, or a wagon-driver. Often the wronged, oppressed immigrant had been a man of substance in the old country and somewhat knowledgeable in matters of the Torah, and here the ignoramus oppressed him and sucked out his sweat in order to get rich. This theme was the central one in the storytelling literature of that era. The social struggle was, in its essence, a family quarrel, though externally it had all the signs of social struggle in general. And again, we can read in the pioneer storytellers about the protest against human oppression and the yearning for human elevation. The pioneer storyteller, like the pioneer poet, definitely incubated in himself Jewish ethics, which he often didn't recognize and thought he was writing the way he did because he was a socialist.

The literature of that era was a goal-directed literature. It had to turn the Jewish immigrant into a person ready for class conflict, and paint for him the bright picture of the future socialist society. It also contained a considerable amount of mockery of the Jewish faith, for its naive belief was that the religious Jew was incapable of class warfare. Formally, the pioneer literature did not concern itself with artistic values — the goal was the main thing for it. The writer took up his pen without the slightest artistic preparation — the driving force in him was the social mission. So the literature of that time was full of miniatures: short stories, short poems. Long novellas or novels, which were published only in the daily press, were in a trashy style, far from realism, full of weird episodes, fantastically exciting, unbelievably Nirvana-like.

But in the fermentation of that era, the yeast settled and there remained pure wine, which we still drink today with great pleasure. It was practical-goal-directed literature, but in many of the writers their artistic blood pierces through the goals. Though we know that era only from contemporary articles and later reminiscences, we can still identify with that life when we read its poems and its stories. The pioneer writers, who did not set any artistic goals for themselves, intuitively, perhaps involuntarily, attained artistic expression.

* * *

The Yiddish literature of the pioneer era was American long before American literature was — American in the sense of realism, the ambience, the shop, and Jewish practical-goal-orientation. To be sure, in the America of the pioneer Yiddidsh writers there was not the spaciousness of the land, the prairie, and big industry, but the narrow Jewish immigrant world was indeed fully present in it. Its ideas were cosmopolitan, but in its artistic essence it carried out a quite different mission: the unification of the Jewish people. Both in poetry and prose, the literature of that time bound together the Jews of Eastern Europe and the Jews of America; the Jew in it was still emotionally and psychically deeply rooted in the *shtetl ;* he created a new *shtetl*-like reality that did not sever its connection with the reality of the old *shtetl*.

The tendentious literature that set no artistic goals for itself plowed the field for its followers, who believed that literature was a goal in itself. While the early immigrant writers had no literary consciousness, only a drive toward self-expression, their followers were already saturated with the consciousness of a Jewish writer's 'mission' to build a great structure of literature. They emphasized artistic words but had contempt for ideas.

Ideas, they felt, muddied the pure wellspring. Words alone were the artistic goal— words themselves were full of ideas. So though they shook themselves loose from their predecessors, the pioneer writers of the 1880s, and reduced them to nothing—literature writers, not artists—there was no doubt that they learned a lot from them. They, the successors of the pioneers, did indeed turn to world literature, especially Russian and German literature, looking for poetic and fictional forms, but they wouldn't have been able to arrive at more refined expression if the pioneers hadn't previously artistically plowed the field.

In their artistic goals they went to extremes, just as the pioneers did in their goals regarding ideas. In poetry they sought not only the depictive ability of words but also the shadows of the words. They wanted to transmit words in a form in which rhythm and words were conjoined; they wanted to elevate the individual poet, with his artistic caprices, with the lack of clarity in him, with the tendentiousness of both his sorrow and his joy. In their artistic laboratory they re-created the Yiddish word, squeezed out its finest nuances, drew fresh purity from the folk-wellspring, revealed such richness and flexibility in the language that it was practically blinding. While Perets could still lament "My poem would sound different if I could sing in a Gentile language for the Gentiles," the poets in New York, in the first decade of the twentieth century , did not lament but triumphed over the Yiddish word. The Yiddish word was, in their hands, like clay in the hands of the potter.

In prose, the course of events was the same, though in a slightly different way. The storytellers of the pioneer period approached a person with a sort of generalized measurement —their person had his own characteristics, but their goal was to depict the whole community through him, so that hundreds like him could learn from him. The story, therefore, was in its essence not about an individual person who was different from all others even though he socialized with them in the same community. The storytellers who appeared after the pioneers were already trying to plumb the depths of the special characteristics of a person, get to his psychic mechanisms, and lead him out of the generalized abyss and into individuality. With their refined word-tools, the most important thing for them was to transmit the nuances of human experience, often psychological confusion and very often unexpected turns that the previous writers, the writers of the pioneer era, would not have permitted themselves even if they had occurred to them. Prose writers also attempted longer novellas, but didn't get very far, simply because they emphasized expression and words, not ideas. Experimentally and artistically, however, they accomplished a great deal—they plowed the field for the long novels that came later.

* * *

From these two contradictory tendencies, there arose a synthesis of full creative maturity. The same generation of writers who at first revolted against ideas and gave precedence to artistry later achieved harmony between both goals. In world literature, the struggle for harmony between ideas and artistry lasted for decades; Yiddish literature in America went through the same process with virtually a single supernatural leap.

Yiddish literature at the beginning of the 1920s faced two historical events: Soviet communism and Jewish redemption. The Bolshevik revolution, which did not remain localized to Russia but penetrated demandingly into every country in the world, couldn't help but capture the fantasy of creative Jewish persons with its psychic course. Communism figuratively seized the Yiddish writer by the lapels and demanded an answer from him: do you accept me or reject me? The Yiddish writers had either come directly from the country where communism had arisen with such world-dominating fervor or from countries on its periphery. In addition, Russian Jewry was then healthy and fresh, and a new stream of Jewish creativity was flooding out of there. For the first time, the song of building, of love of country, of connection to the fate of a land, wafted from Yiddish storytelling. It was new, it was fresh—it brought cheer in a purely writerly manner.

I must confess that I and others like me, who were ideologically anticommunist from the beginning, were also artistically influenced by the new pulse and driving rhythm in the Soviet-Yiddish literature of the early years. We were ideological opponents of Sovietism, but as writers we envied the writers in Moscow, Minsk, Kiev, and Kharkov their love of a land, their artistic joy, and their full relationship as family members at the great historical wedding.

The theme of Jewish redemption was the echo of the "country under construction" that resounded after the Balfour Declaration. I say echo, and I think it is necessary to make clear why the redemption theme with respect to Israel reached Yiddish literature as an echo. Emotionally and psychically, Yiddish writers had never ruptured their bond with Israel, but the political idea of Israel—Zionism, and even the pioneers—did not excite them artistically. There were many reasons for that, most importantly the writers' identification with the idea that the Jewish future lay in the lands where Jews resided. In that respect, they met on common ground with religious Jews, to whom Messianism was never a political idea but a faith and an experience. The "country under construction," however, had a creative influence on Yiddish literature from the beginning of the 1920s, via a detour that was itself hidden from it: hidden Jewish historical documents flooded the literature with refreshing purity.

Under the influence of the "country under construction," Yiddish writers turned—not with their faces, but with deeply artistic consciousness— to Jewish historical channels, to folk-wellsprings, to the spiritual essence of Judaism. The echo demanded no less from them than did the direct sound of communism. So though they didn't respond ideologically or politically, they found exaltation in it. It was absolutely the historical call of the "country under construction" that brought the Yiddish writers to great national immersion, nationalistic fervor, Jewish artistic unrest, and Judaism in its broad national sense. That was the source of the great novellas— new forms, rhythms, even pictures and song-like qualities. More deeply, however—through experience, immersion, and the return to essential Jewish ideas—Israel had a decisive influence on our literature. Even the writers who responded more sensitively to Sovietism than to Israel drew their national artistic fervor from the historical Jewish road toward an independent country in Israel.

All three phases of Yiddish literature in America were squeezed into about eight decades, a small span of time for a literature to go from its beginning to its high-point, especially since the beginning was in a chaotic immigrant environment in the process of transplantation from one part of the world to another. If we look back on those years, the abundance of Yiddish creativity is a miracle and a riddle to us. In loneliness, in isolation from the broad Jewish currents, amid constant announcements of destruction, Yiddish literature put forth the heroic resistance of creativity. Where did it get the inconceivable strength? Yiddish literature drew its strength from the eternal Jewish source that has stood by us throughout our entire exile: the idea of one Jewish people throughout the world. The Yiddish writers in America always had the experience of having a point of attachment outside the borders of the land, of building a creative structure for the whole people in all the countries of the Diaspora. The Yiddish writers were also conscious that they were part of the Jewish creativity over a span of thousands of years. They were not isolated, they were linked to generations of Jewish writers. They were contributing their own spiritual treasures to the great spiritual treasury of our people.

(From the essay *Yiddish Literature in America*)

Avrom Tabatshnik (1901-1969), in addition to being a poet, was one of the finest and most incisive critics of Yiddish literature. He was famous for a series of recorded interviews with Yiddish-American poets. He was also a teacher in Yiddish secular schools.

~

Avrom Tabatshnik

Tradition and Revolt in Yiddish Poetry

The title of my lecture, as you already know, is *Tradition And Revolt In Yiddish Poetry*. The truth is that the lecture could have been called something else, because only the last two words of the name are important, namely "Yiddish Poetry." All names, all theses, all approaches and viewpoints are, in the end, no more than an excuse to be able to speak again and again about Yiddish poetry, perhaps the only bit of consolation that still remains to us. Yiddish poetry, its course, its development, and its achievements are our prideful heritage and our miracle, and definitely the words "the more one speaks about it, the better" apply here. Nowadays, the number of those who speak about it a lot is limited, and this lecture will therefore be more an outline of something than a detailed picture. Nevertheless, the name is not just a 'vehicle' — both tradition and revolt are current issues in literature and are pertinent to its course, to its dynamic, and to its development.

The truth is that we no longer hear about revolt in our literature today. Unfortunately, our time for literary revolt and striving for new forms has passed. We are acquiring new forces, but we hear nothing about new movements in the formal sense. In general, our period of new movements didn't last very long. Poets who began in our literature as representatives of modern schools have long since outgrown those schools. *Di Yunge*, for example, were, in the beginning, a group of poets with a certain group image. Some 35-40 years ago, one could more readily speak about the character of the group as a whole than about the achievements of its individual representatives. Later it became the reverse; not only did H. Leyvik (who came to the group somewhat later) and Moyshe-Leyb Halpern very rapidly outgrow the group, but also Y.Y. Shvarts and Yoysef Rolnik. And even

284

Mani Leyb and Ruvn Ayzland, who are to this day the official standard-bearers of *Di Yunge*, have taken a giant leap forward.

The same is also true of the *Inzikhistn* (Introspectivists.) What sense does it make today, for example, to speak about Yankev Glatshteyn as an *Inzikhist*? Not only has Glatshteyn's poetry outgrown the theories and credos of *Inzikhizm*, but also his current approach to poetry is different. In Glatshteyn's critical articles, one can find dozens of definitions of the art of poetry and dozens of statements about the music of words, the plasticity of poetic images, that are the opposite of the theories and also the practices of the one-time *Inzikhists*.

On the other hand, it has happened with us that older poets fascinated by the new movements became younger, so to speak: for example, Yehoyesh and H. Royzenblat, may he live for many years, and even Avrom Lyesin, a poet who never chased after fashions and wrote his artistic poems long after we had finished revolting and storming. Both Lyesin and Yehoyesh, in their later years, became not only more mature and more artistic, but also more modern. Lyesin even has a poem called *Imaginary Things*. And Avrom Reyzn, the dean of our poetry, who is in many respects the father of modern Yiddish lyrical poetry—did he not learn about the art of words from those who began as his students or even his imitators? We cannot speak, therefore, about revolt and tradition among us in the same sense as we speak about them among other people and languages. In general, we cannot measure our poetry by the measure of other literature, nor classify it according to the classifications of those literatures. Our poetry has developed with the speed of supernatural transport. In some 50-60 years, we have had to experience as much as other literatures have in two or three times that time.

We shouldn't forget that it's not so long ago that we began to create the language of Yiddish poetry, and the process is still far from finished. Movements that appeared with us at the same time as, or under the influence of, movements in other literatures have an entirely different significance for us, for the reason mentioned. For example, what was decadence for the Gentiles was renaissance for us, and what was a decline for the Gentiles was an advance for us.

Even in the case of poetry with an openly social character, it's different with us. When a Nekrasov came to Russian poetry with his citizen-motif, with his 'journalistic' language, a Tolstoy could scream bloody murder that he was destroying the tradition of Pushkin. Even if that was not true with respect to Nekrasov, in general, poetry, which is often didactic and tendentious, did represent a lowering of artistic standards for the other peoples of the world. But can one say that about our social poetry? Not only can one not say that about the poems of Rozenfeld, Lyesin, Frug, and Perets, but even not about the poems of Vintshevski, Bovshover, and Edelshtat. From whom, truthfully, did they represent a decline? Did people write better before them? They were, after all, the poets who "chewed up and tore up 'Jargon' " and made a literary language out of it. And just as with the phenomenon mentioned, things are different with us in the matter of tradition. Can one say, for example, that the fathers and grandfathers of our poetry have exactly the same significance for our current poets as the fathers and grandfathers of the Gentile poets have for them?

Do we have anything similar to a Shakespearean tradition or a Pushkin tradition? When Itsik Manger says, for example, that he derives his tradition from Velvl Zbarzher or Avrom Goldfaden, is that the same as when T.S. Eliot says that he derives his tradition from the English metaphysical poets? In the case of Manger, it's more in jest than in earnest. In him, it's more a question of stylized antiquarianism than a certain tradition. And it could not have been otherwise: some fine appearance our poetry would have if it had stuck to the forms and styles of its fathers and grandfather!

But if the younger poets didn't have anything to hold on to, they did have something to turn away from; if they didn't have anything to attach to they did have something to tear away from. At the time *Di Yunge* began their revolt, the older Yiddish poetry already represented a significant entity—there was someone to struggle against, someone to gird their loins against. Whatever opinion we may have today about our older poetry, we should remember that for both the poets and the critics and readers of that time, it was true, or rather authentic, poetry. Concerning Yehoyesh' first book, *Collected Poems*, I. Leontieff published in *Di Tsukunft* a review with the title *The Songs of Yehoyesh the Poet*. True, he pointed out certain faults, but he didn't doubt for a moment that Yehoyesh's poems were 'songs' in the highest poetic sense of the word. Yehoyesh's *Unsung Song*, which Glatshteyn has recently ripped to pieces, was considered a masterpiece of form and diction at that time. As late as 1915, Moyshe Olgin was delighted with *The Unsung Song*.

We should therefore remember that historically speaking *Di Yunge* were contesting against not just anyone but against poets whose works were then considered the highest and last word in poetic art. No one could have imagined that after the poems of Rozenfeld and Yehoyesh there could be anything better or more beautiful. *Di Yunge* therefore had to fight hard, put up with the greatest mockery and even persecution. They were considered not only 'decadents' but simply barbarians and corrupters of the Yiddish word. *Di Yunge*, however, triumphed in the end, and their triumphs and accomplishments were of an epoch-making character—they forever changed the character of Yiddish poetry. After them, no one could write as they had before them. The linguistic boldness and poetic novelties that a Moyshe Nadir, a Moyshe-Leyb Halpern, a Mani Leyb, and a Zisho Landoy brought to Yiddish poetry, in comparison with the poetry of the previous poets, were not only more fruitful but also more modern and more radical improvements than the novelties and boldness of the later *Inzikhists* were with respect to the poetry of *Di Yunge*.

The revolt of *Di Yunge*, though it set out purely artistic goals and so keenly avoided social questions, was nevertheless, in essence, an expression of deep social changes in Jewish life. New forces had to arise in Jewish life, new spiritual resources had to develop and old ones had to revive, profound changes in the relationship between the individual and the community had to develop, a new sensitivity had to mature, new cultural needs had to develop, and a new viewpoint about the meaning and goals of life had to develop so that such a thing as the revolt of *Di Yunge* could occur. It often happens that precisely the more radical revolutions in art are reactionary in their social significance, and that precisely the return to very old traditions is progressive and democratic, popular in character.

What certain 'Marxist' critics among us decried as "reaction and darkness" was actually a deepening of our thousand-year-old spiritual tradition, a maturation of artistic-feeling, a refinement of taste, and a liberation and exaltation of the individual. It represented becoming inspired by popular religious movements, which were themselves an expression of the highest inspiration, an enrichment of fantasy through those elements of folk-creativity that were themselves the product of great fantasy. Literary or any other movements and tendencies that enrich the life of humanity are not reactionary. But just as our modern literary tendencies did not bring "reaction and darkness," so did they also not bring Dadaism or Nihilism.

On the contrary, it can be demonstrated in our literary history that the more modern Yiddish poetry became, the more it oriented itself toward such subtle and refined poetic tendencies as symbolism, impressionism, and neo-romanticism; that the more refined and subtle it itself became, the closer it came to those little chambers of the Jewish soul in which is located the '*or-hagnuz,*' the hidden light, as Dovid Ignatov, one of the principal leaders of *Di Yunge*, titled one of his works. Conversely, the more didactic, old-fashioned and conventional, the less refined our poetry became, the less Jewish it was in its artistic specifics and its rhythms and images, the less it expressed not only the Sabbaths of our lives but even the everyday reality, which later poets, such as Y.Y. Sigal, exalted to a poetical Sabbath-holiness, to the beauty and holiness of an ancient religious legend.

So you will ask: was Lyesin distant from the deeper Jewish sources? Lyesin, the great national poet, the fiery patriot, Lyesin who "went to the scaffold with all the martyrs," was he distant from the deeper Jewish sources? Yehoyesh, the brilliant student, the translator of the Bible, the poetic author of dozens if not hundreds of poems on Biblical and Talmudic themes— was he distant from Jewish sources? And can one even say that about Moris Rozenfeld, who wrote so many fiery national hymns? So the first thing to remember is that Yehoyesh and Lyesin also later became part of modern Yiddish poetry. Second, Lyesin's somewhat old-fashioned poetry, his rational-declarative method, his resoundingly hammered-out verse, often came into conflict with the quieter mystical and metaphysical elements in his spirit. Third, we are not talking here about themes, about national orientations, or even about national hymns and odes to the Jewish people, but about something that is more delicate and deeper, something that expresses itself not with a declarative "I believe," but which can be felt in the form—no, more than that, is itself form.

Take, for example, Yehoyesh's poems on Biblical and Talmudic themes. In what way are they different from the poems on the same themes by the now half-forgotten Russian poet Lev May? What Yehoyesh and even

Lyesin brought to the table was a sometime less and sometime more successful paraphrase of a Biblical episode or a Talmudic legend. How far
they were, however, from the fantasy, poetry and style of such a legend!
Compare, if you will, a poem on a Biblical or Talmudic theme by a modern Yiddish poet with the poems on the same themes by our older poets;
compare Leyvik's poems about Rabbi Akiva with Lyesin's declamatory
poem about Rabbi Akiba; Leyvik's poems about Cain and Abel, or about
Joseph and his brothers, or about Saul, with Glatshteyn's poems about
Saul, David, Abishag, and Ezekiel; or Manger's Biblical poems with the
Biblical poems of Yehoyesh and you will see who is closer to the spirit and
the fantasy of Midrashic commentary. Not for nothing does Manger title
one of his books of poems *Itsik's Midrash.*

The more modern and even modernistic Yiddish poetry became, the
freer in its rhythm, the subtler in its music, the more artistic and refined in
its images, the more Jewish it became; I would even say more *khasidic*, in
Reb Nakhmen Bratslaver's sense of the word. Even the first revolt in Yiddish poetry, the revolt of *Di Yunge*, was an expression of a return to the old,
"barely surviving sources," as Perets calls them, a return to the religious
fantasy of the Jewish person, to his exalted sorrow and joy, to his yearning
for the Messiah and the myth of redemption. One can see that not only in
Leyvik but also in Moyshe-Leyb Halpern, the rebel, the blasphemer. One
can see it in his images; in the free course of his apocalyptic visions and his
caricatures, which contain so much Jewish Purim-theatricality; in his mas-
culine rhythms, which contain so much of the traditional Talmudic
melodies.

And not only in Leyvik and Moyshe-Leyb, but also in Mani Leyb, about
whom people like to say that he, the master of Yiddish idiom, is not a Jew
at all but a disguised Russian, God help us! Certainly no one can deny or
minimize the influence of Russian poetry on Mani Leyb. Nevertheless, no
one among us has brought out in such a unique and beautifully artistic way
the poetry of Jewish faith as has Mani Leyb. If Leyvik (in poetry, of course)
follows the tradition of those mystics among us who were not content to
wait for the Messiah but wanted to bring him by force, then Mani Leyb is
our poet of the quiet faith of our people, the poet of the belief that is expressed in folk-tales that God does not forsake us, that the miracle is not far
way, that it will happen at the last moment.

In Mani Leyb, Elijah looks just as the people have imagined him and brought him to life. It's not the Elijah who flies to heaven in a fiery chariot, but the Elijah who wanders about the earth disguised, often as a peasant. And take a second figure in Mani Leyb, the figure of the poet, "the incomparable whistler," as Mani Leyb calls him — who and what is he if not a crusader, a soother, a rocker-to-sleep? He is after all, almost somewhat of a disguised Elijah. Do you see the similarity between the two:

His eyes full of love and sorrow,
on his lips the dearest smile,
in a fur from a peasant borrowed,
through poor homes Elijah goes 'round the while.

And the poet goes around among the same houses and "whistles like a magical flute all the songs about poverty," and as he whistles this, "Jews stand and listen, hear, and silently swallow their tears, for their hearts are overjoyed because they know about poverty." Rozenfeld sang: "On a silent willow hangs the dream of my people." The modern Yiddish poets have taken the dream down from the silent willow and given it tongue, expression

What is true about *Di Yunge* (and when I say *Di Yunge* I mean also the young poets in Europe, whose chief representative was Dovid Eynhorn) is also true about the *Inzikhists* in America and the so-called Expressionists in Europe. The *Inzikhists,* despite their ultramodernism, or rather because of it, were mostly oriented toward Jewish tradition. They didn't do it in such a sublimated way as *Di Yunge*, they did it in a more direct, open, consciously ideological way.

Our most important exponent of Yiddish expressionism in the 20s was Moyshe Kulbak. Expressionism in Kulbak went hand in hand with a deepening of Jewish myhology. Kulbak, about whom Dovid Eynhorn has recently said correctly that he was the one who finally succeeded in finding the Jewish landscape, the specifically Jewish image, saw even the Russian revolution as a "bloody giant with golden tablets". And as for Arn Tseytlin, one of our modernistic poets, not only his themes and his religious mystical concepts are Jewish, but the sharply hairsplitting zig-zags of his poems, the austerity of his verse, the hinting, the flushed interpretations, and the wonderfully clever comparisons, are all Jewish. I also believe that Uri-Tsvi Grinberg, an important representative of Jewish modernism in the 20s, is no exception to the rule: the more modern our poetry was in form, the more Jewish it was in spirit.

Melekh Ravitsh, however, is somewhat of an exception. He puts more emphasis on the ethically universal than on specifically Jewish themes. He himself recently said about himself that he is a "realist and nationalist". In essence, however, he is some kind of mixture of an ancient Essene and a modern Dukhobor. If we had an ascetic tradition, we could assign Ravitsh to it.

Perets Markish, though he was in Poland in the early 20s, belongs more to the Kiev group, according to his origins. In his early poems, he was under the influence of Russian futurism and imagism. That, however, didn't stop him from being Jewish, not only in his themes but also in his style. Even in his earliest poems, disheveled and over-enthusiastic as they are, one feels the generational rootedness. Not only in his *Heap*, but also in his other poems of that period, the striving toward a Jewish style of imagery is apparent. It is appropriate in general to remark that Jewish poets who were under the influence of Yesenin built their often ingenious and imaginary images out of elements related to Jewish liturgy and ritual. One can see that even in the Hebraist Shlonski. If Yesenin, in his images, smoldered with incense, sparkled with the gold of priestly banners and vestments, and rang like the brass in churchbells, our imagists blew the *shofar,* wrapped their images in leather *tfiln* strips, and decorated them with Torah crowns, ark curtains, prayer shawls, and silk shirts. Even more than in Markish, purer and more circumscribed, one feels the striving towards a Jewish style in the older poets Dovid Hofshteyn and Osher Shvartsman, and more quietly and directly in Kvitko, Fininberg, Reznik, and Shtaynman. Fininberg's first book, titled *Blue*, I believe, is saturated with Jewish symbolism and mysticism.

None other than the later, and for a time official, Soviet critic, Professor Y. Nusinov, in a lecture about the Kiev group that he gave in the earliest years after the Russian revolution, said:

"It must be emphasized that though literary works among the Kiev group were evaluated according to the standards of literature the world over, Yiddish literature has still rarely achieved such a national historical stature as precisely in the works of the group itself, especially the works of Bergelson, Der Nister, Shteynman, Hofsthteyn, and Osher Shvartsman. The last three have linked our national past with the revolutionary tomorrow in a particularly remarkable way."

Bergelson, in his literary articles of that period, emphasized 'Jewish elements,' and in that regard designated Der Nister as a model for the younger Yiddish poets of that era. As soon as the poets of the Kiev, Minsk, Kharkov, and other groups blended into the single stream of Soviet Yiddish poetry, and, in the words of Kvitko's poem, "quarreled with the grandfathers and fathers," things changed. It is not appropriate to make light of Soviet Yiddish poetry. Just the fact that among the Yiddish poets in the Soviet Union were a number of the most talented poets we have had mandates a serious and extremely serious approach.

Soviet Yiddish poetry scored many accomplishments, not only in the earlier, freer years, but even in the later years. One has to be able to read Soviet poetry—it is often a poetry of forced converts. Between one paean to Stalin and another, one often finds, in a good Soviet poet, precious lyrical and artistic passages. And even from the standpoint of Jewishness, not everything is so simple. If the scholarly, the religious and even the national Jewish tradition was lacking, one felt, however, a social tradition of the Jewish masses. "Common folk from Niezhin who study Torah with Vilna Litvaks," to use an expression of Mani Leyb's, are Jews too. In the works of an Izzy Kharik, especially his early works such as *The Swamps of Minsk*, one feels the explosion of the collective energy of the Jewish masses, its bitterness and protest, which was expressed earlier in an organically flaming way in some of the poems of Moris Rozenfeld, and in a truly artistic way in some of the stories of Itshe-Meyer Vaysenberg, There is something of Sholem Aleichem in Itsik Fefer's early poems. Fefer, from his village of Shpole, jumped into the turbulence of the Russian revolution, just as Motl, in *Motl Peysi dem Khazns,* jumps from his father's sick room into the Spring outdoors. Fefer rejoiced in the revolution, rejoiced in its Red Army regiments, its blond Komsomol members who went to the front, just as another youth in Sholem Aleichem rejoiced in emigration on the eve of Pesakh.

However, as much as we may want to praise Soviet Yiddish poetry, which has now become a "Jewish treasure without heirs" in its own land, one cannot deny that after it "quarreled with the fathers and grandfathers" it lost more and more of the fruitful soil in which modern Yiddish poetry had grown. It is, in the end, a poetry of front-line soldiers and front-lines without a spiritual hinterland. In the final analysis, a large part of Soviet Yiddish poetry lacks durability and generational span. Who knows how many of the thousands and thousands of poems that Soviet poets have written we will be able to rescue for the general treasure of Yiddish poetry. True, at the time of the war, when Russian poetry began to celebrate Russian heroes, Soviet Yiddish poetry began to sing about Judah the Maccabee and Bar-Kokhba. It is also true that at the time when one could openly boast about one's Jewish pedigree and openly weep about the Holocaust, the poems of Markish, Hofshteyn, Fefer, and to a certain extent Halkin, acquired more substance, warmth, and integrity. But one shouldn't exaggerate in this respect—the Yiddish poet in Russia was already too frightened, too bureaucratized, too long in harness, for us to feel a free, creative breath in his work, even with regard to things that moved him deeply.

And what is true with respect to Soviet poetry is even more true about the so-called proletarian poetry in America, which was never distinguished by much talent. It is sufficient today to leaf through the few dozen books of the proletarian poets to see how all of it, with few exceptions, is already outmoded today, how it is all gray, boring, and poor.

Unfortunately, I cannot dwell on the generation of poets that came after the period of revolt and renewal in Yiddish poetry. In that generation, one finds poets with real talent, poets who already have to their credit significant work, not only the poets in America but also the poets who appeared in the 20s in Poland, Galicia, Romania, and other parts of our Diaspora. Their number, however, is too large for me to be able even to just mention their names, to say nothing of characterizing them.

By the way, today's conference should have presented several lectures exclusively dedicated to the generation that is still far from having been evaluated by our criticism. Generally speaking, it is a generation that did not publish any new artistic manifestos, did not create any schools, and did not make any revolutions in Yiddish poetry. After all, not every generation is destined to make artistic revolutions, and that is not necessary to the course of a literature. It is enough that poets appear who can utilize and reinforce the new things that were introduced by their predecessors. And this generation of poets has done that. It has continued what the previous one began, with significant alterations, of course. What we must especially keep in mind when we speak of this generation, however, is the fact that it was faced not only with an older poetry but definitely with an artistic tradition. And that brings us to the second point, or thesis, of my lecture: that the true creators of an artistic tradition in our poetry were not the classical writers, as with other peoples, but precisely the modernists—not the fathers, but the sons and grandsons.

This tradition is still a young one, and enough room and possibilities remain for innovations and further fulfillment. At the same time, however, there are signs that this tradition is in the process of being not only crystallized but also fixed and frozen. And that is a danger. Tradition can in time become convention and cliché, and instead of stimulating new forces it can breed epigones. Here, for example, we see how the previous deep and fruitful turn toward the Jewish spiritual tradition begins to degenerate into boring obsequiousness and empty Jewish self-adulation that obligates us to nothing.

We hope that the Yiddish poets of today are not yet the last ones, and that there will yet come to us poets who will want to both strengthen and revolt against the artistic traditions that have been created among us in the last four or five decades.

I want to return for a moment to our pioneers and classical writers. Is it true that what they accomplished in Yiddish poetry no longer has any value for us? No, that is not true. They too created a tradition, perhaps no less than our modernists did. It's only that it does not consist in the forms of their poems, of which the majority, unfortunately, are permanently outdated, but in the spirit, the ideals that inspired them. The older Yiddish poetry is old in form but young and powerful in spirit. It has a belief in humanity, a healthy optimism, a hope for a bright tomorrow, and a trust in human common sense. It is distinguished by its social feeling, by its clear, rational, and positive view of life. Those are all things we lack so badly today.

And when new Yiddish poets come who feel the need to return to a more sober and critical consideration of things and events (as we refuse to stop hoping will happen), they, weary of the arcane, will be able to return to the openness of our older poets, and having before them the artistic traditions of modern Yiddish poetry, will also be able to give the themes of wordliness and openness a modern and subtle artistic expression.

Alef Kats (1898-1969) was a lyric poet of great skill. His viewpoints varied at different times from *In Zikh* to proletarian concerns and back again. He wrote a great deal about New York, and also wrote many poems, stories, and plays for young people.

~

Alef Kats

Yiddish Poem

Yiddish poem,
seethe!
Shout—don't be silenced!
Sing with every letter and limb.
Cry—and sing your tune.

You must cry—you're fated to;
a wail is sown within you.
Ten times six hundred thousand galls
burn in your innards.

Ten times six hundred thousand people
call, demand: "Don't forget!"
Envelop them in your flames,
in the lines of your miracle.

You are the heir of the calls—
carry the shout abroad.
Give the sounds words and bodies—
carry their woe abroad.

You are a relative of prophets;
in your destruction comfort blooms.
Cry of woe but sing of survival,
because for this you were created, poem.

295

Yisroel Yehoyshua Zinger (1893-1944), the elder brother of Yitskhok Bashevis Zinger, was a distinguished novelist whose work (in translation) was appreciated by readers throughout the world. The piece presented here is an excerpt from one of his greatest novels, *The Family Karnovsky*. His sudden death at the age of 51 was widely mourned in the Jewish community.

◇

Yisroel Yehoyshua Zinger

Yegor

In no way could the youngest member of the Karnovski family, Georg Yoakhim, whom they called Yegor for short, acclimatize himself to the new land.

*   *   *

Like a person bitten by a mad dog that, though dying of thirst, is afraid to take a swallow because of fear of water, so was Yegor dying to get to-gether with people but was afraid of them because they had once insulted him so badly, and he was eating himself up alive in his loneliness.

Dr. Karnovski, knowing of the boy's fear of people, did everything in the world to put him in contact with people. Like a capable physician who knows that terribly ill patients are often healed by introducing into their bodies the bacteria that had poisoned their blood, he too tried to heal his son with the things he was afraid of. With Karnovskian stubbornness, he drove him into the new life. With Karnovskian stubbornness, Yegor resisted his father and hid in his corner, like a mole in the ground.

At first, Dr. Karnovski tried to woo Yegor with kindness. He did every-thing possible to make the boy comfortable in the new land, to give him a taste of the new life the way one gives medicine to a sick, stubborn child so he will get better. He took him to places of amusement and parks, to beautiful streets and colorful bridges to show him the good features of the city, to sell him on the new home. Early in the morning, he awoke him from sleep and drove him out of his bed, for which Yegor had such a weak-ness, and called on him to accompany him on his strolls to the seashore. Yegor turned his face to the wall and pulled the covers over his head.

"Sleepyhead — the sun is shining outside," his father tried to whet his appetite.

"What do I care about the sun? I'm sleepy," answered Yegor from under the covers.

"Yegor—we'll hire a rowboat."

Yegor thought about that for a while. Rowing had always been his greatest pleasure. But the pleasure of resisting his father, who was to blame for all his troubles, was greater than the pleasure of rowing, so he didn't accept his father's offer.

"I didn't sleep all night because of the noise of the God-damned city," he grumbled. "Let me sleep now."

Precisely because his father was so fond of praising the new city and enumerating all of its virtues, its bigness and beauty and freedom, Yegor called it nothing other than God-damned — reduced it to a big nothing.

He was more bothered by the noise and tumult of the city, the uncomfortableness of the new residence and the cramped quarters and poverty, than his parents were. Instead of getting used to the new life, he was angry at it, despised it. The angrier he got at it, the more it plagued him, annoyed him. His irritable head was open to every noise in the night, every rustle and commotion. The sound of automobiles driving by woke him from even the deepest sleep. Not having anyone to whom to vent, he used to go into his parents' bedroom in the middle of the night and rail against the city to which they had brought him.

"God-damned city," he cursed, "I'll go crazy in this accursed city!"

Dr. Karnovski tried to appease him with logic.

"Listen, young man, the city will not accommodate itself to you—you'll have to accommodate yourself to it. Be understanding, logical."

Yegor didn't want to be logical. Nothing made him so bitter as when his father told him to be logical. Precisely because he had no answer for his father's logical words, the words irritated him.

"You're always with your logic!" he grumbled.

Seeing that the father's words of logic didn't help, Tereza tried to soothe him with softness.

"Be sensible, child," she pleaded with him. "We didn't come here of our own free will. You know that very well."

"I don't want to be sensible," said Yegor angrily.

He used to go to sleep late at night and sleep till well into the day, often till noon. No matter how late he got up, he then crept around all day in his pajamas, rumpled and bitter at having gotten up late. He constantly lay next to the radio, seeking to catch some news about 'back there.' He understood nothing of the new language, which he had learned so readily in the old country and had thought he understood, and for that reason he didn't want to hear a word from the radio speakers and singers and comedians and news announcers, all of whom had only one goal; to irritate him with their incomprehensible shrieks and laughter. Because of that, he used to sit for hours and tinker with the radio, turning the dial till he caught something of the 'back there.' That was something cozy and personal and understandable. In the same way that he avoided the new language, he avoided the street and the playing and yelling boys and girls who filled it. He could sit for hours at the window and watch their games and their running and chasing, but he was afraid to go down to them. His mother couldn't bear to see Yegor sitting alone at the window, and she pleaded with him to go down to the street and join in the games. He didn't listen to her. His father insisted that he had nothing to fear from the boys in the street, because the boys here were not like 'back there'. Yegor got furious.

"Who's afraid?" he yelled in order to drown out his father's accurate words. "I'm not afraid of anyone."

But he was indeed afraid. There was no way he could rid himself of his old fear of getting together with boys, a fear of being laughed at and insulted. Every laugh by a person filled him with the suspicion that they were making fun of him. The fear of the possibility of being insulted filled him in time with aversion towards those who might insult him. In each of them he foresaw an enemy, a possible oppressor.

Seeing that a kind approach couldn't tear Yegor away from the nest in which he hid himself, Dr. Karnovski tried a strict approach. He drove him by force out of the house and into the street, so he could get a taste of it. Yegor had to surrender. But he went unwillingly, with careful steps, like an unskilled skater on the ice. Precisely because he was so careful with his English, to please the youngsters in the street, his tongue stuck in his mouth from the very first words he tried to speak. The youngsters in the street understood his grammatical and very distinctly enunciated English, in which he also stammered, less well than Uncle Harry's youngsters did. Running around in their torn sweaters with numbers embroidered on the backs, with shirts sticking out of their pants, wearing overalls, even half-naked, chasing, yelling, throwing themselves onto the ground and grinning broadly, they had absolutely no time or patience for the dressed-up, resentful young man who was wandering around them uncomfortably.

"Hell—catch the ball, catch it!" they called out to him so he should catch the ball which flew just past him.

Yegor had to do just one thing: throw himself onto the ground, catch the ball, and throw it farther, which would immediately have made him part of the gang, but he didn't understand the words, the likes of which he had never encountered in his English textbooks, and he questioned the boys with the phrase those books said to use in such a case.

"Beg your pardon, sir?" he asked with a marked German accent.

The "beg your pardon," and the "sir" in addition, threw the excited youngsters into such gales of laughter that they forgot about their ball.

"Katzenjammer," a jokester gave him the name of a hero of a comic strip, "sauerkraut."

Yegor ran away, back into the house, like someone being shot at. Just what he had been so afraid of had happened. They had laughed at him, mocked him in front of everyone, and thereafter he avoided going near the yelling, tumultuous youngsters in their embroidered sweaters. He watched their games, their laughter and joy, and their skill at running around, enviously. As always, he masked his envy with hatred and contempt. He took great pleasure in seeing someone slip and fall when someone else threw him the ball badly.

When the school-season approached and Dr. Karnovski started talking about a school, Yegor was completely overcome with fear. More than anything else, he was afraid of school walls and school rooms, the places where they had once insulted him so badly. Just hearing the word "school" struck fear into his heart. With each passing day, he lost his appetite more and more. He slept poorly and cried out in his sleep at night. When he was supposed to go to school for the first time, he developed a high fever. Tereza got frightened and called her husband over to the boy's bed. Dr. Karnovski looked at him and saw that Yegor was not deceiving him—his temperature was indeed elevated. However, he knew that it wasn't from any illness but from anxiety, from fear, and he told him to get dressed and go. Yegor looked at his father with hatred.

"It's all right with me," he murmured, "but when I get sick, you'll be to blame."

Tereza was upset about Yegor's words, and she looked pleadingly at her husband. Dr. Karnovski stuck to his guns.

He administered the bitter medicine to his son by force, sure that it would bring him healing and peace.

"He'll get used to the boys," he prophesized to Tereza. "That will cure him."

The fever passed, as Dr. Karnovski had foreseen, but Yegor didn't get used to the school. They placed him in a lower class because of the several years of school he had missed and because of his unfamiliarity with the new language. Older than all the boys around him and a head taller than anyone else in the class, he felt very embarrassed about his overgrown size and his educational backwardness, and about the surprised look on the faces of the smaller boys, who looked at him in wonderment—the one who was older and taller than everyone else. From the very first answer he had to give the teacher, he became anxious because of his accent and he tried to say the words as well and clearly as he could. The more clearly he spoke, the more comical they sounded. They reminded people of the language of the comedians who spoke English with a German accent. First one boy couldn't contain himself and burst out laughing. After that, all the others, both the boys and the girls, joined in the laughter. Out of excitement, Yegor began to stammer. That further increased the laughter of those around him.

Mr. Barnett Levi, the English teacher, immediately stopped the noisy laughter. Tapping his pencil several times on the desk and wiping his glasses so they sparkled with cleanliness, he interrupted the lecture in English and made a speech in front of the class in his soft, baritone voice. That had always been Mr. Levi's instrument, that voice of his. Himself quite short and chubby, with big glasses on his dark black eyes, curly black hair, and a fleshy, hooked Jewish nose, he didn't have much chance of being a darling of the class, amid the mixture of Irish, Jewish, German, Italian, and Negro boys and girls. But as soon as he opened his mouth and spoke the first words through his fleshy lips, everyone listened to him intently and with interest. It caressed like velvet, that voice of his, coming unexpectedly from that undistinguished, chubby little person. Because of that voice, he seemed taller, more important, and handsomer to people. Listening to his voice, the female students fell in love with him. Mr. Barnett Levi knew the power of his voice and put all of his clearness into it to stop the laughter of the boys and girls.

"Quiet, quiet, quiet!" he caressed with the velvet of his voice.

He didn't get angry, teacher Levi—he just caressed. Instead of getting angry at the class because they had laughed at a new schoolmate, he preferred to start describing the reasons that had forced the new pupil to leave his fatherland, where his own language was familiar and easy, and come over to a new country, learn a new language, and go into a lower class. Even more than the boys, the girls were moved by their teacher's words.

Satisfied that he had quieted the class so well, inspired by his own words, Mr. Barnett Levi looked with smiling, dark eyes through his sparkling clean glasses directly at Yegor to show him his sympathy and empathy. In order to end the matter on a light note, to make up to the pupils for his serious words, he made a joke: that though the new pupil's accent was not completely American now, he could improve it with time so much that he could even become a teacher of English, as he himself, Barnett Levi, had become though he was the son of an immigrant Jewish tailor.

He winked at Yegor, which meant that they understood and empathized with each other. But instead of replying with a smile and thankfulness, as Mr. Barnett Levi had expected from the one he had protected, the new, overgrown pupil looked at him with alienation.

"I am not a Jew, sir," he said bitterly to the teacher, who had tried to include him as a fellow-believer.

During the whole time that the teacher had spoken to the class about him with so much empathy, Yegor Karnovski had felt no thankfulness to him, his protector, but only anger and contempt. He had never liked those curly-headed, short, bespectacled, brainy people whose race cried out from their faces, and who had made him think that he too was one of them. They immediately reminded him of the caricatures they had made 'back there' of ones like him: curly-headed, big-nosed, bespectacled, and intellectual. The fact that this curly-headed, bespectacled person with the compromising name Levi, the kind they were ashamed of 'back there' and should have been ashamed of here, was protecting him, Georg Yoakhim, a Holbek on his mother's side, insulted and debased him. Worst of all was that Mr. Levi had presented him to the class as a Jew, as his equal. Yegor did not want to be a fellow-believer of that curly-headed, bespectacled Levi. And he told him so, right in front of everyone, so they should know it once and for all.

For a while, Mr. Barnett Levi felt uncomfortable that the tall, older pupil whose part he had taken so strongly had made a fool of him in front of the class. Like any Jew who sniffs out another Jew, no matter how much he disguises himself, he too had sniffed out the Jew in that young man. But he knew that the class was not the place to have a discussion about it, and he made the whole thing into a joke in order to smooth out the uncomfortable matter:

"We'll leave the matter to the race-specialists on the other side of the ocean," he said, "We don't concern ourselves with such researches and we'll go on to the lesson."

From then on, there developed a two-way antipathy between the pupil Yegor Karnovski and the teacher Barnett Levi. The hatred that Yegor had had toward teachers since one of them had insulted him he loosed upon the teacher Levi, who had tried to take his side. He also hoped thereby to find favor in the eyes of the blond, blue-eyed pupils in the class, whom his heart drew him to approach, though at the same time he was afraid of them.

Yegor Karnovski divided the pupils in the school into two categories: the first group wwere the blond, blue-eyed ones, whom he wanted to get close to, be one of, but was afraid that they would insult him for his past Jewishness, as those like them 'back there' had so badly mocked him and insulted him; the second group were the dark-skinned and dark-eyed ones, whom he was not afraid of but had contempt for and didn't want to be one of, precisely because deep inside himself he felt a relationship to them. Toward the first group, he felt exaggerated inferiority—toward the others, exaggerated haughtiness. The boys in the school sensed both things in him, the fear and the haughtiness; playful, happy, running around, making noise in their games during recess, free, mixed together, they often took digs at one another for their nationality, called one another "wop," "sheenie," or "nigger," but then quickly forgot about it while catching the ball or running and chasing one another, and they were not suspicious of one another.

The cautiousness of the new pupil, his reticence, his inferiority and haughtiness, his shame and pride, his debasement and superiority injected bitterness, discomfort, and difficulty, and they shunned the too-tall, too-clever pupil with the comical accent.

Seeing their unfriendliness toward him, Yegor tried to take revenge on his colleagues by ridiculing their country and praising the land he had come from. Knowing deep inside himself that it was a lie, he praised to the skies everything about the old country, its soldiers and policemen, its sailors and sport-champions, to which those of the new land couldn't even be compared. Being afraid to take part in the games and the races, in which he had never been good from childhood on, he said he didn't want to play because the American games weren't worth a God-damned penny and it was beneath his dignity to make a fool of himself. That greatly insulted the boys, and they challenged him to fights to see who could deliver the better blows, America or Europe. Yegor didn't accept the challenges, and the boys called him "coward" and "blowhard." For that reason, he often pretended to be sick and came late just so he wouldn't have to look at the teacher Barnett Levi and wouldn't have to get together with the playful, happy boys and girls. To spite the teacher Levi, he didn't want to put his mind to his lessons and didn't do any homework. Dr. Karnovski understood that Yegor was pretending to be sick, and he told him so. Yegor became his mortal enemy because he was able to see through him completely. He couldn't hide anything from his father's dark, piercing eyes, which penetrated his bones. Yegor was afraid of those dark Karnovski eyes, hated them.

(From the novel *The Family Karnovski*)

Yehude Leyb Teler (1912-1972) spanned the worlds of poetry and journalism in Yiddish and English. In addition to publishing several volumes of poetry, he was a regular contributor to the Yiddish *Morgn-Zhurnal* specializing in political commentaries.

~

Yehude Leyb Teler

The Song Of My Family

I seek in myself the traces of my family.
Where in me is my grandmother,
who stood long days
next to a dark windowpane
and chattered old-fashionedly
with her God?
And my mother,
who cried about a story in the newspaper
and never ignored
an outstretched hand?

I seek in myself the traces of my family.
It's a long, difficult sleigh-ride
of "how"
and "what"
from my grandfather to me.
Different stimuli
upset my dreams,
different worries
harness my thoughts,
but my tongue and nose
have probably still retained
his tastes
and his desires.

I seek in myself the traces of my family.
Who knows the nights

of my great-grandfather's pious days?
Have I inherited from him
my crazy dreams,
where the moon is flecked with blood
and my own body is a trap?

I seek in myself the traces of my family,
the years my father spent in foreign lands
in panic about burning cities
when his wife was at the other end of the mail.

Draw the curtain, douse the wick—
my family is an angry legend.

New York Through the Jewish Soul

The big-city streets,
joyously wonderstruck
like houses that await
the return
of the men
from holiday evening prayers.
Winds gnaw
like a cycle of cantorial chants.
Skyscrapers flicker
like pagan idols
facing a sun
of scoured Jewish brass.
Evening fear
falls on me
like a prayer-shawl,
and I understand the meaning of my days
with crystal clarity,
as if touched by the pointer
of the reader.

Nokhem Bomze (pen name of Nokhem Frishvaser) (1906-1954) published his first book of poetry at the age of 23, in Poland. He served in the Red Army during the second World War. He was the editor of the Lodz journal *Yiddish Writings*. He emigrated to New York in 1948. He was in the process of editing posthumous volumes of Mani Leyb's poems when he died at the age of 48.

◦

Nokhem Bomze

O Friends of Mine in Big Noisy New York

O friends of mine in big noisy New York,
through all the streets, avenues, and squares,
in the middle of a bright day
let's stop and honor
the funeral of a person,
Itsik Kalmen,
the oldest member of a Workmen's Circle branch,
on his way to Mt Carmel cemetery.

Oh how many sorrows he endured
across cities, lands, and oceans!
Oh how many deaths hovered over him
at every moment of an hour
and every hour of the day
in big noisy New York!

So let us be silent before his casket
for the ninety years he lived,
for the corpse of Izzy Charles
(Itsik Kalmen in the old country)
on its way to Mt Carmel cemetery.

O friends of mine in big noisy New York,
let us pray that the deceased be destined,
in his last moment,
to make it without pitfalls

through the New York streets
on his last road to the ground.

Sunset In The City

Between Ninth and Tenth Street, in the city,
in the evening, the sun hung—
a gigantic wheel
near the earth.
And it came to pass
that at just that fearsome moment
all the gates opened up
and people raced and ran
on the way to their homes.

Only I and my sorrow and a child walking along
admired the strange sunset.
For the duration of that moment, as if for long years,
I stood thus,
till the elevated train
rode over the sun.
Concealed and gone, no longer here,
the sun in the terror of the evening hour.

All night long I kept thinking
about the death of the sun
on the soil of New York.

Arn Tseytlin (1898-1973) was distinguished from most other Yiddish writers by his interest in mystical and religious themes—his poems were completely suffused with the religious quest and with the doubts and conflicts of the religious soul.

~

Arn Tseytlin

Song of the Good Deed

What is opinion? An opinion is not worth anything.
Today it's like this
and tomorrow it's just the reverse.
What is love? Is love worth anything?
It's love today
and tomorrow it's just the reverse.
What is woman? She is contrariness.
Today she's like this
and tomorrow the opposite, full of contradiction—
that is woman.

What is poetry? Whoever trusts it
will lose the game.
Words mislead you—images fool you.
Good deeds—only they last,
and from them
beams radiate without end,
without measure.
Good deeds, as if in numberless mirrors,
reflect in all the worlds at once.
They bear your stamp on them
and they radiate
and reflect your image
in all the worlds.

The Jew in Me Weeps

The Jew in me weeps, the Jew in me sheds tears:
"Have you, Aaron, son of Esther, angered your Creator?
With what, pray tell, will you come to the next world?
How many good deeds do you have to your credit?

"What will you bring with you? The songs?
Will they be your protector and shield?
Even if you are the greatest singer,
is that the answer, Aaron, son of Esther?

"Is that why your Sender sent you?
Is that the most important thing, is that the most important thing?

"How many misfortunes have you lightened?
How many pains have you eased?
How much darkness have you brightened?"

The Jew in me weeps, the Jew in me sheds tears.

Faith

Wherein does faith reside? You wish to know
where it lives? Ask despair.
Through its realms the paths run—
faith lives on ruins for everyone.

Upon the sparkling foundation
of a building that has burned down,
its tears run down, one by one.

The tears reflect a dawn
that brightens in the sky
above it and the ruins.

In its tears, the dawn grows bright
as it sits and wrings its hands.
And if you have not known despair,
you'll not find faith in any land.

Cosmic "No"

I asked myself: Shall I commit suicide?
And a voice answered me: "No!"

And the voice was outside me
and as deep within me as a star in the river.

And the "No" was as deep
as the bottom of a deep and radiant "Yes."

And the voice was a fresh breath of snow
and the aroma of the river and of hay

and the taste of a first frightened kiss
and the naked nerve of desire

and the tears of sin in the abyss of cities
and the wings of purest prayer.

In the distance, space barely trembled,
like a bluish skin on a plum.

There was a rising of branches, a flying, a going,
and all of this was just one word: "No!"

The Secret: Man

Don't tell me that Man is a beast.
Compared with Man, the beast is an angel.
Does a beast build crematoriums?
Does it throw children into the fire?
Does it take pleasure in murder?
Don't tell me that Man is a beast.

Don't tell me that Man is a beast.
He's still more than an angel.
He is the word of Isaiah,
he is the protest of Job,
he has a desire for a new world.

Don't tell me that Man is a beast.

The Mystery of Yiddish

The sacred Hebrew language is eternity, as is Jerusalem;
it's the language of mystic revelations,
of true prophecy that comes to pass,
of the Song of Songs and the Psalms—
the language of the living God.

And Yiddish? The *kabala* says:
Israel is the reverse of Amalek—
Amalek, conversely, is the reverse of Israel;
there is in that an entire world.
If your heart hears,
let it understand my words.
I want to reveal a mystery to you
regarding the *kabala*-secret that resides in Yiddish.

I interpret Yiddish kabalistically!
The language of the reverse Israel, Amalek,
we reversed;
we transformed it into Jewish groans and Jewish tears,
into Jewish sorrow over the exile of God;
with raisins and almonds
we transformed it into Jewish wisdom, *khasidic* stories,
and heartfelt prayers.

By making it as motherly as our women's prayers
and as fatherly as *khasidizm,*
we reversed the reversal
through Yiddish.

Shloyme Shvarts (1907-1988) was sometimes called "The Poet of Chicago." His poems were lyrical and emotional, and often melancholy and autumnal. His later poems make reference to the Holocaust and Jewish refugees, and also to legends about Biblical subjects.

~

Shloyme Shvarts

Chicago

1.
Bright city, my city,
all dressed up.
My city,
sly and vandalistic.
I bring to you
from among the stones
a flower that has blossomed massively.

I know that every stone
is an individual emissary
of the great fire—
miraculous, cliff-like, legendary stones
rich with winds;
hewn-out citadels,
renewed and protected
near the ever-blue river.

The day bows
closer and closer to your shore,
and in the evening
says its *mea culpa*.
Then your stones
become secretive martyrs,
girded against the nocturnal stream
by their mute relatives.

2.
As if I were seeing you
for the first time,
I am constantly amazed by your size.
Your giants,
your hacked-out-of-steel guards,
warn and protect.

The city is drawn to the river,
and I am drawn,
in all your nights,
to the waves
that give birth to poems.

Through tin and stone
sprinkled with stars,
flowers bloom
in your courtyards.

So I remain your faithful singer,
made happy
by both sorrow and song
amid your sated granite.

Hallelujah

The street speaks a telegraphic tongue;
the moon,
in a calculated message,
announces a new dream.

Tell me:
am I really
now the last in the Jewish Diaspora?

On dawn-lit walls
in my city,
with pious moments of joy
in the ecstatic morning—
my song, my riddles,
don't let yourself be deceived
in the flickering neon lights.

You won't die.

You speak to me with the freshness
of newly baked goods,
with Divine incantations
amid excited trees,
with a tremulous hurrah
to my generation,
amid the noise of propellers.

My Jewish song flies
with glowing notes
to distant generations.

Itsik Manger (1901-1969) was a unique figure in Yiddish poetry. While living a Bohemian and somewhat dissolute life and wandering from country to country, he was nevertheless a beloved bardic figure who combined in his poems inspiration, playfulness, lyricism, and optimism. Many of his poems were on Biblical themes, and his modern reinterpretation of the Megillah of Esther was admired by both critics and the general readership. Many of his poems were set to music, and are still widely sung today.

~

Itsik Manger

Since Yesterday

Since yesterday, I live on another planet;
only my love and my song are with me here.
So what if my cherry tree has blossomed?
Without regret or tear, I stand naked before my mirror.

But I have one desire: to hear, to hear, to hear
the rhythm of all that breathes or takes flight.
I'm such an admirer of the cosmic fair,
whose magic lantern casts a brilliant light.

Where I was born and where I've wandered
I've forgotten—don't remember the above.
Fuzzy in my memory are all the familiar addresses.
I live on another planet, with only my song and my love.

I have but one desire, to hear, to hear, to hear
the choral sounds of the most distant stars.
I'm an admirer of that kind of cosmic symphony.

The Song of the Golden Peacock

The golden peacock flies away
to the East, to look for yesterday.
Tri-li, tra-la.
He flies and flies through mountain heights

and meets a Turk upon a mare.
He asks the Turk, in just this way:
"And have you seen yesterday?"
The Turk just frowns, and tries to think:
"Not seen or heard yesterday."
He pulls the reins, they ride away—
his laughter echoes all the day.
"A golden bird—there's just no way!"

The golden peacock flies away
to the North, to seek yesterday.
Tri-li, tra-la.
He sees a fisher by the sea
who spreads his nets and sings his piece,
and in his song a fire burns,
a child is sleeping in its peace,
a blonde girl's spinning at her wheel.
The golden peacock asks him then:
"And have you seen yesterday?"
The fisher frowns and tries to think:
"Not seen or heard yesterday."
His laughter echoes all the day:
"A golden bird—there's just no way?!"

The golden peacock flies away
to the South, to seek yesterday.
Tri-li,tra-la.
He sees a Negro in the field,
who's fixing tents with golden straw.
He asks the Negro, just this way:
"And have you seen yesterday?"
The Negro grinds his snow-white teeth,
and flashes him a charming smile,
but makes no answer, just says "What?
A golden bird—most surely not!"

The golden peacock flies away
to the West, to seek yesterday.
Tri-li, tra-la.
He meets a woman dressed in black
who's kneeling at a grave, so sad.
He asks her nothing, knows himself:
the black-clad woman who weeps today
next to the grave beside the road
must be the widow of yesterday.

Near the Road Stands a Tree

Near the road stands a tree,
bowed in contemplation.
All the birds have flown away
from their leafy station.

Three flew East, three flew West,
the rest flew South together;
left the tree there all alone—
to brave the stormy weather.

"Mother dear," I said to her,
"please don't try to stop me.
My intentions are, you see,
to be a bird there on the tree."

"I'll sit there upon the tree—
croon it softly into sleep.
Through the winter comfort it—
sing to it 'O tree don't weep'."

Mother says: "O dearest child,"
and she weeps a bitter tear,

"on the tree you'll freeze to death—
that's my deep and solemn fear."

So I say: "O mother dear—
please don't weep—your eyes get red.
In the twinkling of an eye,
I'll be a bird, just as I said."

Mother weeps: "O Itsik dear,
take this shawl in God's sweet name.
It will help to keep you warm,
and you can perch there all the same."

"Take galoshes with you too—
winter's cold, with wind and rain.
Put your wool cap on your head
so my cares won't be in vain."

"Take your winter-vest as well—
put it on to warm your breath.
I'm sure you do not want to be
a guest within the house of Death."

I try to flap my laden wings—
too many things she's put on me.
I haven't got the strength I need
to lift them up onto the tree.

So I look so sadly now
into my mother's tearful face.
Her love did not allow me to
become a bird and take my place.

Dora Teytlboym (1914-1992) was another of the great women Yiddish poets. Her reputation never became as great as that of some of the others, partly because she was strongly identified with left-wing proletarian groups—this was a negative for a considerable proportion of the general Yiddish readership.

∾

Dora Teytlboym

The Last Road

They rode, rode, rode
in closed trains,
sealed trains—
disheveled, faint,
accompanied by mockery and hate
on roads paved with blood and tears.

They rode, rode, rode
through dense Polish forests
redolent of earthy depths, rustic, cold,
with tangled, concealed, hidden secrets
overgrown with shadows of ancient times.

They rode, rode, rode
from East, West, North, and South,
summer and winter, winter and summer,
day and night, night and day,
through snowy fields
and fields of flowers,
mothers, children at the breast,
fathers, sons with hands for working—
and didn't know
they were going toward slaughter.

They rode, rode, rode,
young and old, old and young,
from yesterday, from tomorrow,

torn from their roots
and robbed of everything they had—
and still they believed, believed:
there they'd be given
a drink of water,
their fill of bread,
and a roof over their heads.
Their enemies had promised, promised,
promised with the mouths of humans
in the language of Beethoven,
Goethe, and Bach.
They rode, rode, rode
to the gate of the last finale,
along the road, the shortest road
from life to death,
measured out precisely,
to the last detail.

They rode, rode, rode
under skies full of black smoke,
and at the gate marked "Work Makes You Free"[30]
they were stripped and driven into the gas-chamber.

Their thirst and hunger were stilled with gas.
The profit, to the last penny,
from each man, woman, and child
was collected accurately and precisely:
locks of black hair, blond hair,
and gray women's hair
in the package.

Trains soaked with blood
rode, rode, rode.

---

[30] The gate of Auschwitz

People, My People

On all the roads of your wandering,
with boiling craters and abysses,
with pyres and scaffolds,
I have followed you
like a shadow.
Like the name of my father,
I have borne your name.
The stalks of your wisdom
on the stormy fields
I have reaped and guarded.
From your wine-grapes
I have absorbed the wine into my limbs.
The bloodied stones you walked on
are moistened with my tears,
like my mother's prayers in her *sidur*.

The endless river of Time
has gnawed and chewed on you for ages
with secret, hidden teeth,
has fed the garden of Golgotha
with your bones.
Like the sky, with the sun blazing like a crown
it bears anew after every night—
just so you've borne your bitter fate
and glowed and burned.
After every catastrophe,
trampled and crumbled,
you have arisen again,
raised yourself even higher,
bloodied and passionate.
In your poverty,
you were so rich!

People, my people—
I don't recognize you any more.
Where is your face?
Who wiped the morning dew from it—
that face, that refined face,
scoured and polished
by the whetstones of the years,
matured and ripened
on the sands of rage.

Who erased and covered up your memory,
pressed the demons of cruelty into your heart?
You were once merciful, after all—
your heart quivered and sparkled with justice.
That's alien to you now—
alien the sorrow of a mother,
the weeping of a child.
You're a fist now,
a bloody fist—
woe, woe is to me!

The ashes of sisters and brothers,
which opened the gate to victory for you,
are sprayed with blood now;
they rock on the eyelashes of dawn.
Who will wash the blood from them?
The ancient dream of millennia,
pierced by a sword,
is rolling around in the gutter.
And you, my people, conquered by victory,
lie prisoner in a deep sleep.
As David once did to Goliath,
they throw stones at you today,
and a rain of stones
cannot awaken you from sleep.

Woe, woe is me!
Deaf and blind you are now, my people,
"and your leaders are misleaders.
With the stammering lips of a foreign tongue,
they confuse your paths."[31]

Abel and Cain

Abel and Cain, Cain and Abel—
I am the mother of both.
Day and night, night and day,
the shame of one,
the sorrow of the other,
I carry in my heart like twins,
for both of you are my sons.

Abel, child mine—
You didn't bloom like a flower
with many Springs destined for you.
You were cut off from the Tree of Life
and prevented from blooming—
your shadow was sheared away,
your path was interrupted,
your dream was trampled.
At night I hear your voice,
rippling and soft
like the wool of your lambs.
It rises from your grave
and, as before,
it rests on my breast.
Abel, child mine—
your last dying tremor

[31] Isaiah 1:23, 3:12

travels across the world
like a storm
and conquers all deaths.

Cain, son mine—
You suckled milk from my breast, after all,
together with my love.
You took your first steps on my body,
you laughed for the first time in my lap,
spoke your first word there.
Day in, day out,
I was reflected in your eyes,
my son.
I wrote your name on the stars.
Pain with pain,
like the first man—
stone rubbed against stone
so a spark would flare
to ignite light for your eyes.
The hard, virgin earth
you nourished with your sweat—
its cruelty, congealed and naked,
you removed and commanded it to bloom.
How can I reflect myself in you now,
as I used to, my son,
when innocent blood
drips from your hands.

Who planted the poison
in your heart, my son—
coupled you with murder?
Like a climbing vine, an alien species,
he lent you strength
and made you his leader.
Cain, son mine,
blessed fruit of my womb,

my today bows me down to the ground
and tomorrow frightens me, frightens me.
Woe to your mother, woe to your mother!
Every stone in the pavement,
every leaf on the tree, asks you:
"Cain, where is your brother?"

Martyrs

Martyrs grow at night
up to the sky
and ignite the stars,
take soft bright steps
so no one should see,
no one should hear.

In shadows long and broad,
veiled and hidden
by rain and snow,
from generation to generation
they go around in the world,
come back to the places
they once signed with blood,
wipe away the dust of Time,
and murmur long-dead words
whose meaning no one knows.
They look into overgrown graves,
slice through sleep,
and mow the grasses of pain.

Martyrs grow at night
up to the sky
and ignite the stars,
which then become
beacons for lost travelers.

Khayim Grade **(1910-1982)** is considered possibly the greatest Yiddish novelist, as well as a fine poet. He was a lifelong rival of Yitskhok Bashevis Zinger but never became as popular as Zinger, perhaps because he did not have the good fortune to be extensively translated into English.

◦∼◦

Khayim Grade

Colorado

Am I on Earth? Am I not on some other star?
The day, like a clear child's eye, looks down on this district
and I look up through a veil of joyful tears.
Red, flaming cliffs! I've met you somewhere before.
But where? On watch or in a hospital bed when I fevered?
Daytime, when the sun was shining, or when it was dark with rain?
I don't know. I know only that you once approached me,
running stormily and wildly like a pride of lions,
and just like the sunset, you disappeared into my memory.
And though it is hard to believe in a garden of gods,
your flying past me has ignited belief in my heart.

Now you've become a bonfire of glowing roses,
you cliffs that I've seen soar.
They say the gods reside in your mountain cracks.
I've named you "Mesopotamia,"
Mesopotamia, the country in the desert
where Father Abraham's laden wedding-camels dozed—
that's what I want to call the caravan of mountain peaks,
and I also call familiarly the army of walkers and riders,
drunk, like me, on the sylvan air and happily celebrating the sunny,
     clear day.

Stand still, my traveling companion! Listen to the noise of the depths!
What sound is that, a waterfall or the wind in the trees?
Only he who has wept bitterly in the night out of disappointment
can feel the joyous mood of the silent cliffs.

327

Only he in whose heart a secret sorrow gnaws
and whose hairy head has been burned up by a thought,
only he can understand what the ancient, swaying forest murmurs
and how sweet it is to die in the shade of the trees.
Forward, my companions! Let's climb higher to the mountain!
We are fated to see further unbelievable wonders today.
Sorrow has only one face beneath its nocturnal veil,
but joy has many faces, my merry traveler.

Blazing red cliffs, like burning towers,
rusty gold Rockies, like heaps of autumn leaves.
Snows and storms have polished you for millennia
and sunshine has melted your golden forms
till you've emerged as a garden of gods.
Now you flicker like a chain of Indian bonfires,
glowing stone-bordered bonfires that give us signs
to guide us even farther across the abysses,
till we all reach the snowy mountain peak.

In the Synagogue

In the synagogue, fumes are coming from the burned-down candles on
the lectern and from the melted large memorial candles in their wooden
boxes. The sunbeams coming in weave themselves together with the dark
red shine of the electric lamp. The streaks of light blind the eyes and cut
across faces like slaughterer's knives. In the sunbeams, a cloud of sparkling
particles of dust swarm as if lost, sinful souls from the world of chaos had
come through the windows into the synagogue's *yom kipur* atmosphere to
find absolution. Heat emanates from bodies and faces, beads of sweat form
on beards and foreheads. White steam comes from the hand-washing bowl
and clouds the brass knobs of the iron bands around the platform. The wor-
shipers roll down their prayer-shawls from their heads onto their shoulders
and wipe the sweat from their necks. Some slip outside to cool off until the
bang on the table that indicates that they are getting ready to say the Memorial Prayer. Even the recluse Reb Yoyel has taken the prayer-shawl off

his head for a while, but hasn't turned his face away from the wall in the Eastern corner where he is standing. Before his eyes hangs a fog of light and tears, and in the fog there hovers a poor, small synagogue in the town of Utian. There he was born and studied in *kheyder* and in the synagogue. His father was a burner in a resin factory all his life. A sparkling darkness, like that of a dense forest, always looked out from his eyes. His father's veiny hands, with their crooked fingers, looked like the trees from which he drew the resin. His mother was the same height as his wife, Hindele. Hindele was by nature childishly happy and impressionable, but if she wanted to insist on something, she could let out a yell too. His mother, however, was a humble and hardworking woman, a servant in fancy houses to supplement her husband's income so their little boy could sit and study Talmud in the Utian synagogue.

When he was fifteen years old, he started to search for a place to study Torah. He wandered from one village yeshiva to another: a year in Lekhevitsh, a year in Kobrin, until he stopped for a longer time to sit and study in Slonim. By then he had not seen his parents for several years and just wrote an occasional letter home. He was then very busy. The more homesick he was, eating by day and sleeping at night on the hard bench in the synagogue, the more pious he became and the more he studied with great diligence to find consolation in the Torah.One time, on the eve of the New Moon of *Shvat*[32], he, together with a *minyen* of old men was celebrating the 'minor *yom kipur*' in the Slonim synagogue. In the middle of the recitation from the Torah, a student friend of his came up to him and said: "Man from Utian—your mother is waiting for you in the synagogue vestibule." At first, he didn't believe it: from Utian to Slonim is a long journey, after all, and his father hadn't written that his mother was coming. Only when his friend repeated it again and again did he believe it, but his strict piety did not allow him to go out in the middle of the reading of the Torah. In that regard, he made the calculation of a fanatically pious man: when they had started to pray, they had asked him whether he had fasted, and he had answered yes; without him there wouldn't have been a *minyen* of fasters, and they wouldn't have been able to read the Torah portion, *Vayikhal,* and therefore he must not go out in the middle of the recitation. So he stayed

[32] One of the Winter months in the Jewish calendar

and listened to the reciter reel off the Torah portion, with the proper ac-
centuations, and was careful not to miss hearing a single word, though his
heart was breaking: his mother was waiting! He wanted even more to conquer the Evil Spirit, and he didn't go out during the silent *shmone esre*.
After that, he remained for the repetition of the *amida*, and later joined the
entire *minyen* of fasters in reciting the hymns, the Penitential Prayers, the
chapters of Psalms, the Great Confession of Rabbi Nissim, and the Con-
fessional—everything, everything till after the mourner's *kadish* and the
aleynu.

During the whole service, the student who had told him his mother was
waiting was wandering around in the synagogue and looking at him with
a crooked, mocking smile. Since he knew that that student was a mocker
and didn't fast on the minor *yom kipur*, he began to suspect that his friend
the jokester had made up the whole story about his mother in order to cause
turmoil during the praying. But when they had finished all the prayers and
he finally came down from his place at the East wall, he didn't find his
mother. A couple of men, among those that always sat near the oven, told
him that while he was praying a short, poor woman had come into the synagogue and asked for him. The woman had said she was his mother and
had come all the way from Utian. But when his friend had relayed to her
the message that her son didn't want to interrupt his praying, she had
watched him for a while from behind the platform and then had gone to
the door. One of the men near the oven had asked why she didn't wait for
her son, and she had answered "My son is a saintly person" and had de-
parted.

Yoyel ran through the synagogue courtyard and down the various little
streets yelling:

"Mama! Mama.!"

He asked for her at the Slonim guest house and the hotel, and asked various people, but she hadn't been seen or heard anywhere. When he came
back to the synagogue depressed after all the searching, a man told him that
he had happened to be in the vestibule of the synagogue when his mother
had come in and put down her little bundle. A little later she had come
back in, picked up her bundle, and left.

Then he felt pangs of pain and shame. He didn't have enough money
to go home in the middle of the semester, and he was ashamed before the

rabbi and the important people of the synagogue. All of them considered him a great student and a God-fearing pious person, so how could he break off his studies in the middle of the semester? Even more than the Slonim Jews, he was ashamed before his mother. After all, she had said of him: "He is a saintly person," so she would have great anguish if he gave up his studies in the middle of the semester. So he stayed in Slonim and promised himself that this time he would go home for Passover at the beginning of Nissan. But in the third week of Adar, a week before he was supposed to go home, he received a letter from his father saying that he now had to say the mourner's *kadish* for his mother.

When he went home for Passover, he got there with a big mourner's rent in his vest. His father told him that his mother had made the trip from Utian to Slonim half on foot, with a horde of beggars, and half on wagons, and hadn't been ashamed to beg while on the way. She had ridden as much as the pennies she had put together would pay for and the rest of the way she went on foot. She did the same on the way back from Slonim to Utian. Yoyel begged his father to tell him whether his mother had forgiven him for not going out to her in the middle of the praying, but his father either didn't want to or didn't know what to answer. He just told Yoyel that after coming back from the long winter journey his mother had developed pneumonia, and when she was burning with fever she had kept repeating:

"My son is a saintly person! My son is a saintly person!"

(From the novella *Leybe Leyzer's Courtyard*)

Reyzl Zhikhlinski (1910-2000) was a somewhat underappreciated poet who may well be the finest of all the women Yiddish poets. She was the master of the very short, unrhymed poem with tremendous impact and remarkable imagery, written on a wide variety of themes, some homey and some cosmic, often with a deeply personal component.

~

Reyzl Zhikhlinski

And Always When The Sun Goes Down

And always when the sun goes down,
I see the Christ of Titian.
Last rays fall
on his pale hands
and limbs,
rushed to a grave
before night
and darkness.
And always when the sun goes down,
I see those
who were gassed,
incinerated—
so many pale, unhappy hands,
a forest of hands,
and not one ray of sun
pitied them,
and no grave was allotted them.

My Story Is Your Story

My story is your story,
neighbor across from me in the subway.
What you are thinking about
I have long since forgotten.
What will happen to you
happened to me long ago.

What you hope for
I smile about
with closed lips.
My fate is shown
in the blue veins of your hand—
yours you can read
in the deep wrinkles on my face.

Ibn Dagan of Andalusia

Ibn Dagan of Andalusia,
the last Jewish poet
in the Spanish land,
in deep, blooming orchards
kissed the face of his beloved.
He sang:
"Flowers grow beneath your feet,
you are beautiful like the sun,
and, like the morning star,
you are the light of my eyes."

Came the expulsion—
all the Jews were driven out of Castille
and Aragon.
About what did he sing then,
Ibn Dagan?
Here history is silent.
We know only
that thousands set off wandering
into the unknown distance.
Thousands died of hunger,
thousands of cold.
Murderers slaughtered them
and robbed them of their money,
And those who survived

sat down by the side of the road,
on the bare earth,
and waited for the Messiah.
He was expected to come
in the year fifteen hundred and three.

Small Autumn Squares

Small autumn squares in New York,
sleeping monuments on high pedestals
amid falling leaves,
lonely men on benches
with long, outstretched legs,
seeking God,
staring looks into themselves,
around themselves,
and pigeons, pigeons with yellow eyes,
on the fading grass.

O small autumn squares in New York,
forgotten by a freezing God
among the stars.

In Times Square

All the clocks in Times Square
ring the message of death.
Electrons race,
announcing the news from all sides:
Latest news from the fronts in Vietnam!
Hurricanes rage in New Orleans!
Astronauts have landed on Mars!
Venus is inhabited!

The stream of people flows endlessly,
passing by, passing by:
the movie-goers,
the happiness-seekers,
the fire-eaters,
the knife-throwers.
But all the clocks in Times Square
ring the message of passing away
alone, alone.

The Knife

"He who has not felt
a knife in his back
does not know
what a knife is"—
says the taxi-driver
who drives me to the train.
I look at his back,
hunched over the wheel,
and my heart freezes—
on the seat where I am sitting,
there sat the passenger
with the knife.
The taxi slides along the New York asphalt,
morning streets rush by.
The buildings, tall pointy daggers,
climb to the sky.
Are they preparing to strike God in the back
and put an end
to the Ten Commandments?

What Wall

What wall can so straighten
our backs
as the Western Wall?

What dust can so extinguish
our burning ashes
as the dust from Mother Rachel's tomb?

What cave can so heal,
collect our tears,
as the Cave of the Patriarchs?

The Kind Hand

The kind hand
that feeds the pigeons in new York,
(and feeding pigeons
is strictly prohibited here,
in big letters
on streets and green squares);

the kind hand
that leads a blind man
across a street—
and the blind man is heavy and dark,
like a mountain;

the kind hand
that pets a homeless dog,
its lonely, bowed head—
that kind hand
will rescue the world
from chaos and destruction.

Malke Kheyfets-Tuzman (1896-1987) was a poet and an educator in Yiddish secular schools. Her poetry was distinctively feminine and often achieved great dramatic strength by directly addressing the reader or God. She was awarded the Manger Prize for Yiddish Literature in Israel in 1981.

≈

Malke Kheyfets-Tuzman

A Letter to My Son at War—1945

Good-morning to you, my son,
or perhaps it's good-evening for you now
or even good-night.
The radio
has brought to our home
victory on all fronts,
and that's good, good indeed,
but a tremor chokes me
in this joyous moment.

That tremor is old and familiar—
through generations, with trembling hands,
like burning candles in the wind,
we've carried it around.

That tremor is old and familiar—
It's the one we felt when God became enraged at us.
A similar joy moved us then,
when weary steps approached redemption:
"You're rejoicing
when the works of My hands
are now sinking in the sea?!"

Do you remember, my son,
How quiet, how silent
everything around us became?
Do you remember?

We were all there,
but you bowed your head
even more deeply than all of us,
and on the sand at your feet
I saw diamonds ignite.
Your tears in the sun
I called, in God-fearing piety,
"blessed by God."

Wandering child of mine,
I know not where you are,
somewhere on a ship or on dry land,
but wherever a radiant eye watches over you
I feel ashamed before you,
and you understand my shame.

The radio has sung out,
announced victory in every corner.
My lips are whispering,
grimacing with pain:
"Blessed be victory for us,
the sad victory."

Like an *Esrog*

I wish you good things—
I wish you things pure and beautiful,
like an *esrog.*

My grandfather, Rabbi Dovid Kheyfets,
would order his *esrog*
from a distant land.
It would arrive carefully packed
in soft, clean whiteness,
in a pretty little box.

My grandfather himself
took care of his *esrog*
so no blemish should affect it, God forbid!
He led each of his ten children
to the copper ladle
to wash his little hands,
smiled at each hand
when it neared the ladle
(when my grandfather smiled,
heaven and the angels sang),
and then slowly placed the *esrog*
into a little hand for blessing.

Therefore,
I forever connect
cleanliness and beauty
with an *esrog*.

Breakfast

At the round table,
she across from him.

Two little glasses of orange-juice—
for him,
for her.

He a sip,
she a sip—
they exchange glasses,
drink, drink to the bottom.

A slice of toasted bread
he cuts in half.
She takes it slowly from his hand,

slowly her fingers touch his.
Cheese and marmalade on the table
beckon.

With eyes half-closed,
they breathe in deeply
the aroma of hot coffee.

But I Can't Sing

You're dear to me, O city of mine, L.A.
but I can't sing to you
as they do,
your innumerable praisers
who write poems about you
in structured and free verse.
They boast, your rulers
who bathe in your riches.
They come for a while and enjoy
the kiss of your sun
and sing praises
to your bubbling springs.

I've gazed at
the wounds
beneath your patterns of flowers,
and my faithfulness
has grown more steadfast.

Like all your treetops
near the edge of poor-street,
I point out your shame through the azure blue to the very sky.
Together with the eggshell-white magnolia blossoms,
I sorrow for your blisters,
which fever with the poison of opium.

Along with your multicolored roses,
I fear your abysses,
where the crooked paths of the universe
are perversely sustained.

I sorrow at your dens
where crime breeds,
and the nests where the plague
robs humanity of your young sons
and devours the fruitfulness
of your beautiful daughters.

City of mine, world-famous one!
You fragrant myrtle-branch!
Your false lovers sing odes
to the small, delicate flower
that grows, most remarkably,
on cactuses and carved gargoyles.
Your false lovers
refresh themselves with the aroma of your eucalyptus.
Your false lovers
snack on your honey, sweet city.
They send air-kisses to you
from departing airplanes;
afterwards, in sonnets,
they'll recall your neon lights.

Rokhl Korn (1898-1982) initially wrote her poetry in Polish but soon switched to Yiddish. The second World War made her a rootless wanderer through many lands, but she eventually settled in Canada. Her early poems had a narrative quality, but her later ones were intimately lyrical and emotional, and specialized in exploring her often sad memories. She also wrote poems about Israel that were laced with Messianic visions.

~

Rokhl Korn

On the Other Side of the Poem

On the other side of the poem is a meadow
on which there is a straw-thatched house.
Standing near, three silent pines —
standing quiet as a mouse.

On the other side of the poem is a bird,
all yellow-brown with breast of red.
It flies here every wintertime —
its color crowns a bush that's dead.

On the other side of the poem is a path —
it's sharp and thin, a hairline slit,
and someone barefoot, lost in time,
now softly walks the length of it.

On the other side of the poem I see wonders
even on a dull, dark day
that pulses, wounded, 'gainst the pane,
its fevered longing to display.

On the other side of the poem — there's mama!
She comes and stands there thoughtfully,
then calls me home, just as of old:
"Enough of games, come home to me!"

You

I am saturated with you,
like earth after a spring rain,
and my brightest day hangs
on the pounding pulse of your first word,
like a bee on the blossoming branch of a linden tree.

And I am above you, like the promise of plenty
when the wheat and rye even out in the fields
and lie with the hope of greenness
on the swept floors of the granary.

And my fingertips drip faithfulness onto your weary head,
like golden-yellow honey,
and my years,
the field your feet tread,
get fat and swollen
with pain, the pain of loving you,
my beloved husband.

I'd Like to Meet Your Mother One Day

I'd like to meet your mother one day
and kiss her hands.
She'd probably find you in my eyes
and all your words, which I've hidden in my gaze.

And perhaps she'd come toward me
with the smile, quiet and wise,
that blooms eternally on the lips of mothers
when they feel their love for their own sons
confirmed by other women.

And perhaps even—
perhaps her gaze would warn me
(mothers always know more than other women)
about the wild sorrow
and arduous happiness
of loving her son.

I'd like to meet your mother one day
and kiss her hands.

Khava Rozenfarb (1923—) was incarcerated in the Lodz ghetto in 1940 and was sent to Auschwitz in 1944. She miraculously escaped and continued to write poems and a masterly 3-volume novel, *The Tree of Life*, which mostly dwelt on the events of the Holocaust.

~

Khava Rosenfarb

First Letter to Abrasha
(Bergen-Belsen, April 29th 1945)

Abrasha, Abrashele, Avremele!

You're alive! You survived! Praise be to destiny, praise be to the world and to life for sparing you!

My head is swimming. I'm going insane with joy!

When will I see you, Abrasha darling? I must see you as soon as possible, and you must get well as soon as possible so you will have the strength for our meeting.

I must also have strength, much strength. I don't know why, but the news about you makes me weak, makes me tremble. It appears that I can't yet bear the suffering of joy. The sparks of faith are burning out my brain.

Abrashele, I have remained all alone. During the selection in Auschwitz, I was separated from my mother and Virka.

I beg of you — perhaps you know something about my father and Nanek? About my Marek? Have you perhaps heard about my mother or Virka? If we were all together in the railroad car on the way to Auschwitz, it's possible that they were later sent to the same camp as you. I'm sure that my father and Marek got through the selection all right. I don't know about Nanek—he was no more than thirteen years old, you know. Although in Auschwitz, right after we arrived in the camp and right after they took the women—shaved, tattooed with numbers, and dressed in stripes—away from the barracks near the gate, I looked back and I can swear that I saw all of you, our men, in the same cabins, from a distance. You waved to us from a window next to the bathhouse—Nanek too. I could swear I saw my mother and Virka too.

I'm here with Malka Cedarbaum (Remember? In our hiding place in the ghetto you used to call Malka "Sheba" or, affectionately, "Malkele Sheba").

345

Baltshe, Malka's mother, also survived. I have stayed together with them and with Sarke and her stepmother, Khanke, the whole time—we were a fivesome in all the marches. But since the day of liberation, I haven't seen Sarke or Khanke. (Remember? You used to say that Khanke was not a stepmother but a sweet mother.)

We are in Block 88, Camp 2 in Bergen-Belsen, not actually in the camp but nearby, in the barracks of our former SS guards. These are fine buildings, a whole little town, in a pleasant forest of oak trees, chestnut trees, evergreens, and acacia trees. The forest had camouflaged the concentration camp so the local populace shouldn't see it. Bergen-Belsen is somewhere near Hanover, they tell me. We were liberated by the British on April 15th, that is fourteen days ago.

Abrasha, it's not possible to describe what went on here when we received the news about you, how my fellow camp-inhabitants fell on me and sobbed together with me. Even the man who 'accidentally'(!) brought the good news shed a tear, though I imagine that his tears had less to do with our joy than with his own sorrow.

For days on end, he, barely still breathing, searched around for his wife and daughter, going from one block of cabins to another—in vain. That's how he came to us. Now he's going back to Brno, to the hospital where he met her. How I'd love to leave with him, to meet you, to search further, but I can barely drag myself around. Besides, he told me there aren't yet any trains or other means of transportation to that land of devils, which is still soaked with blood. The accursed war still hasn't ended, you know.

He himself, that guest of ours, dragged around the liberated regions on a horse, which he had 'liberated' from a German peasant. But now he's so exhausted and depressed that he would first have to 'liberate' a little will and energy to go on. The 'darling mama', Baltshe, Malkele's mother—Remember? You were the first to start calling her that in our hiding-place, and that's what I and the others girls called her in the camp. She was one of the few mothers in the camp, you know—practically forced our guest to lie down on the bunk that became free in our room today. He has tuberculosis and looks like a ghost. The same could be said of us. Remember? In the ghetto, you used to call us, the three girl-friends—Malkele, Sorke, and me—the three Graces or the three Muses. Today, our 'grace' would make an outsider faint! And if we are Muses, we are dark, witch-like Muses, who are searching with candles for the author they will never find.

I'm actually writing this note to you while our guest is sleeping. (He told us that his name was Shedletski, and that before the war he was the owner of the garden restaurant *Capri,* on Pietrikov Street. So how come that you, the world-famous restaurant-patron, first met him in the hospital?) I will give him this note to take with him, and I hope that a troop of American or British soldiers will pick him up on the way back and take him on one of their Jeeps or truck, and that you will read these words of mine very soon.

Abrashele, I beg of you—don't wait a single minute. Answer me immediately. There are other DPs besides our guest who go around searching for their near and dear ones. I meet them outside and in the living quarters with their pasty faces and bald heads. It's hard to imagine that our men must also look like that. That's why we look at one another so closely. They will, of course, be happy to take along a note. They say, too, that UNRRA is setting up offices where there will be lists of all the survivors of the camps, to make it easier to find people (and to make not finding people more definitive). I've heard that one can already send letters via UNRRA.

It's extremely difficult for me to write, Abrashele. My heart is beating wildly and a fever grips my body and my head. I feel that I'm going to faint — sort of like being terribly drunk. Today is the first time I've held a pencil in my hand. (Back to civilization!) It keeps slipping from between my fingers, and it's a shame to put it down. I have so much to tell you that I'm almost gripped by fear. Who knows whether I'll have the strength to do it. I must confess to you that tears are clouding my eyes. I haven't cried in centuries.

Abrashele, my eternal friend, have pity on me and write me immediately about my father, about Nanek and about Marek. When were you liberated and how? I asked our guest what's the matter with you, but he, that absent-minded skeleton, didn't know what to say.

I kiss you. Darling Mama and Malkele send greetings. They ask whether you know anything about Vove and Gabi.

Your Miriam

P.S. I've heard that they're still fighting in Berlin. Still, I'm hopeful that Generals Zhukov and Konev will not make us wait long. I believe they've captured forty thousand Germans. They also say here that Mussolini was killed yesterday by an Italian partisan.

(From the novel *Letters to Abrasha*)

Beyle Shekhter-Gotesman (1920—) is the sister of the great linguist and philologist Mordkhe Shekhter. She is multitalented: poet, painter, and musical composer. She writes lyrical but often trenchant poems with a strong personal component, and often illustrates them and writes music for them as well. She is one of the most popular of living Yiddish poets.

~

Beyle Shekhter-Gotesman

My Home, New York

You're ashamed to say
that the coal-dust,
the gasoline fumes,
the wild tumult,
the fast driving
is your home—and you love it.
You don't want to admit
that your life too,
like the asphalt pavement,
has become congealed, stone cold,
not saying a word to anyone for days—
and that this has become your way of life,
even your desire.
And what is there to boast about ?
Those who don't understand it
will not agree with me,
and the others believe
that it's the best of all homes.

Rock-And-Roll Music

Through the window, my garden looks in—
neatly trimmed, bright, and summery,
but from the next room, there hammers
my children's rock-and-roll music.

Deep in dreams, the roses smile—
still the ancient, sweet romance.
But won't they be deafened
by the resounding rock music?

My heart trembles for the garden—
it seems to stretch out quite rhythmically.
I just hope I don't lose it too
to the rock-and-roll music.

I want to go out and save whatever I can,
but something holds me back by force.
Willy-nilly I hop around.
What else: the rock-and-roll music!

Leyb Borovik (1914-2006) lived through concentration camps during the Holocaust. He was a quiet, introverted, and often sad poet whose poems reflected his personality and interests.

∾

Leyb Borovik

All My Paths

All my paths
lead to you.

All my dreams
mirror you.

My days pass
in yearning for you.

Though I said good-bye
long ago, at the pyre,

I still hear your voice:
"I'm a part of you."

All my bones ache—
how sad it is without you.

I languish here,
far away from you,

but for love I accept my pain
in faithfulness to you.

With all my soul,
I belong to you

till I die
and rest next to you.

Shadows beckon bleakly to me:
"No survival for you;

in the shadow of death
she watched over you

and, out of love,
gave her life for you,

and you did not have
enough courage, woe unto you;

all your trials —
no virtue of yours;

no punishment
can redeem your sins."

Your blood accompanies me
on my path to you.

My pain pales
at the sight of you.

You whisper softly:
"I know how holy I am to you,

but do not believe
that I'm forever separated from you."

Did flame then have no dominion
over you?

"I am as before, as before,
in the valley here with you."

Since the traces of you
are long since wiped away,

let my elegy
be a memorial to you.

This is my prayer:
let me come unblemished to you.

The Forest

Wrapped in anguish and fear,
it prays to the Creator,
the forest.

See, Eternal One, its pain
and judge it with understanding,
the forest.

O all-righteous Judge,
receive its earnest prayer,
the forest.

In its hour of need, Creator,
withhold not Your mercy
from the forest.

In stormy weather,
shield, good Protector,
the forest.

Bind, O God, the thunder,
that it not ignite flames
in the forest.

Let not its crown be devoured—
strengthen and nourish
the forest.

O God, who controls the seasons,
judge it with compassion,
the forest.

Yoni Fayn (1914—) is a multitalented writer and artist. His paintings are of world-class caliber and have been exhibited in museums around the world. His writings, including both poetry and prose, are of superior quality, as demonstrated by the samples published here.

~

Yoni Fayn

The Closed Door
(fragment)

Julian Piast lived on the fourth floor in a tenement. The stairs were steep and dirty. From a dark corridor, private city-life billowed out through half-open doors: radios played, children cried, women chatted, dogs barked, girls sang, and men coughed and cursed.

The odors of onions, garlic, olive oil, mothballs, and cat feces filled the damp, tired air.

I knocked on Piast's door (the bell had been torn out.) A man wrapped in a gray housecoat opened it. I recognized the poet immediately: the same bold, high, bird-like head on a long neck; the same sharp, long nose; the same thin, slit-like lips; the same searching eyes, now half-blind with sadness.

"Come in," the poet said. "From your letter I thought you were a lot younger. What can a man of your age expect from poetry?"

The room was small and almost without furniture — just a table and three chairs. Two narrow windows without curtains looked out on a red brick wall. The floors were crooked and the boards squeaked with every step.

The poet sat down on one of the chairs and was silent. I had the feeling that he had completely forgotten about me.

Not waiting for an invitation, I sat down but didn't know what to say.

"How long have you been in America?" he asked suddenly. His voice, clear and sharp, was bigger than the old man.

"Less than a year," I answered.

"Do you want to remain here? Is America now your country?"

"I don't know."

"Was Poland your country?:

355

"Yes, once upon a time."

"And now?" His pupils hung there, near my face, like two dried cherries.

"Without Jews, how can Poland be my country?"

Piast didn't say anything. He stood up and slowly moved to one of the two windows. His back was straight, and his long hands in the housecoat sleeves hung down like sick birds.

I stood up and went over to the other window. The red wall was full of shadows. I felt Piast's eyes on me. They were scrutinizing me. Suddenly, the slit between his lips moved and he started to speak:

"The pine-trees and the elders haven't changed in Poland, and the Polish language is the same as it was. The wolves howl as they did hundreds of years ago, and the wounds they make are the same. And the church bells announce fires in the same way as before. Why then, is Poland no longer your country?"

"My people died there."

"But Poland was never a Jewish country," Piast interrupted. "Did only Jews make it feel close to you? The earth, the clouds, the lakes, the smell of new-mown hay, the chains of the martyrs, Tsimkevitsh, Slovatski, the heaven of miracles—without Jews all of that is nothing at all for you?"

His voice was without doubt too big for the dark, forgotten little room, but it took me back to Poland, and I hastily cried out:

"Tell me, yes tell me with your hand on your heart, what would Europe mean to you without a bunch of Polacks?"

The poet reeled back, as if from a heavy blow, and barely managed to stammer:

"It's a sin, a great sin against everything that lives or will be born, to speak such words. From what darkness have you emerged to dare to carry these words to human lips?"

He went back to the little table and sat down. I felt that he didn't want to look at me, so I didn't move from the window.

"How can you say such a terrible, crazy thing out loud? What devil possesses you?"

Though Piast's question was directed to me, I saw only his back and I answered that back:

"I don't have to imagine Poland without Jews—it's a fact. A people lived on Polish ground for centuries, and suddenly—gone, no longer there. An emptiness remained after it, and a little later the emptiness was filled and life goes on, exactly as if nothing had happened."

"Why have you come to me, " Piast cried, turning toward me.

I went over to the little table.

"Sit down," the old man commanded," and tell me why you've come to me."

I sat down and tried to speak calmly:

"I came to tell you what you meant to me in my youth. I—I've never stopped reading you. I've come to a poet."

"Nonsense—I'm not the only Polish poet. And who isn't great when one reads him in one's youth? Tell the truth—what are you doing here, in my private and quiet darkness? What do you want from me?"

I was silent.

"You've come to me, because I'm descended from Jews. That and not something else is the real reason."

"Perhaps, " I stammered.

"No, not perhaps. That alone and nothing else is the real reason. But don't you know that I've avoided Jews much more than antisemites? With them, with the antisemites, I fought for my right to be a Pole. And what is a fight without sleepless nights, without wounds? But victory didn't elude me—without me, something would have been missing in Polish poetry, and above all, I'm alive on the lips of schoolchildren. But with Jews? With them, in my opinion, I've had to fight constantly for the right not to be a Jew. I can tell you with my hand on my heart: With respect to Jews, I've felt more lost and helpless than with respect to the wildest antisemites. To fight against undeserved hatred has all the elements of a great historical drama, but to fight, so to say, 'heroically', against an undeserved love is no more than a farce. And since I didn't want to be the hero of a farce, I ran away from them—ran faster, perhaps, than decency permitted."

"But your poetry spoke to my generation. You, more than anyone else, saw the dark forces of a wild, scream-filled century, and your premonitions were expressed in the purest biblical form. We Jewish readers may have understood you better than anyone, because we had a wounded ancient memory. Is that not enough to earn our love despite all your reservations?"

Piast was looking at me in astonishment as I spoke, just as if he no longer recognized me. When I finished, he was silent for a moment, and then he spoke up, enunciating every word with exaggerated clarity:

"I didn't want to cause you pain, and I also didn't want to insult you. I was sure that you would draw the only logical conclusion from my words: Jews owe me nothing, and I owe them nothing. We have absolutely no point of contact. I never left them—they never existed for me as a living creative reality. Jews, in my opinion, are not a people."

"So what are they?"

"A concept of a people in the brain of a fanatic; an organized opposition to the rules of human history; a sickness that declares itself an ideology. Do you want more definitions?"

"If everything you've said is true, how is it that we have outlived so many peoples who lived according to the rules of history?"

Julian Piast bust into laughter.

"I wondered when you would come out with that boast. As they say, if you wait long enough, you'll get to see everything."

My coming to Piast had doubtless been a mistake, but to get up now and leave would look like running away. The truth be told, I was more curious than hurt by his words. Perhaps this angry , wise man knew something that I had not perceived in my whole life.

He again began to speak:

"The whole tirade about your outliving empires and peoples is no more than an empty delusion. Remembering destruction doesn't mean living. The most beautiful legends are shallow compared with the living folk-organism; your legends are worth more than you are. Normal peoples inhabit their own ground and write books; only for you is your Book your ground. As long as the great Book lives, you will continue barely gasping as a theory of a people, but since the French Revolution, the Book has begun to lose its dominating force, and as that happens, your theory is becoming converted into a pathetic anachronism. The democracies are slowly digesting you, in a calm and systematic manner, according to the rules of evolution. Dictatorships, and especially those paradigms of absolute power, Hitler and Stalin, kill you according to the rules of uncompromising evolution. To the tired, sober mind of democracy, you are a relic that vexes it from time to time but shouldn't be taken too seriously. To the primitive, atavistic mind of totalitarianism, you are a rebel against the principles of history, a sinful seed. In the final analysis, you can see that despite the fact that human history creates poets, it remains consistently antipoetic, and that poets who become important figures remain without a people, because poetry is anti-historic."

"Do you mean to say that history and poetry never meet?"

"Of course they do," laughed Piast, cracking his knuckles drily. "The axe of the executioner and the throat of the dreamer meet, and the result is always the same."

"But whose side are you on?"

Julian Piast almost jumped out of his chair. It got dark in the room. He lighted the lamp and considered me from a distance. The lamp filled the space with a sparse, sad yellowness.

"Your question is an insult to me," he said quietly, looking not at me but at the celing with the forlorn little lamp. Then he walked over to me, laid his hand on my shoulder, and started speaking with unexpected gentleness:

"St. Augustine said it before me, and much, much better than I can say it: 'My way is my love.' Newton discovered the gravity of physical bodies, Augustine the gravity of love. Love gravitates to God. In Him is our resurrection. He is the third way. In Him, history dissolves in poetry. Do you understand?"

The poet remained silent and didn't take his hand off my shoulder. I didn't answer, and since his hand had started to get heavier, I believed he was trying to provoke me. As if he had read my thoughts, he exclaimed again.

"I still have enough strength to stand on my own feet. Come, come—I want to show you something."

He took me by the hand and led me into what must have been the bedroom It was a tiny room, no larger than a prison cell. The mattress that lay on the floor took up more than half the space. On the wall, over the mattress, hung a gigantic wooden cross made out of rough-hewn wood and put together with nails. Under the cross hung a parchment with long, irregularly inscribed letters. Since the little room didn't have any light and the rays from the dining room barely illuminated the parchment, I couldn't read the words.

"It's not poetry," said Piast, still holding my hand in his. "You might call it: *A Short Summary of a Diary.*"

He had, it seems memorized the text, because despite the darkness he began reciting with the drawn-out, regular intonation of a prayer:

After all the roads
that led
to an abandoned railroad station;
after all the loves
that have, without honor,
grown old;
after all the furnished rooms
and hotels, where shadow
is the final reality;
after all the whitewashed
hospitals and sanatoriums
where illness
is the final truth;
after all the encounters
with old friends
who have forgotten
when they died;
after all the songs
that keep polishing themselves
for a dead masked-ball;
after all the totalities
that are a composite
of cigarettes-holes
in a lonely pillow,
I come, Lord, to your wounds.
In my kneeling is my rising;
in my dying is my ascent.

Julian Piast let go of my hand. He waited for me to say something. I replied:

"Your lines are poetry, not some third way. And how could it be otherwise? Without poetry, human history would become a prison."

The poet shook his head in dissatisfaction and went into the third room. Not looking at me, he murmured.

"History is a prison even with poetry. The key to the locked door is in the hand of the Crucified One, and not in free blank or rhymed verse."

He sat down again on the chair. He looked tired and pale. It was time to go.

"Good night," I whispered.

"No," the old man started shaking his head. "Say what you want to say. We will never meet again."

"The Church has swallowed you up. Will the Poles, too, swallow you up, with no reservations?" I asked, almost against my will.

"What do you think?" the poet smiled—an old, tired, sparrow-hawk with a sliver of light on its beak.

"I don't know. I know only that Jews will never leave me outside."

"Outstanding, outstanding!" exclaimed the poet. "Finally we have a definition of the concept 'people': it's a house you can go into with muddy feet."

"And if your feet have frozen, you can crawl in on your belly," I interrupted him.

"You Jews have always had a weakness for melodrama. I want to go to my people the way I go to a church, dressed in my finest and not on my belly."

I went to the door. The words "you Jews" and "melodrama" had suddenly lost their innocent character and they made my skin crawl. I could hardly believe my ears: to be able to equate great things with small things?

I reached the door and turned around to say good bye. Piast, as before, was sitting and looking in my direction.

"You shouldn't have come" he said.

"I came with the best of intentions."

"No, you came as a Jew, as an emissary and demander for something you call history. What is your history as an individual?"

From my earliest years, like all Jewish children in Poland, I lived with my parents and with our history. But how, for example, can one express an intrinsic gentleness, knowledge from the heart, and a strange mixture of ancient hunger and ancient satisfaction while standing on one foot. But I had to say something, so I whispered:

"My history, our history, is a road where a vision of the future interprets the past, and where today is only a bridge connecting both them."

"Words, words—no more than words," Piast cried out. He thought for a moment and then added:

"Good night, unhappy man, good night. Go with God."

I slowly closed the door behind me. In a few minutes, the visit took on the photo-like flatness of something that had happened long ago.

*   *   *

Coming home from Piast's place, I tried to write down our conversation, but nothing came of it. I just wrote down, insofar as I remembered it, the poet's 'prayer.' Today, on the day of his funeral, I thought back to our meeting, and with no difficulty at all I recorded the general outlines of our conversation. In the course of the two years that had passed, certain details had surely been erased. Nevertheless, I am more precise in describing Piast's words than my own. I was too overcome to remember everything that had been ripped out of me.

I've returned to that visit in my mind more than once. What did I want from the poet? I came back with all sorts of answers. Not one of them satisfied me. Perhaps I'll never untie the knot. But when I leave the past and ask myself: "What do you want from Piast today?" I answer, almost without thinking: "Nothing."

Quite Simply

I'll tell you quite simply:
a fire burns, water flows,
and only a man who finds himself alone
does not live in vain.

High doors decorated with portieres
frighten me more than an open grave,
and a book with words in love with words
is for me a cage, not a house.

Though I've achieved very little,
and haven't understood very much either,
I've lived in terrain
too perpendicular for airplanes to fly in.

Yesterday and today meet for me
in a cube of sugar between my teeth,
and my hand, which shaves me in the light,
can understand me in the dark too.

I'm thankful for things without names
and for names without things,
for tears that come without my knowledge,
and for knowledge locked in silence.

I'm thankful to be able to be thankful,
for hurrying, though no one has invited me,
for gentleness that can bypass harshness,
for eagerness to make up in the middle of a fight.

I'll tell you quite simply:
even the darkest hour has its wick,
and if my life is no more than a match,
I'm thankful for the little flame built into a match.

Yitskhok Bashevis Zinger (1904-1991) was an enormously talented writer of short stories, dramas, and novels who became more famous in the non-Jewish world than any other Yiddish writer. His work was recognized by the award of the Nobel Prize for Literature in 1978. His rise to worldwide popularity began when the Nobel Laureate Saul Bellow translated his short story *Gimpel the Fool* into English in 1953. His themes were often somewhat erotic, which lessened his popularity among older, more conservative Yiddish readers.

~

Yitskhok Bashevis Zinger

The Psychic Journey

A.

This is the way it happened: One hot day in September, I was standing on upper Broadway in front of a fenced little garden and throwing food to the pigeons, as I do every day. The pigeons there know me already. When they see me coming with a bag, they start to fly in from several blocks around. The police know me too. They say it's forbidden to feed pigeons outdoors, but they sort of pretend not to see. I even remember one time when a gigantic policeman came up to me and said:

"Why does everybody bring food for the pigeons but nobody thinks they need to drink? It hasn't rained in New York in weeks—the pigeons are being devoured by thirst."

To hear such words from a policeman was an experience for me. I immediately went home and brought the pigeons a plate of water, but I spilled half of it in the elevator and the other half the pigeons themselves spilled.

This time, on the way to the pigeons, I noticed in an item in the newspaper saying that a new issue of *The Unknown* had come out. I immediately bought a copy, because people grab up that merchandise in the neighborhood where I live. For some reason, on upper Broadway there are a lot readers who are interested in telepathy, clairvoyance, psychokinetics, and immortality of the soul.

As I was standing there and throwing handfuls of food, I noticed that a number of the pigeons had somehow begun to hesitate about whether they should continue to eat my food and others had even moved to one side. That astonished me, because as one who knows pigeons I know that pigeons never get full. I gave a look and saw that three steps from me a woman was standing and throwing seed to the pigeons. I was used to com-

364

petition in every field, but never before had a competitor come and stand so near me. I took another look and I began to laugh. The woman was holding the recent issue of *The Unknown* under her arm. On that hot summer day, she was wearing a black dress and a broad-brimmed black hat. Her shoes and socks were also black. After a while, she raised her head and I saw a face that looked young to me, or at least not old, with sunken cheeks, a narrow nose, and a longish chin. She looked Italian or Spanish. She had to have been a foreigner, because no American dressed like that on a hot summer day, even at a funeral. It also struck me that her dress was longer than women usually wore. I said to her:

"Competition, ha?"

She smiled, but her black eyes remained serious, and even strict. She said:

"Don't worry, sir. More pigeons will come. Here they come!"

And she pointed prophetically to the sky. Yes, a whole army of pigeons had flown in from downtown. The little garden soon got so full of pigeons that some of them jumped over others and tried to push themselves into the center of the feeding area. Pigeons, like khosids, love to push themselves. After the two of us emptied our paper bags, we went over to a garbage-can, and I said, like a gentleman:

"*Après vous* (after you)." After a moment, I added: "I see that we both read the same magazine."

She answered with a foreign accent, and with a deep voice:

"You don't know me, but I have seen you feeding the pigeons many times, and I want you to know that those who feed pigeons never know want. The few cents that you spend on those creatures will bring you much good fortune and will help you in many crises."

"How can you be so sure?"

She began to explain to me, and we were now walking together. I suggested to her that we should go in for a drink, and she answered:

"I'd be delighted, but I don't drink any alcoholic beverages, only fruit juice and vegetable juice."

"Come—if you read *The Unknown*, you're one of my people."

"Yes, I read the magazine every month, and a bunch of other such periodicals that I receive from England, Canada, Australia, and even India. I used to read such a magazine from Hungary, where I come from, but people get put in prison there for believing in the higher forces. Is there such a magazine in Hebrew?"

"You know Hebrew?"

"No, only a few words."

"Are you Jewish."

"Yes, on my mother's side, but for me there are no separate peoples and religions, just one kind of human being. The separation comes about because we've lost the sources of our spiritual energy and because a disharmony of our psychic evolution has developed. When we send out waves of love, brotherhood, mutual help, and peace, those vibrations create greater closeness and identification among all of God's children, human and animal. You saw how the pigeons flocked to me. They usually stay around the Central Savings Bank on Broadway and 62nd Street, which is too far away for pigeons to see what's happening in the 80s. But the balance of cosmic consciousness in them is in complete equilibrium and therefore..."

We went into an air-conditioned restaurant and sat down in a booth. She introduced herself:

"Margaret Fugazy. It's remarkable," she said, "you always feed the pigeons around one o'clock, when you go to lunch. I feed them in the morning. I fed them today, as always. Suddenly some sort of voice commanded me to go out and feed them again. Now at six o'clock the pigeons are not particularly eager to eat—they're starting to get ready for their nocturnal rest. The days are getting longer, and we are in a different constellation of the solar cycle, but I know that when a voice starts repeating the same announcement over and over, it's a manifestation of the world forces. I came out and saw you feeding the pigeons too, also not at your usual time. How come you were late this time?"

"I also heard a voice."

"You're psychic?"

"I'm joking."

"You must not joke about such things!"

Sitting with her for some three hours, I heard a lot of details. Margaret Fugazy had come to the United States in the 50s. Her father was a doctor. Her parents were no longer alive. In New York, Margaret got close to an old woman, a medium, more than ninety years old and half-blind, and the two of them lived together. The old woman died at the age of 102, and

Margaret gave courses in yoga, concentration, thought stimulation, bio-rhythms, and, most important, self-awareness and how to connect with the "I am." Margaret said to me:

"I've watched you feeding the pigeons for a long time and haven't known who you were, but someone told me that you were a writer and a vegetarian and I began to read your work. That led to a telepathic communication between us, even if it was one-sided. I'll tell you something that will astound you, but I hope you won't take it amiss. I've visited you in your home several times, not corporeally but when I was traveling in the astral plane. I tried to attract your attention, but you were sleeping sweetly. That usually happens with me just before dawn. Only once did I find you awake, and you spoke—perhaps not to me— about the mysteries of *kabala*. That was a great gift for me, because for years I've been looking for a teacher who would initiate me into *kabala*. When I had to return to my body, I gave you a kiss. You probably thought it was a dream.

"You know my address?" I asked.

"The astral body doesn't need addresses!"

I remained silent for a long time. Then Margaret said:

"If you want, give me your telephone number. Astral visits entail a certain danger. When the silver cord ruptures, then ...." She didn't finish the sentence, apparently frightened by her own words.

B.

On the way home, at one o'clock in the morning, I said to myself that I mustn't get involved with this person. I had a bellyache from the soybeans, raw carrots, molasses, peas, and celery juice that Margaret had served me for dinner. Her advice about how to eliminate psychic pressure, frustration, and sleeplessness, and how to control dreams, emit the alpha waves of rest, the beta waves of intellectual activity, and the theta waves of trance gave me a headache. It's all Dora's fault, I thought. If she hadn't left me and flown away to her daughter Sandra in the kibbutz because she was getting ready to give birth to her first child, I'd now be spending time with her in a hotel in Bethlehem, New Hampshire, instead of remaining in hot New York and suffering from hay-fever. I was afraid to walk the few blocks from Columbus Avenue and 96th Street to my studio apartment in the 80's and I tried to hail a cab, but for some reason all the cabs passed me by even though they were empty. Had Margaret cast a magic spell on me or were my nerves to blame? As I was riding up in the elevator, I was assailed by all kinds of fears. Perhaps I had been robbed meanwhile. Perhaps the thieves, out of revenge for not finding any jewelry or money in my place, had torn up my manuscripts. I opened the door and I was struck by a blast of heat, as from an oven. I had forgotten to lower the Venetian blinds, and the sun had baked the apartment all day. I had left a light on in my clothes closet, and there could have been a fire. Since Dora had been in Israel, nobody had cleaned up in my apartment. I immediately started sneezing from the dust. I was too negligent and too lazy to change my bed-linens. Dora had pleaded with me to go to Israel with her, but I had no intention of sitting in some far-flung kibbutz near the Syrian border and waiting for Sandra to give birth.

I undressed quickly and lay down in bed, but I couldn't get to sleep. My throat felt scratchy and my ears were full of water. My anger at Dora seethed in me, and I fantasized all sorts of plans for revenge. Perhaps I would marry that scraggly Hungarian and send Dora a cable telling her she no longer had anyone to come back to. Since Margaret was paying me astral visits and kissing me in addition, it would be easy for us to become a couple.

It was just before dawn when I fell asleep, and I was awakened by the ringing of the telephone on my night-stand. The clock showed twenty after ten. I picked up the receiver— surely it was one of my Yiddish readers— and wheezed:

"Yes?"

I heard a woman's voice.

"Did I wake you? This is Margaret, Margaret Fugazy. Morris—may I call you Morris?"

"You may even call me Potiphar"

"Oh just, listen to him! What happened this morning is a sign, if any sign is needed, that our nocturnal meeting was not just an accident, but a fateful event, planned and carried out by the hand of the Lord. Let me tell you before anything else that when you left me yesterday I was very worried about you. You promised me you'd take a cab, but I know—don't ask me how I know—that you didn't listen to me. Today, before dawn, I suddenly found myself in your apartment again. What disorder! What dust! And when I looked at your pale face and listened to your choked breathing, I decided that you absolutely must not stay in the city at this time of year. But on the other had, I didn't want our increasing closeness to be marred at the outset by separation. Today, very early, my telephone rang, and it was an old lady friend of mine calling, also a Hungarian, a Jewish girl—Lily Wolfner. I hadn't heard from her in more than a year, but yesterday, before I fell asleep, I suddenly and for no reason whatsoever started to think about her, and that's always a sign to me that I will hear from the person. At exactly nine o'clock, my telephone rang, and I was so sure it was her that I said: 'Hello, Lily!' Lily Wolfner owns a travel bureau. She arranges excursions to Europe, Africa, Japan, and also Israel. Her excursions always have a cultural character. The leaders are psychologists, writers, artists, and rabbis. Twice I was a leader of such a tour, with groups that were interested in psychic research, and I'll tell you about my wonderful experiences some other time. I said to her: 'Lil—what made you think of me ?' And she told me that she had a group for me, one that planned to visit the Jewish land during the High Holidays, but in relation to an advanced course in self-awareness, and she offered me the position. I don't remember now how, but I mentioned your name and that you had promised to give me an esoteric insight into *kabala*. I beg you—be patient and don't interrupt me. As soon as she heard your name, she became simply hysterical. 'What? He lives here in New York and you've eaten dinner with him?' To her you're completely legendary. I'll make it brief: she proposed to me that the two of us should be the leaders. She'll meet all your demands. These are rich women — most of them, of course, readers of your works. I told her I'd talk to yo, but that first she had to make sure the women wanted it. Not a half-hour had passed when she called again. She had already managed to get in touch with her clients and they had jumped at the prospect. Morris— one has to be blind not to see in all this the hand of Fate. Lily is a businesswoman, not some sort of mystic. She told me: 'You two together could conquer the world. You're a fantastic couple!' I was so shaken by all of this that I forgot about our little angels, the pigeons. Morris, I want you to know that the past few months have represented a deep crisis in my life, spiritually, physically, financially—in every sense. I was closer to suicide than you can imagine. When I sat down next to you yesterday with the bag of food for the pigeons, I knew somehow that my life was in your hands, however weird those words may sound to you. I therefore beg you, on my knees—don't say no, because your "no'" would be a death knell for me."

During this long monologue, I tried several times to interrupt, but Margaret didn't let me get a word in, I wanted to answer her that I was miles away from being a leader of a tour, that I was not a specialist in *kabala*, and that I had no intention of dragging around in Israel with a bunch of rich women who wanted to combine tourism with mysticism. But I remained silent, bewildered by my own weakness or compassion.

After a few moments, Margaret exclaimed:

"Morris, wait for me. I'm coming to you!"

"In the astral plane?" I asked.

"Cynic! In the flesh!"

C.

Who said it? Perhaps nobody: "The drama of every person is a melodrama." I have both acted in that melodrama and observed it. I was now sitting in an air-conditioned bus that was traveling from Haifa to Tel Aviv. We had spent *rosh hashone* in Jerusalem. We had already been in Eilat and Safed, in the occupied territories, near the Suez Canal, on the Golan Heights, in a number of kibbutzim , and wherever they take tourists. We had driven about three miles from the kibbutz where Dora was located. Wherever we stopped, I gave a lecture about *kabala* and Margaret gave advice about love, health, and business; how to use the subconscious to achieve all sorts of goals; and how to meditate. She chattered about "delta brain waves" and "the chain of meditative stimulations", about "the resonance of the tantric personality," and the mirror of "the discoveries in Ur." She conducted astrochemical analyses for the women; cast their horoscopes; showed them how to find the third eye, the pineal eye; and revealed the mysteries of Atlantis and Lemuria and Tibet and Mount Shasta. I attended séances where she hypnotized the women, and most of them fell asleep or pretended to be asleep. Margaret apparently believed in all kinds of nonsense. At night, when she visited my room, she brought along a Ouija board and a special pencil and paper that she used for automatic writing—when in a trance, Margaret wrote mirror-script. She swore that my mother had revealed herself to her and had told her to watch over me, because I was born under the sign of Sagittarius, and that was a sign that one of my enemies, who was born under the lucky sign of Scorpio, would begin a dispute with me that might lead to bad consequences.

I had stumbled into a situation that embarrassed me. To be sure, so far I hadn't run into anyone I knew, but I still had a week more to stay here. Every few days we stayed in a different hotel, and it could easily have happened that someone would recognize me. Quarrels and intrigues began among the group of women. One woman had lost a brooch and suspected one of the other women. The women started cooling toward Margaret and her lectures, and their enthusiasm for *kabala* had also evaporated. One woman complained to me, not without reason, that my interpretation of *kabala* was too subjective, and was in fact a kind of philosophy of literature. According to our plan, the group was now supposed to stay a few days in Tel Aviv, where the women would have time to shop, then spend *yom kipur* in Jerusalem, and then on the following day, return to America from Lod Airport. Because I had quietly toyed with the idea of surprising Dora at the end of the tour, I had asked Lily Wolfner before our departure from New York to provide me with an open return-ticket so I wouldn't have to go back together with the group, and I had paid her the price differential. I told Lily that I had literary business in Israel. I didn't say anything about that to Margaret, and the crafty Lily also didn't tell her.

On the last days in Tel Aviv, the women were so busy with shopping for all sorts of bargains, and also with visiting relatives, that no time remained for lectures. Margaret had found a relative in Tel Aviv who she thought had died in the concentration camps, a woman of eighty, deaf and half-lame. She lived in an old-age home. Because a lot of tourists had arrived, we didn't get the hotel in which we were supposed to stay, according to the program, but only a small hotel instead, and that aroused a lot of agitation and complaints. But the day before *yom kipur*, after breakfast, when the group was supposed to go from Tel Aviv to Jerusalem, I had to reveal the secret, because I was supposed to remain in Tel Aviv for *yom kipur*, actually in the same hotel where we were staying. The constant traveling around had put me in a very depressed mood. I wanted to be alone for a day.

I had expected a reproach, but Margaret made an absolute scene. She cried, screamed that Lily Wolfner and I had plotted against her, cursed, and warned me that the higher forces would take revenge. She threatened me and flooded me with curses. She called me all kinds of names and predicted that a great catastrophe would befall me because of my falseness. Suddenly she cried out:

"If you're staying in Tel-Aviv, I'm staying here too. I'm not Jewish and I don't have to pray at the Western Wall on *yom kipur*. My work is finished, just like yours."

"If you stay here you'll lose your ticket" I reminded her.

"Tomorrow, after *yom kipur*, I'll take a taxi from here to Lod, " Margaret answered.

When the women heard the news that their leaders were staying in Tel Aviv on *yom kipur*, they started to ask all sorts of questions and making sarcastic remarks, but the bus was already waiting in front of the hotel and there was no time left for a long discussion. Margaret assured the women that she would meet them after *yom kipur*, very early, at the airport. Some of the women kissed me when they said good-bye. Others shoved me aside or ignored me. After the bus left, I showed Margaret in the contract, in black and white, that my work had ended the previous evening. I had every right to remain in Israel as long as I wanted. But Margaret rejected all of my responses.

"You have some woman here that you want to fool around with," she complained, "but all your plans will come to naught."

She pointed her index finger at me, and I clearly sensed that she wanted to cast a magic spell or the Evil Eye on me. My own belief bewildered me, and I tried to appease her with promises. Just as the hotel had been completely full till that morning, it was now empty. Everyone had left for Jersusalem. Margaret had no difficulty getting her room back, and after a while she went to unpack her clothes again. While she was dong that, I tried in my room to make telephone contact with the kibbutz on the Golan where Dora was staying, but I couldn't get connected. Because all the guests had left for Jerusalem, the hotel in which we were staying had not prepared a pre-*yom kipur* meal. I am not a *shul*-goer, but I fast on *yom kipur*, so Margaret and I had to look for a restaurant. When Margaret heard that I fasted on *yom kipur*, she exclaimed:

"I'll fast too. If God is punishing me with such shame, I must have sinned greatly."

"You're ostensibly a Christian woman, but you yammer like a fishwife", I said to her.

"I'm more Jewish in my smallest fingernail than you are in your whole body."

When we came back to the hotel in the afternoon, all the shops were closed. We were supposed to buy food for the pre-fast meal but we couldn't get anything. Evening fell. The streets became empty. Even the American embassy near the hotel seemed to me to be *yom kipur*-quiet. Angrily, Margaret came into my room and we went out onto the balcony, which overlooked the ocean. The oblong sun, a purple melon, was slowly sinking in the west. It cast fiery reticular patterns on the waves. The beach was empty; birds were walking in the sand. The closeness that had developed between Margaret and me during the trip had been ruptured, and we had become like a couple that had already decided on a divorce. We stood for a while apart from one another and watched the sun ignite *yom kipur* candles in the ocean before it was extinguished. A few stars twinkled in the sky for a while longer. Margaret's dark face became brick-red, and from her dark eyes there looked out the melancholy of those who have torn themselves away from everything and are trying to settle their accounts with the world. Margaret said:

"The air here is full of spirits..."

D.

In the evening, we were both sitting at the Ouija board, and it predicted one dark prophesy after another. Later I confessed to Margaret, told her the truth about Dora. Early the next morning, we went for a walk, first on Ben-Yehuda Street and then on Rothschild Boulevard. We talked about going into synagogue, but the synagogues we passed all looked packed— men were standing outside in their prayer-shawls. About ten o'clock, we headed back to the hotel, and we decided not to go out again till evening. We had talked everything out, and I lay down to read a book about Houdini, about how he had fought the occultists. I had always considered him a person with mysterious powers. Margaret sat at the table and played solitaire. From time to time, she knitted her brows and cast a dark look at me. Later she went to her own room and told me that since she hadn't slept the whole night thinking about my staying in Israel and my confession about Dora she would try to sleep now. She warned me not to wake her. In the middle of the afternoon I heard an alarm and I was astonished that the military forces would carry out such a drill on *yom kipur*. But I also knew that the State of Israel had actively come into being about two o'clock in the afternoon. I also knew that I was hungrier this *yom kipur* than I had been on any previous *yom kipur*. I read, dozed, and devoted myself to a sort of *yom kipur* spiritual stock-taking. In all past years, I had pursued pleasures, but they had always gone amiss. My lovers all immediately got too serious and developed the female depression. I never did justice to them, and they had innumerable pretensions toward me. This excursion had humiliated and exhausted me. My hay-fever didn't even get better.

My room became full of shadows. By my calculation, the Jews in the synagogue had already finished their prayers. A bit later, the first star appeared in the sky, and then another. The door opened and Margaret came in silently. She slipped in like a shadow. We had fasted not 24 hours but 28 hours. We went down by elevator. The lobby was empty and half dark and the French doors were covered with dark cloth. Behind the reception desk sat an elderly Jew who did not look like a hotel official. He was reading a Yiddish newspaper. I went up to him and asked:

"Why is it so quiet here?"

He raised his eyes reproachfully from the crumpled newspaper and asked a question in return:

"What do you want—that we should dance?"

"Why is it so dark here?"

The Jew scratched his beard.

"Are you trying to play the fool or what? There's a war going on in this country, a bitter war!"

The Jew began explaining to me: The Egyptians had crossed the Suez Canal and the Syrians had entered the Golan. It seemed that Margaret understood a little Yiddish, because she began wailing:

"I knew it! Felt it! The punishment! The catastrophe!"

I nudged the outside door open. Hayarkon Street was enveloped in darkness—all the windows were draped with cloth. There was a stillness like that of a small village in Poland. This was not like the end of *yom kipur* in Tel Aviv, when all the restaurants and cabarets are packed, but like the night of *tishe b'ov* in a small village in Poland. In the few automobiles that stole past, the headlights were not lit, or were covered with some kind of paint or paper. We walked the few steps to Ben Yehuda Street, and all the shops were closed. It was clear now that we wouldn't get any food anywhere. We went back up to my room and Margaret discovered a radio set into my nightstand. The news broadcast was full of bad news. It appeared that civilian air transportation was suspended. All the armed forces had been quickly mobilized. An officer was appealing to the populace not to panic. I found in my packed valises a bag of cookies and two apples, and we broke our fast with that. On the day before *yom kipur*, Margaret had ordered a taxi for five o'clock that morning, to take her to Lod. But would the taxi come? And would there be a plane to America at Lod? According to the news from the Golan front, I had the feeling that the kibbutz where Dora was located was in the hands of the Arabs. The Russians had provided them with fast tanks and the newest airplanes. Margaret now began to try and convince me to go with her to Lod early in the morning if the taxi came, but I answered that I had no intention of lying around for days and nights in Lod. I predicted that thousands of tourists would flee there from all corners of the country. Margaret asked:

"And dying here is better?"

"Yes — better."

We had slept a whole day, and now we stayed awake till two o'clock in the morning. Margaret seemed more shocked about my so called conspiracy than by the war. Her only consolation, she claimed, was that she had foreseen it all in the depths of her soul. She now predicted that Dora and I would never meet again. She even hinted that this war was one of the punishments that the Lord had prepared for me. Since time was an illusion and everything is determined, sometimes the punishment could come before the crime. That had happened to her many times, she said. The angel that protected her had years earlier prepared the conditions to prevent the enemy from gaining power over her. Those who had tried to cause her pain had later been killed or maimed or had ended up in an insane asylum. Before Margaret left to go to sleep, she nevertheless consoled me by saying that she would pray that my unjust behavior should be forgiven. Even though the *yom kipur* day was over, the gates of repentance were not completely closed.

E.

I had fallen into a deep sleep. I opened my eyes. Someone had awakened me and was shaking me:

"Morris! Morris!"

It was dark. I didn't know where I was, who was waking me, and who I myself was. It took a while till my amnesia passed. I heard Margaret telling me, with a hoarse and solemn voice:

"Morris, the taxi is here!"

"What taxi? Oh, yes."

"Morris, come with me. The taxi will wait!"

"No, Margaret, I'm staying here."

"Is that your decision?"

"Yes, that's my decision," I answered, not knowing myself why I was deciding that way.

"If that's your decision, then be well and good-bye!"

She kissed me with rough lips. Her mouth smelled of fasting. She closed the door behind her and immediately became a piece of history. Only after she had left did I grasp the motives for my behavior. I didn't have a reservation, as she did, but an open ticket. Besides, I had told the women from the excursion that I was staying in the country, and it seemed to me that it was inappropriate for them and for myself to run away like a coward. Dora and I had once toyed with the fantasy that I would remain with her on a ship that was sinking. The other passengers would be pushing to the lifeboats, screaming, crying, and struggling, but Dora and I would remain seated in the dining-room, with a bottle of wine that the waiter had set on the table before the panic broke out. We had enjoyed our happiness and one would rather die than push and shove and beg for a little bit of life. Now that fantasy had become somewhat of a reality, but Fate had decided that we should die separately.

I closed my eyes and simultaneously dozed and thought waking thoughts. After a while, I started to dream. When I woke up, it was daytime. The sun had just risen, but several men and women were already doing gymnastics on the beach. Others were splashing in the water or swimming. I started laughing at those optimists who were developing their muscles the day before death. I had gone to sleep hungry, but I woke up full. I stuck my hand in the pocket of my jacket, which was hanging on a chair, and touched my passport and the airline ticket. I had had no reason to take a large amount of money with me, but I had brought two thousand dollars worth of Traveler's Checks and a checkbook. Those people down there by the ocean had provided themselves with muscles before their death, and I had provided myself with dollars. I had slept very little during the previous two weeks. We had constantly been in a hurry, packed and unpacked valises, kept looking at the clock. Now the time had come for resting. I went back to my bed and put in some time sleeping. Later, I shaved and bathed leisurely. I had a number of friends and acquaintances in Israel but I had decided not to show myself to anyone. What would I tell them I was doing here? When had I come? I didn't want to tangle myself in new lies. I put on fresh underwear and a fresh suit. I turned on the radio to hear the news. The enemy had surged forward. Our casualties were heavy. Other Arab countries were preparing to attack. Russia was sending gigantic shipments of ammunition. I again tried to contact Dora's kibbutz, and I was told it was impossible. The fact that the telephone was working at all and there was electricity and hot water in the bathroom struck me as a miracle.

I went down by elevator and saw a number of guests in the lobby. The previous day I had had the impression that the hotel was empty, but here were men and women standing and speaking English among themselves. All of the male hotel officials had apparently been mobilized, and women had taken their places. Breakfast was being served in the dining room. As unbelievable as it seemed, bakeries had baked rolls that night—they were warm from the oven. I ordered an omelet and received it immediately. Outside, the sun was shining and the sky was summer blue. I knew that in my place someone else would have approached the American tourists, gotten information from them, and become one of them. But for some reason, I was not enthusiastic about speaking to them and their wives and listening to what they had to say. Besides, they were speaking so loudly that I could hear what they were saying anyway. In Lod, people were lying around outdoors with their baggage and no one could help them.

After breakfast, I went for a walk on Ben Yehuda Street. There was no trace of war. Automobiles were racing back and forth with the same energy as always. The shops were open. A Jew with a white beard, wearing a rabbi's hat, was carrying palm leaves and a citron. On a balcony, someone was busy putting up a *suke*. Newspapers had been printed that night too, though thinner than usual. I bought a paper, sat down at a table in a sidewalk café, and ordered cheesecake and coffee. I had always considered myself a timid person and I had always been a great worrier. I was sure now that if I had been in New York reading about what was happening in Israel, I would have panicked. But everything in me was quiet. Overnight, I had become a fatalist. I had brought a bottle of sleeping pills with me from America, and I had razor blades with which I could slice open my arteries, but for now the cheesecake was tasty and the coffee had a strong aroma. The sun was warm, not hot, but it seemed to me that there was indeed some change in the sky: shadows were falling from above, as at the start of an eclipse of the sun. A little pigeon flew in and set itself down near my chair. It threw it a crumb but it didn't eat. This was an Israeli pigeon— small, brownish, and skinny. It was shaking its head about a truth that was as old as the land: if one is fated to live, one will live; if one is fated to die, that's no catastrophe either. Is there, then, such a thing as death? It's something thought up by human cowards.

The day passed in strolling around, reading the book about Houdini, and sleeping. The supermarket on Ben Yehuda Street was packed with customers; there was even a line outside. Women, despite all the prohibitions, were buying out everything they could get. But I had gotten bread, cheese, and fruit in a smaller shop. During the day, peace reigned; at night, the war returned. The city became empty and dark. In the hotel, all the guests sat in the television room. There the war was storming, with tanks, cannons, jet planes, and explosions and fires from bombings. The commentators all confirmed the same thing: the danger was far from over. After a while, I went up to my room and went out onto the balcony. The ocean was full of waves and foam and was roaring with the restrained roar of a cosmic lion that was full for the time being but could get hungry at any moment. Military jets roared overhead. Because the city was dark, the sky was full of stars. To me, they looked uncomfortably near. A cool wind blew the sulfur-and-pitch smell of biblical wars into my nostrils. They were all here again: Adam and Amalek, Ammon and Moab, Gog and Magog, Esau's generals, and the tribes of Israel, and they were fighting the eternal war between God and paganism. I could hear the clang of their swords and the rattling of their chariots. I sat down on a straw chair and deeply inhaled the aroma of eternity.

I had dozed off and I was awakened by the blaring of a thousand shofars. The door of my room had opened by itself. I knew that there were no bomb-cellars in the hotel. I sat down on the edge of my bed, ready to live and ready to die.

F.

Ten days later, I came back to America. Not long after that, Dora came back the grandmother of a little boy. I told her I had spent several weeks at a small college in California, where I gave lectures. Dora had fled to Tel Aviv with her daughter and the family, and there she had stayed at a hotel on Allenby Street, not far from my hotel. The circumcision had taken place on the second day of *sukes*. Usually, Dora put me through an inquisition after every trip. She thought that my lectures were no more than a pretext and an opportunity to meet with other women, but this time, ironically, she accepted my words without suspicion or questioning. I again fed pigeons, but Margaret had disappeared. She neither telephoned me nor wrote to me, and as far as I knew, she had not paid me any astral visits.

One day in December, when I was strolling with Dora on Amsterdam Avenue, looking to buy a used book-case, a young man shoved a flyer into my hand. It was cold and it was snowing, and he had no coat or hat and his shirt was disheveled. He looked like a Spaniard or Puerto Rican. Usually I didn't accept such flyers, but there was something in the young man's appearance that made me take the wet pile of paper. He didn't look like just a hired distributor of flyers, but like a fighter for truth. His black eyes expressed the zeal of someone who was ready to sacrifice himself for something. I stopped and read, in large letters, the name Margaret Fugazy over a picture of how she had looked at least twenty years earlier. I read:

"Are you ill? Are you having business problems? Problems in your family life? Are you in a predicament with no way out? Come to Madame Margaret Fugazy, for she is the only one who can help you! Margaret

Fugazy, a world-famous medium, studied yoga in India and *kabala* in Jerusalem and specializes in ESP, occult forces, UFO mysteries, self-hypnosis, cosmic wisdom, spiritual healing, and the secrets of Tibet. Advice is given to you in strict privacy. The first visit is only two dollars."

Dora tugged at my sleeve.

"Why did you stop? Throw it away!"

"Wait, Dora, Where did he go?"

I looked around, but the young man had disappeared. Had he been waiting just for me? Dora asked:

"Why are you so interested? Who is this Madame Fugazy? Do you know her?"

"Yes, I know her," I answered, not knowing why.

"Who is she? One of your witches?"

"Yes, a witch."

"From where do you know her? Did you fly with her on a broom to a Black Sabbath?"

"Do you remember *yom kipur*, when you went to your daughter in the kibbutz? While you were there, I flew with her to Jerusalem, Safed, and Rachel's Tomb, and we studied *kabala* together."

Dora was used to my chatter, playful words, and absurdities, and she cleverly went along with me:

"Really? What then?"

"When the war broke out, the witch got frightened and flew away."

"She left you alone, ha?"

"Yes, alone."

"Why didn't you come to me? I'm a witch too."

"You too had disappeared."

"Poor child! All the witches abandoned you. But now you can get her back, that big bargain. She's advertising. Isn't that a miracle?"

We stood there bemused. The snow was falling thick and dry; it was hitting me in the face like hail. The sky grew black and Dora's black coat grew white. In the whirling snow, a single pigeon tried to fly. It flapped its wings but fell back. Dora shook herself.

"That young man looked weird. Certainly a witch too, and all of that for two dollars! Come, let's go home on the subway, not on a psychic journey...."